# CONCORDIA

*Norman C. Habel*

CONCORDIA PUBLISHING HOUSE

# COMMENTARY

## Jeremiah
## Lamentations

SAINT LOUIS    LONDON

Concordia Publishing House, St. Louis, Missouri
Concordia Publishing House Ltd., London, E. C. 1
© 1968 Concordia Publishing House
*Library of Congress Catalog Card No. 68-19474*
MANUFACTURED IN THE UNITED STATES OF AMERICA

# CONTENTS

# PREFACE

The preparation of commentaries on the Bible is a continuing task of scholarship and faith, for the unchanging Word of God must speak to the varying needs of each age. Furthermore, new knowledge of ancient cultures and languages adds to the insight into the world and meaning of the Bible. A commentary is thus a means of listening to the text.

The Concordia Commentary offers its readers a running narrative interpretation of the Revised Standard Version of the Bible. Writers are free to criticize the translation since their work is based on the Hebrew, Aramaic, and Greek texts of the original Bible. Footnotes and foreign language expressions are generally omitted. Brief bibliographies provide direction for further study.

The writers of this series accept the Bible as the source of faith and the directive for life. They pursue their task in confessional commitment to Biblical revelation. Yet in their role as Biblical scholars it is their function to subordinate personal reflection and private or sectarian views to the unique and original direction of the text.

This commentary, therefore, is addressed to the devout who may often be mystified or frightened by the Bible's vastness and depth. The commentary attempts to provide a contemporary understanding of the ancient text rather than to develop practical implications for modern life. Theological, historical, and literary interests are uppermost. However, the writers are aware not only of the difference between the past and the present but also how little basic human problems have changed and how directly helpful the Biblical perspective and commitment remain.

The contributors to this series hope that their words may bear worthy witness to that Word which alone abides.

WALTER J. BARTLING AND ALBERT E. GLOCK

*Editors*

# Jeremiah

# INTRODUCTION

Anyone who hopes to read a book such as Jeremiah with acumen and profit ought to begin with a number of preliminary questions and guidelines. The books of the Old Testament are not modern documents but ancient texts from a distant world. As the author of one of these texts Jeremiah needs to be introduced to the reader of today. Several points of introduction are especially significant: What was Jeremiah like? What kind of world did he face? How did his book arise? What was God's word to Jeremiah? What kind of language does Jeremiah use? How do we interpret Jeremiah? What are some of the basic emphases of the prophet that shape the message of the book as a whole? These are but some of the questions we might pose, and the partial answers offered here are only brief summaries. Jeremiah is a long and complex book that can be fully appreciated only after years of study. It is hoped, however, that these introductory remarks will serve as signposts for the reader as he begins.

*The Character of Jeremiah*

The Book of Jeremiah and the man Jeremiah are obviously two different entities. In the case of Jeremiah, however, we know much more about the prophetic figure whose word and work are recorded in the book that bears his name than we do in the case of most other prophets. To know Jeremiah as a person helps us to understand many of the things he says and does. Jeremiah was a man of dangerous extremes, a man who lived at odds with the world around him and sometimes with God Himself. As a result he speaks his messages in black-and-white challenges to the living situation. He pulls no punches, and he would probably be disturbed if we were to press the letter of each of his pronouncements today. We must learn to feel the spirit of this passionate martyr and servant.

Jeremiah was a lonely man who felt an uncontrollable urge to scream the message of God to his people. He couldn't help himself. "The word came," and he shouted. If he tried to hold back a message, he felt an irrepressible eruption from within himself (see 15:17; 20:8-9). That Word, moreover, came to him in a rational way. He rejected the dreams and professional techniques of the false prophets as inefficient ways of determining God's will (see 23:16-32). The Word "came" to him! A message of God would reach him at the most unexpected moments. An almond rod, a steaming pot, a potter at work, a chance remark of a drunkard may have passed unnoticed before others. For Jeremiah, however, God spoke through these things (see 1:11-14; 18:1-11; 13:12-14). At the same time he spoke through Jeremiah. His life and actions were a living sermon, primarily of God's wrath. He was filled with divine indignation (15:17) and forced to live as a rejected representative of God (16:1-9). This meant loneliness and cruel hardship, rejection and persecution. It led him to make one of his forceful affirmations that for 23 years no one listened to his preaching (25:3-4). His whole life is a series of dramatic rescues at the hand of unexpected people. He survived where others did not. (26:20-23)

Jeremiah also belonged to the people of God whom he had to condemn throughout most of his career. He felt their need and felt the horror of their downfall long before it happened. He lived the fate in anticipation and went through vicious agony in doing so (4:5-31) He was fully aware of the urgent preaching of doom that God demanded, and yet he often wished that things would work out differently (see 28:5-9). His personal feelings were not always identical with God's demands. God's promises of protection for Jeremiah as God's chosen spokesman often seemed to break down. In his personal writings Jeremiah exercises his right as a prophetic intercessor by protesting God's actions and accuses God of negligence in the execution of His righteous will. God had apparently forgotten His promises. In the passion of his personal inner turmoil Jeremiah is ready to call God a deceiver, an unfair tough guy, a mirage (see 20:7-18). This boldness and forthrightness is evident throughout the book and colors its message. The sensational methods of communicating this message by the use of symbolic actions and language often loaded with double meaning is also consistent with the character of Jeremiah (see 9:1-13; 27:1-7) Jeremiah was an extremely sensitive and emotional prophet, whose life virtually became a living sermon to rebellious Israel.

13

*The Times of Jeremiah*

Jeremiah lived in a crucial period of ancient Near Eastern history. That era, in general, was marked by political instability. The Northern Kingdom of Israel had long since become a part of the great Assyrian Empire, now inherited by the Neo-Babylonian Empire. Judah was little more than a petty nation caught between the clashing world powers of Egypt to the south and the Tigris-Euphrates valley to the east. Judah's political existence was always in danger. In the day of Jeremiah the people would have to face possible extinction as a nation and a people, a fact of which Jeremiah was acutely aware. The Babylonian army under Nebuchadnezzar destroyed the city of Jerusalem in 587 B. C. and broke up Judah as a national entity. In a series of deportations many of the people were exiled in distant parts of Babylon. Jeremiah's preaching is, at least in part, an interpretation of this period of history. The following table is provided as a working outline for the history of Jeremiah's age.

640 – 609 B. C. – Josiah rules Judah (2 Kings 22:1 – 23:30)
627 – Jeremiah becomes a prophet (Jer. 1:2)
621 – The reforms of Josiah
612 – Nineveh, the capital of Assyria, falls to the Babylonians
609 – Josiah is killed by the Egyptian army at the battle of Megiddo
609 – Jehoahaz rules Judah for three months (2 Kings 23:31-35)
609 – 598 – Jehoiakim rules Judah (2 Kings 23:36 – 24:7)

| 605 | —Babylon defeats Egypt for the supremacy of the Near East at Carchemish |
|---|---|
| 604 | —The scroll of Jeremiah is read (Jer. 36:9) |
| 598 | —The first fall of Jerusalem and the deportation of Judahites to Babylon under Nebuchadnezzar |
| 598—597 | —Jehoiachin rules Judah for three months and is deported to Babylon (2 Kings 24: 8-17) |
| 597—587 | —Zedekiah rules Judah (2 Kings 24:18— 25:30) |
| 594 | —Revolt and unrest in the Babylonian Empire |
| 587 | —End of the Babylonian siege of Jerusalem. The city is destroyed and more people are deported to Babylon |
| 586—583 | —The governor Gedaliah is murdered, and some Judahites flee to Egypt, taking Jeremiah with them |
| 582 | —The third deportation of people to Babylon |

Jeremiah was active throughout this course of events. Early in his career he may have had a part in the reform of Josiah, but later he described its results as a shameful sham. Prior to 605 B. C. Jeremiah preached primarily messages of doom and forecast the advent of an enemy from the north. After 605 he explicitly named Babylon as the chosen agent of Judah's downfall. Following the first deportation of Judahites, Jeremiah also preached to those in exile, including also some messages of hope. During the final years of Jerusalem's siege Jeremiah's advice was to surrender to Babylon so that Jerusalem and many of its inhabitants would at least survive. And when things were blackest, Jeremiah's message of hope was heard by the desperate. Jeremiah remained with the survivors in Judah and continued preaching to them even when they took him forcibly to Egypt. The Book of Jeremiah is a selection of pertinent messages that Jeremiah addressed to specific historical situations which the nation and people of Judah faced in that age. These messages must be understood in the light of those historical conditions.

*Interpreting Jeremiah*

The interpretation of a prophetic book like that of Jeremiah is not a simple task. It is one thing for us to read the words of the text and quite another to know precisely what they meant for the audience Jeremiah was addressing. Still another consideration is the import and meaning of these passages in the light of God's New Testament Word. How, then, is the reader to study Jeremiah so that he will remain faithful to the intent of the prophet and the message of God from Jeremiah? The following procedure is offered as a simple guideline. It does not profess to cover all of the possible phases of Biblical interpretation.

First, using the divisional units given in the outline of this commentary, read a section of the text of Jeremiah several times. These units represent a logical or formal division in the original text.

Second, determine, if possible, who is speaking, whom the speaker is addressing, and the specific historical, social, political, or religious situation to which he is addressing his message. Wherever possible, this information will be given in the commentary, even though there is sometimes room for difference of opinion. The preceding summary of "The Times of Jeremiah" is designed to aid the reader in this phase of studying Jeremiah. Since the materials of Jeremiah are not arranged in chronological order, the reader must not assume that adjacent sections are necessarily from the same period. John Bright's *History of Israel* is one of the best works for studying the background of the prophetic period.

Third, ascertain the kind of literature or literary formulation involved. Poetry and poetic language must be read differently than simple prose narrative. When the text reads, "I am making my words in your mouth a fire" (5:14), the poetic imagery is obvious, and the words are not taken literally. Within the general categories of prose and poetry there are numerous other kinds of literature represented in the prophets. Biographical summaries, autobiographical notes, prose sermons, letters, and historiography are among the prose forms found. The oracle is perhaps the most common form among the poetic materials. The oracle is a divine utterance which the prophet as the spokesman and messenger of God announces publicly in the name of his God. Such oracles are often relatively short messages that may be introduced by the formula "Thus says the Lord" and concluded by a corresponding fixed expression, "says the Lord" (e. g., Jer. 2:2-3). These formulas, however, are often absent. In many cases a number of oracles will be combined either in a loose collection or as part of a larger literary unit. The commentary takes these literary features into account where they are of special relevance for understanding a passage.

Fourth, search the passage in question for terms or expressions that seem to have some major importance or some kind of significant history behind them. Thus

17

if the writer is using a lament psalm to express his message, the worship life of Israel may provide valuable background information for understanding the text. If the prophet mentions the covenant, the exodus, or Baal, for example, he is using expressions that have a long history behind them and are loaded with important religious overtones. At times it will be necessary to search among the customs and literature of the ancient Near Eastern world to discern the implications of a certain passage. At other times parallel references elsewhere in the Old Testament will clarify the intent of a verse as the text of the commentary testifies.

Fifth, in the light of the above, determine the primary point the prophet wishes to make. The reader should then ask how this particular message fits into the total message of Jeremiah and into the testimony of Scripture in general. Is there a corresponding New Testament word that affirms, interprets, or in some way fulfills the particular oracle of Jeremiah being read? By studying a passage in connection with its New Testament counterpart, a richer meaning can be gained (see the discussion on pages 24 – 26). At a number of crucial points the corresponding New Testament word is given in the text of the commentary.

In the last analysis it is only through his personal faith that the Christian reader can appropriate the word of the prophet as being valid. The mystery of God speaking in the prophetic message must still be affirmed through the prompting of His Spirit, who guides us into all truth. By the work of that Spirit the prophetic Word will speak to the needs of the listening Christian reader.

*The Book Called Jeremiah*

In studying Jeremiah it is also helpful to know

something of the composition and probable growth of this work. For the Book of Jeremiah seems to be far more than a simple collection of oracles that Jeremiah wrote down in an obvious chronological arrangement. The growth of a Biblical book such as Jeremiah is illustrated admirably by the evidence Jeremiah affords. We have commented on the forceful way in which Jeremiah insisted that he was one of the genuine prophets of God to whom the Word came. And men of faith acknowledge the truth of this mystery. Another striking fact is the way in which God employed the various processes of history to create the Biblical Book of Jeremiah, which records the works and words of Jeremiah. To appreciate the growth of the Book of Jeremiah, the following outline of its structure may prove useful:

| | |
|---|---|
| Editorial Preface | – 1:1-3 |
| Scroll No. 1 | – 1:4 – 25:13 |
| Biographical Records | – 25:14 – 29:32 |
| Scroll No. 2 | – 30:1 – 33:26 |
| Biographical Records | – 34:1 – 45:5 |
| Scroll No. 3 | – 46:1 – 51:64 |
| Appendix | – 52:1-34 |

Jeremiah begins with an editorial preface stating that the materials of the book date from the call of Jeremiah to the fall of Jerusalem in 587 B. C. Portions of the book, however, stem from a date after 587 B. C. Apparently this preface was added before the final stage of the book's growth. Scroll No. 1 is mentioned in 25:13. It contained primarily oracles of judgment. 25:1 dates this scroll in 605 B. C., which is the same date as that given for the scroll read to Jehoiakim (36:1-3). Presumably they are one and the same scroll. However, not all of Jer. 1 – 25 could have been a part of that

19

scroll, since some of the material in Jer. 1–25 is later than 605 B. C. (see 21:1 and 24:1). It would seem, therefore, that there were additions made to the first scroll from time to time. Scroll No. 2 is referred to in 30:2. Its contents are described as words of hope and restoration. This scroll is therefore often alluded to as the little book of comfort. The extent of this book is not specified, but the content of Chs. 30–33 fits the preface description of 30:1-3. Jeremiah 30–33, therefore, seems to have been a separate scroll embracing primarily oracles of hope. A third scroll of oracles is found in Chapters 46–51. The topic of these oracles is the foreign nations. Once again they are arranged not chronologically but topically. The biographical records between these three scrolls are almost entirely prose narratives reporting about Jeremiah's activity. These records are more chronological in their sequence than the poetic materials of the three scrolls. Inasmuch as Baruch was Jeremiah's personal scribe and knew the details of Jeremiah's life intimately, many believe that Baruch is the author of these records about Jeremiah and that he was the person who collected the materials of Jeremiah to preserve them. Jer. 51:64 states that the words of Jeremiah end at that point. The Appendix of Jer. 52, therefore, seems to be a later addition by another author. A glance at 2 Kings 24:18–25:30 reveals that the majority of Jer. 52 is word for word identical with the text of 2 Kings at that point. This evidence suggests that some scribe copied from Kings (or a common source also used by the writer of Kings) in order to carry forward the story of the fate of Judah in exile, some features of which took place after Jeremiah was taken into Egypt as an old man. Here and there the text seems to indicate that some oracles of the book

are the inspired work of prophets later than Jeremiah
(e. g., 33:14-26), although the evidence of the texts in
question can sometimes be argued two ways. Of special
interest is the fact that the order of the scrolls we have
isolated in the Hebrew text (which the RSV follows)
differs from that in the Greek text of the Septuagint
translation. This fact suggests that the various scrolls
of Jeremiah existed separately before they were put
into one large collection of scrolls. In any case the above
discussion illustrates briefly some of the features of the
Book of Jeremiah that indicate its structure and how
its broad features developed. The arrangement of the
smaller units of poetry and prose within the various
chapters of each scroll or biographical record requires
a detailed analysis that cannot be pursued here. The
reader is asked, however, to watch the divisional head-
ings of the commentary and to search for signs within
each division that suggest that a particular section is
a self-contained unit and must be interpreted as such.
For in some cases a specific unit may have had no
original connection with its present context.

In short, when a Christian reader approaches a book
like Jeremiah, he will naturally acknowledge the mysterious element of God's involvement in the entire process of imparting and preserving the text of Scripture.
At the same time he will not blind his eyes to the evidence of historical situations and processes that are
normal in the compilation of an ancient work of this
nature. The reader who wishes to hear the text speak
to him must be ready to accept all the elements of the
text as God-given directives for appreciating its character and message. Some will be introduced to the name
Yahweh for the first time in this book. Yahweh is the
name of God revealed to Moses in Ex. 6:3 and used

21

regularly by Jeremiah and the prophets. This name is rendered LORD in the RSV. For variation the expressions God, Lord, and Yahweh are used in this commentary. The term Israel also calls for comment. It is often used in Jeremiah and this commentary in the traditional sense of God's chosen people even when the inhabitants of the southern kingdom of Judah are involved.

*The Message of Jeremiah*

In analyzing the various portions of Jeremiah, it is also valuable to relate the individual concerns of the text to the wider context of Jeremiah's theology and thereby gain a deeper appreciation of his preaching. Jeremiah's message involved more than Judah's fate. His word was spoken to change the course of history, "to pluck up and to break down, to build and to plant," the kingdoms of the world (1:10). Nevertheless, his message also addresses us, and as men of faith we dare not escape and cannot ignore his insistence on sin, judgment, and grace as three sharp and relentless forces that shape our lives before God. He calls us to recognize these forces as vividly in our own history and society as he did in his.

The Book of Jeremiah confronts the reader with a wide range of ideas and concerns. From this wealth of material a number of overriding considerations need to be recognized in order to grasp the central import of Jeremiah's proclamation. Jeremiah begins with the discovery that none of God's people are righteous and faithful to the ancient covenant Israel made with Yahweh (5:1-5). He describes this unfaithfulness especially in terms of husband-wife relations. He repeatedly appeals to Judah to repent (4:1-4) but dejectedly admits that the sin of God's people is so deeply ingrained in their character that nothing can help them (17:1-4; 13:23). The entire life of the Israelite nation has become a mere sham; hypocrisy has become second nature to her people. Her prophets are sham prophets and her leaders blatant hypocrites. Judah felt secure because of her many religious institutions and traditions. The temple, the ark, the chosen city, the Davidic dynasty, the priesthood, the Sinai covenant, the election of Israel as God's people, and so forth, were seen as automatic guarantees of God's eternal grace and protection in the promised land. Jeremiah's message challenged this delusion. Israel's repeated rebelliousness meant that her people had forfeited all God's gifts and forbearance. They had become so corrupt they could not change. Total doom and complete destruction was the inevitable course of divine action. Yahweh would break Judah and Jerusalem so that they could not be mended (19:11). Even the intercessions of Moses and Samuel would prove futile in that situation (15:1). God's people would have to acknowledge God as God in and through His wrath. There was no alternative. Those who wanted to save their lives when the day of wrath came were advised to submit to God's directives on that day and surrender to the enemy.

The Babylonians were designated as the divinely ordained agent of Yahweh's condemning activity against His people. Nebuchadnezzar is the servant of Yahweh Himself (25:9). This judgment is described in a great panorama of poetic imagery. One passage even describes that horrible day as a return to the world of that chaos and darkness which existed before the creation of light on the first day (4:23-28). In such imagery we must guard against an overly literal understanding of

23

the wording and learn to capture the mood of the prophetic spokesman as he dramatizes the future. The message of Jeremiah does not mitigate the force of Yahweh's anger in judgment. As a nation Judah was destroyed, and as a religious community the people were forced to reevaluate all the institutions and traditions they cherished. Some people survived, purely by the grace of God. This remnant was not more righteous than those who died or were deported (24:8-10). Jeremiah, however, declared an unbelievable future for these survivors. God's undeserved love stimulated a new beginning. God was willing to start again with the "refuse silver" known as Israel. His love was prompted not by any repentance that Israel had wrought by itself but by Yahweh's own pangs of heart (31:20) and because He Himself was willing to implant in His hard-hearted people a new heart (24:7) and to heal their wounds (30:17). The day of Israel's re-creation is described in terms of her glorious past. That day would be tantamount to a repetition of the great exodus experiences of the past (31:1-6). At that time a new David would arise to rule the new age in peace and prosperity (23:5-6). Yahweh would establish a new covenant with His people, in which the liberating power of forgiveness would so transform the lives of men that all would have first-hand knowledge of Yahweh and obedience to His will would be spontaneous and natural (31:31-34). The exile over, life would return to normal again. (32:9-15)

The content and form of Jeremiah's message is governed largely by the situation and traditions of his audience. God spoke to them in terms of their needs and their language. This is true also of the hopes and promises of Jeremiah. Thus we read of "vineyards upon the mountains of Samaria" (31:5), a reunion of Judah and Israel (31:27), or an unbroken line of Levitical priests (33:18). The New Testament asserts that the Old Testament promises of God find their true fulfillment in the person and work of Jesus Christ. These promises need not only be understood in the narrow sense of a prediction, nor do they imply that all possible ways of fulfillment were made clear to the hearers of Jeremiah. Fulfillment can be seen as the outcome of God's plan for saving mankind through His reign in Jesus Christ. The promises of God were powerful words that propelled the redemptive program of God forward. The advent of Jesus Christ is the goal, climax, fulfillment, and center of that saving plan, or program, of God which extended through centuries of complex history and traditions. Both the giving of the ark of the covenant and the promise of its disappearance in favor of better things were part of that plan (3:16). This promise of God's perfect rule through a true Israel was an essential part of Israel's faith that was vindicated in the coming of Jesus Christ. According to Heb. 1:1-4, Jesus Christ is the final Word of God concerning man's salvation. The words of the prophets were messages along that way of salvation; they lead up to Him; they provide the setting and the situation for His coming; they are the saving Word from the past to which the New Testament Word corresponds in a variety of ways. Accordingly the New Testament application of a prophetic word to Jesus Christ may not always appear to correspond exactly to the literal sense of the prophet's words. The immediate fulfillment of an Old Testament hope may even seem to be bypassed by God in favor of fulfillment in His ultimate plan of redemption in Jesus Christ (e. g., 33:19-22). Yet the promises of a David whose rule would be perfect, a covenant where all

25

past ills would be eliminated, and a day when God's will would be known perfectly to Israel all reveal a dimension of hope implanted by God in His prophets that reaches beyond the immediate situation to a glorious new day of God. With the advent of Christ that day dawned. The promises of the prophets were the pre-dawn light. And just as the sun is far brighter than the beams that precede its rising, so the coming of Jesus made clear the true goal of the promises of the prophets. Jesus Christ came as the perfect David, as the Divine Mediator of the new covenant, as the eternal High Priest, as the true Israel of God, and as the Suffering Prophet far greater than Jeremiah. Jeremiah testifies to this plan of God in terms of his distinctive message of sin, judgment, and promise for the chosen people of God.

*Bibliographical Aids*

Volume 12 of the *Layman's Bible Commentary* (Richmond: John Knox Press, 1960) is by Howard Kuist and treats the Book of Jeremiah in a manner similar to this commentary. Perhaps the best recent introduction to Jeremiah is found in the commentary on Jeremiah by John Bright in the *Anchor Bible Series* (Garden City: Doubleday, 1965). The commentary on Jeremiah by Elmer Leslie (Nashville: Abingdon, 1954), now in paperback, treats the oracles of Jeremiah according to their chronological sequence. Leslie considers many oracles to be later than Jeremiah's time. *The Book of Jeremiah* (New York: Macmillan, 1960), by H. Cunliffe-Jones, also provides a profitable discussion of selected oracles and difficulties in Jeremiah. A fine topical discussion of the issues of Jeremiah is to be found in a somewhat older work entitled *Jeremiah:*

*His Time and His Work* (Oxford: Blackwell, 1951) by Adam Welch. The traditional conservative approach to the interpretation of Jeremiah is illustrated in the commentary of Theo. Laetsch, published by Concordia Publishing House, St. Louis, in 1952. This work is packed with rich exegetical and theological insights. For more technical articles and works the reader is directed to the article and bibliography of James Muilenburg on Jeremiah in *The Interpreter's Dictionary of the Bible* (Nashville: Abingdon, 1962).

27

# OUTLINE

29

# A Historical Preface

## Jeremiah 1:1-3

¹ The words of Jeremiah, the son of Hilki'ah, of the priests who were in An'athoth in the land of Benjamin, ² to whom the word of the LORD came in the days of Josi'ah the son of Amon, king of Judah, in the thirteenth year of his reign. ³ It came also in the days of Jehoi'akim the son of Josi'ah, king of Judah, and until the end of the eleventh year of Zedeki'ah, the son of Josi'ah, king of Judah, until the captivity of Jerusalem in the fifth month.

The preface to the Book of Jeremiah is a concise superscription to a collection of the "words" or preaching of the prophet Jeremiah delivered prior to the captivity of Jerusalem under Nebuchadnezzar in 587 B. C. Segments of the book clearly stem from a later date (Chs. 40 – 44, for example). Jer. 51:64 marks the end of another collection of Jeremiah's works. The probable editor of the preface is Jeremiah's secretary Baruch, who had previously been involved in the preservation of Jeremiah's sermons (see Ch. 36). This editor asserts

37

that Jeremiah was commissioned in 628 B. C., or 627, in the 13th year of the lauded King Josiah (cf. Jer. 22:15-16; 2 Kings 23:25), and pursued an active ministry under the revolting Jehoiakim (609 – 597 B. C.) and the vacillating puppet king Zedekiah (597 – 587 B. C.). The brief and insignificant reigns of Jehoahaz (609 B. C.) and Jehoiachin (597 B. C.) are not mentioned. There is no reason to believe that Jeremiah's father Hilkiah is identical with the famous priest who discovered the law book (2 Kings 22), for Jeremiah's family belonged to a colony of priests in Anathoth, some four miles north of Jerusalem. The probable ancestors of these priests were deposed from official priestly duties in Jerusalem by King Solomon and banished to Anathoth (1 Kings 2:26). Jeremiah's priestly heritage may help to explain the pungency of some of the prophet's oracles against the professional religious classes in Jerusalem. The main point of this preface, however, is to stress that Jeremiah was inspired by God, or as the editor puts it, that the Word of Yahweh came to Jeremiah in a specific historical era. In the subsequent call narrative Jeremiah explains this experience in his own words.

# The Account of the Call of Jeremiah

## Jeremiah 1:4-19

### GOD CALLS JEREMIAH AS A PROPHET    1:4-10

<sup>4</sup> Now the word of the LORD came to me saying,
<sup>5</sup> "Before I formed you in the womb I knew you,
and before you were born I consecrated you;
I appointed you a prophet to the nations."
<sup>6</sup> Then I said, "Ah, Lord GOD! Behold, I do not know
how to speak, for I am only a youth." <sup>7</sup> But the LORD
said to me,
"Do not say, 'I am only a youth';
for to all to whom I send you you shall go,
and whatever I command you you shall speak.
<sup>8</sup> Be not afraid of them,
for I am with you to deliver you,
                              says the LORD."
<sup>9</sup> Then the LORD put forth his hand and touched my
mouth; and the LORD said to me,
"Behold, I have put my words in your mouth.
<sup>10</sup> See, I have set you this day over nations and over
    kingdoms,

39

to pluck up and to break down,
to destroy and to overthrow,
to build and to plant."

The call of a prophet was a singular experience. The prophet thereby sensed a driving compulsion from his God to act as He directed regardless of the consequences. The account of Jeremiah's call follows a pattern common to the calls of great men of God such as Moses (Ex. 3:1-12), Gideon (Judg. 6:11-18), or Isaiah (Is. 6:1-13). According to this pattern God first confronts the chosen individual with the appropriate means of revelation. In the case of Jeremiah this means is the Word. "The word of the Lord came to me" is an assertion that the will of his God Yahweh penetrated and controlled the mind of the prophet. Yahweh thereupon defines the precise relationship of the called man to his God. Jeremiah was molded as though God the Creator were a potter at work in his mother's womb. There and then God personally selected him and reserved him for His own use. Three verbs in v. 5 call for comment: "form" is used in Gen 2:7 to describe God molding man as a potter would a vessel (cf. Jer. 18:1-4), and in Is. 49:1 a special call "from the womb" is affirmed; "know" may refer to God's intimate choice of someone (Gen. 18:19); and "consecrate" means setting apart for a peculiar purpose. The task or commission of the individual follows next in the call pattern. Jeremiah is given the unenviable role of "prophet to the nations." He, like Moses, Gideon, and others before him, registers his objections to God's commission. He insists that his youth and lack of experience as a public speaker make him ineligible for the job. In line with the usual call pattern, the reply of God rejects the prophet's excuses and promises him the ability, authority, protection, and courage he needs to act as God's instrument. This answer is reinforced in the prophet's mind by a mysterious awareness of the Creator's hand making contact with his own lips. Jeremiah can hear God saying, "Whatever I command you you shall speak," and "I have put my words in your mouth." These words are a direct assurance that he is in the succession of true prophets like Moses, for these words fulfill the promise of Deut. 18:18. The final verse of the call is rather staggering. Jeremiah must now realize that the word which he speaks will not only affect him and his people but will have the inherent power to change the course of history, to destroy nations and to rebuild them. Moreover, Jeremiah has been officially appointed to this task, as the Hebrew for "set over" implies. He has the royal authority of Yahweh the King.

## VISIONS CONFIRMING JEREMIAH'S
## CALL AND MESSAGE                                    1:11-19

¹¹ And the word of the LORD came to me, saying, "Jeremiah, what do you see?" And I said, "I see a rod of almond." ᵃ ¹² Then the LORD said to me, "You have seen well, for I am watching ᵇ over my word to perform it."

¹³ The word of the LORD came to me a second time, saying, "What do you see?" And I said, "I see a boiling pot, facing away from the north." ¹⁴ Then the LORD said to me, "Out of the north evil shall break forth upon all the inhabitants of the land. ¹⁵ For, lo, I am calling all the tribes of the kingdoms of the north, says the LORD; and they shall come and every one

ᵃ Heb shaqed   ᵇ Heb shoqed

shall set his throne at the entrance of the gates of Jerusalem, against all its walls round about, and against all the cities of Judah. <sup>16</sup> And I will utter my judgments against them, for all their wickedness in forsaking me; they have burned incense to other gods, and worshiped the works of their own hands. <sup>17</sup> But you, gird up your loins; arise, and say to them everything that I command you. Do not be dismayed by them, lest I dismay you before them. <sup>18</sup> And I, behold, I make you this day a fortified city, an iron pillar, and bronze walls, against the whole land, against the kings of Judah, its princes, its priests, and the people of the land. <sup>19</sup> They will fight against you; but they shall not prevail against you, for I am with you, says the **LORD**, to deliver you."

A call is often followed by omens from God designed to confirm the individual's conviction that God has spoken to him in a special way (see Ex. 3:12; Judg. 6:17; Ezek. 2:9 ff.). God's outstretched hand touching his lips was one such sign. Aroused by the Word of God, Jeremiah also becomes aware of additional experiences that confirm his call as a prophet. He first sees an almond rod. If one of us had seen that rod, it would probably have been of no significance. Jeremiah, however, becomes conscious of a deeper meaning in what he sees. This meaning is revealed through a play on words. The Hebrew word for almond is *shaqed* (see the footnote in the RSV). This word immediately suggests an almost identical Hebrew word *shoqed* which means "on the alert" or "on the watch." The prophet now understands the divine clue. God is "on the alert" to insure that His Word will come to pass. Another clue may also be implied in this vision. Inasmuch as the sign is a rod and not merely a branch, it suggests that the Word which God is watching is one of judgment (cf. Num. 17:10) just as it is in the symbol of the pot, which follows. That these visions were seen immediately after the call of Jeremiah, however, is not demanded by the context.

The "boiling pot" was an ominous sign that God's stringent judgments against His wayward people would soon pour out from the north. The north was that quarter from which hostile armies frequently invaded Palestine. This impending evil from the north is defined as a calamity that will befall Jerusalem. It will be as though various nations from the north assemble for a trial in Jerusalem to hear and execute God's verdicts of judgment against His own people. Such an omen was enough to scare a seasoned prophet, to say nothing of a hesitant young priest. God therefore repeats His commission to preach whatever He commands and renews His promise of unlimited protection under attack. Jeremiah would be impregnable like a well-fortified city.

# A Presentation of God's Case Against His People

## Jeremiah 2:1 – 4:4

The authoritative character of the material in this division of the book is underscored by the repeated expression "says the Lord." The principal theme of these oracles is the divine reproach of God's people for having broken covenant with Yahweh, their Overlord, through numerous evils. International alliances and marriages led to a false trust in alien powers and the public acknowledgment of the pagan deities from the nations concerned (cf. 2:18). Various forms of Baal worship with their array of fertility rites had again become popular. The insidious corruption of idolatry had even infected the professional religious classes (2:8). Many vile practices of this era removed by the reform of Josiah (621 B. C.), which was based on the "book of the law" discovered in the temple, are described in 2 Kings 22 – 23. In general the perverse days that preceded that reform seem to provide the grievous situation presupposed by the various units of Ch. 2. Egypt and Assyria, rather than Babylon, are the powers with which Israel is concerned (2:18). Most of the oracles in 3:1 – 4:4, however, were probably delivered soon after the reform of Josiah, which seems to be alluded to in 3:4 and 3:10. In addition the strong element of hope in these oracles may indicate a relatively early date before Jeremiah became aware of the inevitability of Judah's doom because of her inability to repent.

## GOD'S COURTSHIP OF HIS PEOPLE          2:1-3

¹ The word of the LORD came to me, saying,
² "Go and proclaim in the hearing of Jerusalem,
Thus says the LORD,
  I remember the devotion of your youth,
    your love as a bride,
  how you followed me in the wilderness,
    in a land not sown.
³ Israel was holy to the LORD,
    the first fruits of his harvest.
  All who ate of it became guilty;
    evil came upon them,

                              says the LORD."


This oracle is a touching portrait of the moving love Yahweh still fosters for the people He must condemn. One already senses here a deep anguish in the heart of Yahweh. He recalls how He first selected Israel as His chosen people in the days of the wilderness wanderings (cf. Hos. 9:10). Despite the repeated unfaithfulness of this people in the desert (for example, Num. 25), God remembers Israel's responsive days. Israel was His bride, precious and sacred. Any who dared to touch this bride were answerable to Yahweh. Like Hosea, Jeremiah employed the image of the marriage relation to express that intimate bond or covenant which Yahweh

45

had established with His people Israel (cf. Hos. 1–3). Israel, alas, had broken this bond and forgotten God's love. But God remembered—with pain.

## GOD'S COURT CASE AGAINST HIS PEOPLE 2:4-13

⁴ Hear the word of the LORD, O house of Jacob, and all the families of the house of Israel. ⁵ Thus says the LORD:
"What wrong did your fathers find in me
    that they went far from me,
and went after worthlessness, and became worth-
    less?
⁶ They did not say, 'Where is the LORD
    who brought us up from the land of Egypt,
who led us in the wilderness,
    in a land of deserts and pits,
in a land of drought and deep darkness,
    in a land that none passes through,
    where no man dwells?'
⁷ And I brought you into a plentiful land
    to enjoy its fruits and its good things.
But when you came in you defiled my land,
    and made my heritage an abomination.
⁸ The priests did not say, 'Where is the LORD?'
    Those who handle the law did not know me;
the rulers ᶜ transgressed against me;
    the prophets prophesied by Ba'al,
    and went after things that do not profit.
⁹ "Therefore I still contend with you,
                                    says the LORD,
    and with your children's children I will contend.

ᶜ Heb *shepherds*

46

¹⁰ For cross to the coasts of Cyprus and see,
   or send to Kedar and examine with care;
   see if there has been such a thing.
¹¹ Has a nation changed its gods,
   even though they are no gods?
 But my people have changed their glory
   for that which does not profit.
¹² Be appalled, O heavens, at this,
   be shocked, be utterly desolate,

                              says the LORD,
¹³ for my people have committed two evils:
   they have forsaken me,
 the fountain of living waters,
   and hewed out cisterns for themselves,
 broken cisterns,
   that can hold no water.


A number of Biblical writers use the setting of a court trial to express God's oracles of reproof against His people Israel (e. g., Deut. 32; Micah 6:1-8). The charge is usually that of breaking God's covenant. Jeremiah first summons all the families of Israel to hear the proceedings. God is the plaintiff. He begins by challenging His people to demonstrate where He had failed to keep His part of the covenant agreement so that Israel was free to chase worthless husbands. (For the covenant commitment of Israel, see, for example, Deut. 30:15-20.) The blame is on one side only. God is astonished that former Israelites did not even inquire about the key acts of salvation, which provided the basis for the covenant and which were designed to evoke Israel's response of love and obedience to Yahweh as the covenant Overlord. In addition Israel had polluted God's

47

good land. Its leaders had ignored God's will. Its prophets had followed worthless gods, which led to futility. God therefore insists that He will press His case. "Contend" in verse 9 is used as a technical term for pressing one's case in court. God maintains further that the crime of Israel would amaze even the heathen. From Cyprus in the west to Kedar in the east no nation had exchanged gods the way Israel did. Israel traded the incomparable God for worthless images. The heavens, who had been witnesses of the ancient covenant treaty with Israel (Deut. 30:19), are now called upon to register their dismay. The verdict is clear: Israel has broken covenant with the living God and has made a pact with artificial and useless substitutes.

## THE INEVITABLE CURSES OF APOSTASY 2:14-19

14 "Is Israel a slave? Is he a homeborn servant?
   Why then has he become a prey?
15 The lions have roared against him,
   they have roared loudly.
 They have made his land a waste;
   his cities are in ruins, without inhabitant.
16 Moreover, the men of Memphis and Tah′panhes
   have broken the crown of your head.
17 Have you not brought this upon yourself
   by forsaking the LORD your God,
   when he led you in the way?
18 And now what do you gain by going to Egypt,
   to drink the waters of the Nile?
 Or what do you gain by going to Assyria,
   to drink the waters of the Euphra′tes?
19 Your wickedness will chasten you,
   and your apostasy will reprove you.

> Know and see that it is evil and bitter
>    for you to forsake the LORD your God;
> the fear of me is not in you,
>                says the Lord GOD of hosts.

These verses seem to continue the message and style begun in vv. 1-3. Through the exodus from Egypt God had chosen Israel as His firstborn son (cf. Ex. 4:22). His sad fate, however, makes him appear to be no better than a slave. Israel's broken crown (v. 16) is indicative of another curse at the hand of Egypt. Apostasy brings its own curses, and evil has a way of destroying its own servants. Israel, too, must realize that the curses attendant upon the original covenant treaty with God (cf. Deut. 27:15-26) would effect Israel's own downfall if the people persisted in breaking their pact with Yahweh by making futile political alliances with Egypt and Assyria, the two major world powers of the day (v. 18). Israel's bitter end would be its own fault. Verse 15 suggests a recent onslaught by foreign powers (lions, cf. 4:7). This oracle may originally have applied to the humiliation of the Northern Kingdom of Israel at the hands of Assyria, but it would also have been appropriate for the people of God in Judah. Both Israel and Judah were vassals of Assyria at various times.

## THE DEPTH OF THE PERVERSITY
## OF GOD'S PEOPLE                              2:20-37

20 "For long ago you broke your yoke
     and burst your bonds;
     and you said, 'I will not serve.'
 Yea, upon every high hill
     and under every green tree
     you bowed down as a harlot.

49

²¹ Yet I planted you a choice vine,
    wholly of pure seed.
How then have you turned degenerate
    and become a wild vine?
²² Though you wash yourself with lye
    and use much soap,
    the stain of your guilt is still before me,
                        says the Lord GOD.

²³ How can you say, 'I am not defiled,
    I have not gone after the Ba′als'?
Look at your way in the valley;
    know what you have done —
a restive young camel interlacing her tracks,
²⁴     a wild ass used to the wilderness,
in her heat sniffing the wind!
    Who can restrain her lust?
None who seek her need weary themselves;
    in her month they will find her.
²⁵ Keep your feet from going unshod
    and your throat from thirst.
But you said, 'It is hopeless,
    for I have loved strangers,
    and after them I will go.'

²⁶ "As a thief is shamed when caught,
    so the house of Israel shall be shamed:
they, their kings, their princes,
    their priests, and their prophets,
²⁷ who say to a tree, 'You are my father,'
    and to a stone, 'You gave me birth.'
For they have turned their back to me,
    and not their face.
But in the time of their trouble they say,
    'Arise and save us!'

50

<sup>28</sup> But where are your gods
   that you made for yourself?
 Let them arise, if they can save you,
   in your time of trouble;
 for as many as your cities
   are your gods, O Judah.
<sup>29</sup> "Why do you complain against me?
   You have all rebelled against me,
                    says the LORD.

<sup>30</sup> In vain have I smitten your children,
   they took no correction;
 your own sword devoured your prophets
   like a ravening lion.
<sup>31</sup> And you, O generation, heed the word of the LORD.
 Have I been a wilderness to Israel,
   or a land of thick darkness?
 Why then do my people say, 'We are free,
   we will come no more to thee'?
<sup>32</sup> Can a maiden forget her ornaments,
   or a bride her attire?
 Yet my people have forgotten me
   days without number.

<sup>33</sup> "How well you direct your course
   to seek lovers!
 So that even to wicked women
   you have taught your ways.
<sup>34</sup> Also on your skirts is found
   the lifeblood of guiltless poor;
 you did not find them breaking in.
   Yet in spite of all these things
<sup>35</sup> you say, 'I am innocent;
   surely his anger has turned from me.'

> Behold, I will bring you to judgment
>    for saying, 'I have not sinned.'
> [36] How lightly you gad about,
>    changing your way!
> You shall be put to shame by Egypt
>    as you were put to shame by Assyria.
> [37] From it too you will come away
>    with your hands upon your head,
> for the LORD has rejected those in whom you trust,
>    and you will not prosper by them.

**20-22** This unit embraces a series of oracles that employ a wide variety of vivid metaphors and images to underscore the total perversion of the lives of God's people. In the first oracle Jeremiah, in the name of his God, asserts that Israel has long been playing the religious harlot by flagrantly practicing the sexual aberrations of pagan fertility cults "under every green tree." The "high hill" and the "green tree" seem to refer to the Baal shrines with their sacred trees set upon chosen mounds or hills scattered throughout the land (cf. Deut. 12:2-3). Israel is next compared to a "choice vine" of God that has become wild and unmanageable (cf. Hos. 9:10). The evils of fertility worship have become so engrained in her character that they cannot be expunged. The sin of Israel is like an immovable stain.

**23-25** Maintaining the same general theme that idolatry is religious adultery, the prophet now describes God's people as a wild animal with an uncontrollable passion for sexual intercourse. By her own confession, "it is hopeless" for Israel to stop "loving" false gods. In the same breath she protests her innocence: "I am not defiled." The lot of Israel is pathetic indeed.

**26-28** Israel had even stooped to worshiping the

52

tree stump, the symbol of the female deity of the Canaanite fertility cult, and the stone pillar, the corresponding symbol of the male deity. By reversing this symbolism Jeremiah satirically depicts the responsible leaders of Israel addressing the tree stump as "my father" and the stone pillar as "my mother." On the day of retribution Israel will be caught redhanded, like a thief in the night. Her countless gods will be helpless then, and Yahweh will be deaf to her cries. Idolatry, insists Jeremiah, will prove the downfall of his people.

**29-32** Despite her rebelliousness Israel has the gall to press a case against Yahweh. The term "complain" renders the same Hebrew word as "contend" in 2:9 and carries a similar judicial connotation. All of God's salutary punishment and loving discipline had proved of no avail. His prophetic agents of correction had been murdered. In imagery reminiscent of 2:2-3 above, Jeremiah depicts God as a husband pleading with his wife. "Am I a wilderness to be shunned by men?" God asks. "Can a loving bride forget the cherished symbols of her status as a newly married woman?" Painfully God remembers, but Israel forgets time and time again. Israel lives as though she were no longer married to Yahweh.

**33-37** Jeremiah develops the same theme by affirming that Israel has become a true professional in the art of religious harlotry. She can even teach wicked women a thing or two; she can exploit the innocent poor in the process and smugly retort, "I am innocent." God in turn will not ignore her flippant ways but has designated Egypt, one of her political "lovers," to put her to shame, just as He had previously humiliated her by defeat at the hands of Assyria (see, for example, 2 Chron. 28: 16-20). The ways of Israel seemed unchangeable, and the fate of the nation seemed sealed.

## God's Disgust at the Sham
## Repentance of His People                    3:1-20

<sup>1</sup> "If<sup>d</sup> a man divorces his wife and she goes from
him
    and becomes another man's wife,
      will he return to her?
    Would not that land be greatly polluted?
    You have played the harlot with many lovers;
      and would you return to me?

                        says the **LORD**.
<sup>2</sup> Lift up your eyes to the bare heights, and see!
    Where have you not been lain with?
    By the waysides you have sat awaiting lovers
      like an Arab in the wilderness.
    You have polluted the land
      with your vile harlotry.
<sup>3</sup> Therefore the showers have been withheld,
      and the spring rain has not come;
    yet you have a harlot's brow,
      you refuse to be ashamed.
<sup>4</sup> Have you not just now called to me,
    'My father, thou art the friend of my youth—
<sup>5</sup> will he be angry for ever,
    will he be indignant to the end?'
    Behold, you have spoken,
      but you have done all the evil that you could."


<sup>6</sup> The **LORD** said to me in the days of King
Josi'ah: "Have you seen what she did, that faithless
one, Israel, how she went up on every high hill and
under every green tree, and there played the harlot?
<sup>7</sup> And I thought, 'After she has done all this she will

<sup>d</sup> Gk Syr: Heb *Saying, If*

return to me'; but she did not return, and her false sister Judah saw it. ⁸ She saw that for all the adulteries of that faithless one, Israel, I had sent her away with a decree of divorce; yet her false sister Judah did not fear, but she too went and played the harlot. ⁹ Because harlotry was so light to her, she polluted the land, committing adultery with stone and tree. ¹⁰ Yet for all this her false sister Judah did not return to me with her whole heart, but in pretense, says the LORD."

¹¹ And the LORD said to me, "Faithless Israel has shown herself less guilty than false Judah. ¹² Go, and proclaim these words toward the north, and say,
'Return, faithless Israel,

says the LORD.
I will not look on you in anger,
  for I am merciful,

says the LORD;
I will not be angry for ever.
¹³ Only acknowledge your guilt,
  that you rebelled against the LORD your God
  and scattered your favors among strangers under
    every green tree,
  and that you have not obeyed my voice,

says the LORD.
¹⁴ Return, O faithless children,

says the LORD;
  for I am your master;
I will take you, one from a city and two from a
    family,
  and I will bring you to Zion.
¹⁵ "'And I will give you shepherds after my own heart, who will feed you with knowledge and understanding. ¹⁶ And when you have multiplied and in-

55

creased in the land, in those days, says the **LORD**, they shall no more say, "The ark of the covenant of the **LORD**." It shall not come to mind, or be remembered, or missed; it shall not be made again. [17] At that time Jerusalem shall be called the throne of the **LORD**, and all nations shall gather to it, to the presence of the **LORD** in Jerusalem, and they shall no more stubbornly follow their own evil heart. [18] In those days the house of Judah shall join the house of Israel, and together they shall come from the land of the north to the land that I gave your fathers for a heritage.

[19] "'I thought
    how I would set you among my sons,
    and give you a pleasant land,
    a heritage most beauteous of all nations.
And I thought you would call me, My Father,
    and would not turn from following me.
[20] Surely, as a faithless wife leaves her husband,
    so have you been faithless to me, O house of
      Israel,
                says the **LORD**.'"

**1-5** This corpus of oracles develops the previous metaphor of Israel as the bride married to Yahweh through the covenant pact of Sinai. The initial reproach refers to an Israelite law that prohibited a divorced woman from returning to her former husband and remarrying him (Deut. 24:1-4). And yet God's bride, who has become a repulsive harlot by her obscene solicitation of false gods like an Arab waiting in ambush, now seeks a casual return to Yahweh, her Husband. "Return" is often a technical term for religious repentance and change of attitude. By this reproach Jeremiah insists that Israel's repentance was only superficial. Even the droughts sent by Yahweh to evoke repentance and to demonstrate the inefficacy of pagan rain gods had been wasted effort (cf. 14:1-10). God's bride had become hard and callous. While she had readily confessed God as "Father," that title which recalled God's election of ancient Israel as His chosen son, she had blithely sinned to her heart's content. This confession had been made "just now," according to the prophet. It apparently refers directly to the famous religious reforms of Josiah (621 B. C.), when all of Judah made a new covenant of allegiance to Yahweh (2 Kings 23:3). The people had made a mockery of repentance (3:1-5). The thought of this unit is continued in vv. 19 and 20, which may have been severed from v. 5 inadvertently.

**6-11** These verses reflect the same general theme and period as the previous reproach. Judah, the Southern Kingdom, to whom Jeremiah is preaching, makes a pair with her sister Israel, the Northern Kingdom. "Faithless" and "False" Jeremiah dubs these two sisters. God had divorced Israel in the north when He had permitted Assyria to take her captive in 722 B. C. (2 Kings 17). She, too, had been guilty of uninhibited harlotry, the worship of pagan gods. God expected that the divorce of her sister would bring Judah to her senses. But no, even Judah's ostensible repentance in the reform of King Josiah was only "in pretense." In a way Israel was "less guilty than Judah." She was at least consistent.

**12-14** Jeremiah senses that God is willing to employ any legitimate means possible to effect the repentance of Judah. The technique used in the following oracles seems designed to stimulate Judah's return by arousing her jealousy (cf. Rom. 10:19; 11:11). An urgent appeal is

57

extended to Israel, the traditional rival and divorced sister of Judah, to return home, to confess her sin of rebellion to Yahweh, her Husband, and to be reinstated as His bride in Jerusalem. The promise is tantamount to a new covenant: "I am your master," that is, your husband; "I will take you" from wherever the Assyrians have scattered you (see 2 Kings 17:6), and "I will bring you to Zion," My house. In the previous oracle Israel had been designated "less guilty" than Judah. Surely Judah would not take these overtures to Israel lying down.

**15-18** Suddenly the text soars into distant flights of hope. The prophet envisions a day when faithful shepherds, that is, kings or rulers, will govern Jerusalem wisely, when all Israelites will be faithful to Yahweh, when all nations will assemble at Jerusalem to worship Him, and when the kingdoms of Israel and Judah will be reunited. The situation is so idealistic that the prophet can even imagine dispensing with the ark of the covenant altogether. The ark had been an empty throne covering a chest for the deposit of sacred objects. It was located in the temple as a symbol of God's rule and advent (cf. Ex. 25:21-22; Deut. 31:26; 1 Sam. 4:4). In this perfect age God would rule in person with Jerusalem rather than the ark as His throne. The way to God via the old institutions of the cult will be eliminated. Perhaps the destruction of the ark at the fall of Jerusalem helped Jeremiah frame this hope. In terms of God's ultimate plan of redemption, this new age begins with the advent of the kingdom of God in Christ Jesus. As Hebrews, Chs. 5 – 10, asserts, Christ brings us directly into the presence of God. The Old Testament cult is now a thing of the past (3:15-20). For the comment on 3:19-20, see page 57 above.

58

## God's Pleading for the Sincere Repentance of His People 3:21 — 4:4

<sup>21</sup> A voice on the bare heights is heard,
the weeping and pleading of Israel's sons,
because they have perverted their way,
they have forgotten the LORD their God.
<sup>22</sup> "Return, O faithless sons,
I will heal your faithlessness."
"Behold, we come to thee;
for thou art the LORD our God.
<sup>23</sup> Truly the hills are a delusion,
the orgies on the mountains.
Truly in the LORD our God
is the salvation of Israel.
<sup>24</sup> "But from our youth the shameful thing has devoured all for which our fathers labored, their flocks and their herds, their sons and their daughters. <sup>25</sup> Let us lie down in our shame, and let our dishonor cover us; for we have sinned against the LORD our God, we and our fathers, from our youth even to this day; and we have not obeyed the voice of the LORD our God."

<sup>1</sup> "If you return, O Israel,

says the LORD,

to me you should return.
If you remove your abominations from my presence,
and do not waver,
<sup>2</sup> and if you swear, 'As the LORD lives,'
in truth, in justice, and in uprightness,
then nations shall bless themselves in him,
and in him shall they glory."

³ For thus says the LORD to the men of Judah
and to the inhabitants of Jerusalem:
"Break up your fallow ground,
    and sow not among thorns.
⁴ Circumcise yourselves to the LORD,
    remove the foreskin of your hearts,
    O men of Judah and inhabitants of Jerusalem;
lest my wrath go forth like fire,
    and burn with none to quench it,
    because of the evil of your doings."

The hope of Israel's repentance is not yet lost in
the prophet's preaching. He could still hear the distant voice of the true Israel, the conscience of his people, lamenting its waywardness (cf. Jer. 31:15). He
could hear the promise of God to heal its spiritual
ills. And he could hear Israel's confession of sins. The
"hills" and "mountains" have reference to the high
places of fertility worship, and "the shameful thing" is
a common designation of the Baal cult, which had repeatedly corrupted Israel from the time of "its youth."
(Cf. Num. 25:1-5; Hos. 9:10)

Such a confession of guilt, however, was not suf-
ficient. Hence there follows in 4:1-4 an urgent plea for
a genuine change of heart. Israel needed a rebirth;
it was not merely a question of turning from false gods
but of a total commitment to Yahweh, a reaffirmation
of the covenant that would make "truth, justice, and
uprightness" dominant in the people's lives. If this happened, Israel would fulfill its promised destiny as an
agent of blessing to other nations (cf. Gen. 12:1-3). Sincere repentance is further defined as a radical change
like ploughing fallow land, a new beginning similar to
the initiatory rite of circumcision whereby the Israelite

entered the covenant, and a painful inner experience that affects the heart of man (cf. Deut. 10:15-16; Rom. 2:25-29). For Jeremiah the heart was the symbol of man's inner religious self, where the ultimate battle of life was won or lost (cf. Jer. 4:14, 19; 17:1; 31:33). Without genuine repentance the wrath of God would burn like a fire against Israel.

# A Presentation of God's Warnings to His People

## Jeremiah 4:5 – 6:30

The materials in 4:5 – 6:30 seem to be an independent collection of sayings that revolve around two major issues: Israel's punishment through destruction and Jeremiah's progressive understanding of his task. The messages in 4:9-10, 19-22; 5:1-6, 14; 6:9-16, 28-30 all concern Jeremiah personally. He is deeply involved in the messages he must preach. What Jeremiah experiences through this involvement is also the word of Yahweh. Some of Jeremiah's tasks are as much for Jeremiah's own benefit as they are for Israel's. And yet Jeremiah relates these experiences. Thus we begin to understand how God speaks through the "discoveries" of the prophet. Jeremiah's words are at the same time Yahweh's words.

The agent of Jeremiah's message of punishment through destruction is the enemy from the north (4:5-7, 13-17; 5:15-17; 6:1-6, 22-23). This foe is vividly described as an ancient and cruel foreign nation with an efficient military force that can crush fortified cities. The description is only partially appropriate for the Scythian hordes that may have ravaged portions of Palestine during this general period. To identify the foe from the north with the Babylonian armies is much more likely in view of their chariot forces and siegework techniques (4:13; 6:6). Babylon arose as a world power in 626 B. C. and first invaded Palestine in 598 B. C. Other oracles from this collection suggest Jeremiah's reaction to Judah's hypocritical involvement in the reform of Josiah (2 Kings 22–23), which began in 621 B. C. (5:11, 21; 6:16-21). In general, therefore, this corpus of messages probably stems from the period between 620 and the death of King Josiah in 609. The experiences of 5:1-6 may have been somewhat earlier, but the prediction of punishment by exile in 5:18-19 seems to belong to a later stage in Jeremiah's preaching.

The years that followed the reform of Josiah were characterized by outward conformity and religious observances but inward corruption and rebellion. Thus very few flagrant social ills are isolated. Rather, Jeremiah accuses Judah of a total inner perversion of heart and of hypocritical allegiances. The words of the true prophet and the ancient law of the priest are not taken seriously. The religious leaders are content to give the people the comfortable answers they desire. Some have even defected from the covenant of Josiah's reform and turned to false gods. Because of this, Jeremiah announces that Yahweh has now rejected Judah as His people. But the people laugh in his face.

## GOD WILL BRING AN EVIL
## FROM THE NORTH                     4:5-18

⁵ Declare in Judah, and proclaim in Jerusalem, and say,

"Blow the trumpet through the land;
   cry aloud and say,
'Assemble, and let us go
   into the fortified cities!'
⁶ Raise a standard toward Zion,
   flee for safety, stay not,
for I bring evil from the north,
   and great destruction.
⁷ A lion has gone up from his thicket,
   a destroyer of nations has set out;
   he has gone forth from his place
to make your land a waste;
   your cities will be ruins
   without inhabitant.
⁸ For this gird you with sackcloth,
   lament and wail;
for the fierce anger of the LORD
   has not turned back from us."

⁹ "In that day, says the LORD, courage shall fail
both king and princes; the priests shall be appalled
and the prophets astounded." ¹⁰ Then I said, "Ah,
Lord GOD, surely thou hast utterly deceived this people and Jerusalem, saying, 'It shall be well with you';
whereas the sword has reached their very life."

¹¹ At that time it will be said to this people and
to Jerusalem, "A hot wind from the bare heights
in the desert toward the daughter of my people, not
to winnow or cleanse, ¹² a wind too full for this comes
for me. Now it is I who speak in judgment upon them."
¹³ Behold, he comes up like clouds,
   his chariots like the whirlwind;
his horses are swifter than eagles —
   woe to us, for we are ruined!

<sup>14</sup> O Jerusalem, wash your heart from wickedness,
   that you may be saved.
How long shall your evil thoughts
   lodge within you?
<sup>15</sup> For a voice declares from Dan
   and proclaims evil from Mount E'phraim.
<sup>16</sup> Warn the nations that he is coming;
   announce to Jerusalem,
"Besiegers come from a distant land;
   they shout against the cities of Judah.
<sup>17</sup> Like keepers of a field are they against her round
      about,
   because she has rebelled against me,
                              says the LORD.
<sup>18</sup> Your ways and your doings
   have brought this upon you.
This is your doom, and it is bitter;
   it has reached your very heart."


5-8 The opening message concerning the imminent foe from the north takes the form of a public alarm sounded in the ears of the complacent people of Judah and Jerusalem. Contrary to the ancient customs in a holy war, Judah is not summoned to fight, with Yahweh as the mighty warrior at its head (cf. Judg. 4:14-15, 7:15-18), but to flight for temporary safety, with Yahweh as the ultimate enemy at its heels. The immediate reason for this alarm is the oncoming catastrophe (evil) from the north (cf. 1:14), which Yahweh has set in motion. This catastrophe is a war of enormous proportions; everything will be demolished! The gift of Canaan, the promised land, will soon be taken back. And when that happens, Judah's current history will have come to a bitter end. In the face of such an unbelievable act of divine anger God's people have only one recourse: to weep!

**9-10** Why should it be so surprising and astonishing to the leaders of Judah that "that day," the day of the Lord, should be one of utter defeat instead of resounding victory (cf. Amos 5:18-19)? Because, in part at least, Judah had been led to expect otherwise. The popular prophets had been preaching the old hollow refrain, "Don't worry! All is well!" (cf. Micah 3:5; Jer. 8:10-11; 23:17). At this point Jeremiah cannot refrain from accusing God of deception for permitting this state of affairs to continue (cf. 20:7). Is Jeremiah's accusation valid?

**11-12** A periodic west wind was important for Judah to winnow its grain. On the impending day of judgment, however, Yahweh's final word would not be a favorable weather report for Judah. From across the "bare heights," where Judah had sought prosperity through the worship of false gods (3:2), Yahweh Himself would send a scorching east wind to bring aridity and death instead of fertility and life.

**13-18** After these two asides (9-12) concerning the character of the day of doom, the theme of the foe from the north is resumed. The prophet preaches as though God were a breathless messenger giving a vivid report of the onrushing foe. "We are ruined," He gasps. Immediately He urges the incredulous people to take the necessary safety measures — heartfelt repentance and reform. But the people remain apathetic and will not listen. "How long are you going to wait?" He screams. The enemy is on the border. The watchmen in the northern outposts of Dan have sighted him. Now he has been sighted further south in Mt. Ephraim. He is approaching rapidly. Hurry up and do something!

Now he is surrounding the cities of Judah nearby. It's only a matter of time before Jerusalem will fall. Now it's too late; she is besieged! And it is all your own fault, He concludes. Like a dreadful boomerang Judah's own "evil" deeds, carelessly flung from a corrupt breast and heart (v. 14) would soon return as "evil" calamities that reach their mark in that same heart (v. 18). For Jeremiah sin is an evil destructive force that man sets in motion but cannot control (cf. 2:19). The same Hebrew word "evil" is translated "wickedness" in v. 14 and "doom" in v. 18.

## GOD WILL DEVASTATE HIS LAND          4:19-31

19 My anguish, my anguish! I writhe in pain!
  Oh, the walls of my heart!
My heart is beating wildly;
  I cannot keep silent;
for I hear the sound of the trumpet,
  the alarm of war.
20 Disaster follows hard on disaster,
  the whole land is laid waste.
Suddenly my tents are destroyed,
  my curtains in a moment.
21 How long must I see the standard,
  and hear the sound of the trumpet?
22 "For my people are foolish,
  they know me not;
they are stupid children,
  they have no understanding.
They are skilled in doing evil,
  but how to do good they know not."

67

²³ I looked on the earth, and lo, it was waste and void;
   and to the heavens, and they had no light.
²⁴ I looked on the mountains, and lo, they were
      quaking,
   and all the hills moved to and fro.
²⁵ I looked, and lo, there was no man,
   and all the birds of the air had fled.
²⁶ I looked, and lo, the fruitful land was a desert,
   and all its cities were laid in ruins
   before the LORD, before his fierce anger.
²⁷ For thus says the LORD, "The whole land
shall be a desolation; yet I will not make a full end.
²⁸ For this the earth shall mourn,
   and the heavens above be black;
   for I have spoken, I have purposed;
   I have not relented nor will I turn back."


²⁹ At the noise of horseman and archer
   every city takes to flight;
   they enter thickets; they climb among rocks;
   all the cities are forsaken,
   and no man dwells in them.
³⁰ And you, O desolate one,
   what do you mean that you dress in scarlet,
      that you deck yourself with ornaments of gold,
      that you enlarge your eyes with paint?
   In vain you beautify yourself.
   Your lovers despise you;
      they seek your life.
³¹ For I heard a cry as of a woman in travail,
      anguish as of one bringing forth her first child,
   the cry of the daughter of Zion gasping for breath,
      stretching out her hands,
   "Woe is me! I am fainting before murderers."

**19-22** Although 4:19-22 may originally have been part of a separate lament of Jeremiah, it gains additional significance from its present context. The message of a devastated land (4:7) had rent Jeremiah's heart, but Jerusalem had neither listened nor tried to understand. The prophet, however, is emotionally involved in his message and cannot restrain himself. He must speak (cf. 20:8-9). The Hebrew equivalent for "my anguish" is "my bowels" or "my womb." The bowels as well as the heart are the seat of the emotions in Israelite thought. The last line of v. 19 gains further emphasis if read, as the Hebrew text suggests, "I myself," or "I personally," hear the sound of the trumpet. Jeremiah cannot just sit on the sidelines and watch or announce Israel's destruction. He is a participant. He himself hears the trumpet (cf. vv. 5-6) and lives through the agony of the battle (cf. vv. 13-17). He is a part of Israel. Thus he can even speak of "my tents" and "my curtains" (v. 20). But suddenly Yahweh is speaking of "my people" (v. 22). It would appear as though Jeremiah is a living example of the inner suffering of God, whose "bowels" also "beat wildly" according to 31:20 (where the same Hebrew terms are used). The cause of this divine anguish is that same dedication to "evil" (cf. 13:23), which had long prevented Israel from "knowing," that is, consciously experiencing, God's involvement in its daily life.

**23-28** Jeremiah's oracle of total devastation in 4:7 is further elaborated in the terms of an alarming vision in 4:23-26. The portrait of desolation now takes on worldwide, or cosmic, proportions, which reflect the language of the creation accounts of Gen. 1 and 2. After the creation week God looked, and lo, "it was very good" (Gen. 1:31). In Jeremiah the picture is reversed. Four times Jeremiah looks, and lo, there is chaos; the earth has returned to the original state of "waste and void" before "light" was created (Gen. 1:2-3), the mountains that reach to the very foundations of the universe have buckled; there is absolutely no life to be seen, and all signs of fertility or civilization have disappeared. Verses 27-28 provide the explanation. God will bring complete desolation upon His land. This desolation will be so horrifying that all of the universe will be sympathetically involved (cf. 12:11). The heavens and the earth will suffer with the land of God's people. It is the end for Judah; God will not "relent," that is, change His mind. He has spoken, and His message of damnation is absolute. It is precisely this message of total doom that His hardened people needed to hear. In the light of this consistent presentation of complete condemnation and destruction the brief words of v. 27b are regarded by many as a later insertion from the hand of a disciple of Jeremiah, who wished to soften the harsh message in the light of later historical developments or oracles of Jeremiah.

**29-31** The personal agony of the prophet (vv. 19-22) and the sympathetic agony of nature (vv. 23-28) are portents of the final agony of Zion herself. Jeremiah can "hear" her dying screams as well (cf. v. 19). In the hour of crisis, when the land is laid waste, all the other cities will flee — but not Zion. She will remain true to her character. She will wait in all her finery to welcome her murderers and expect to save herself by seducing them with her usual harlotrous devices. Her lovers are her political allies, and her harlotrous techniques her disgusting foreign policies (cf. 2:18). But the unsavory murder (stoning?) of Zion the harlot will spell the end of all her duplicity and faithlessness.

70

## GOD MUST DEVOUR HIS PEOPLE          5:1-19

[1] Run to and fro through the streets of Jerusalem,
   look and take note!
  Search her squares to see
   if you can find a man,
  one who does justice
   and seeks truth;
  that I may pardon her.
[2] Though they say, "As the LORD lives,"
   yet they swear falsely.
[3] O LORD, do not thy eyes look for truth?
  Thou hast smitten them,
   but they felt no anguish;
  thou hast consumed them,
   but they refused to take correction.
  They have made their faces harder than rock;
   they have refused to repent.

[4] Then I said, "These are only the poor,
   they have no sense;
  for they do not know the way of the LORD,
   the law of their God.
[5] I will go to the great,
   and will speak to them;
  for they know the way of the LORD,
   the law of their God."
  But they all alike had broken the yoke,
   they had burst the bonds.

[6] Therefore a lion from the forest shall slay them,
   a wolf from the desert shall destroy them.
  A leopard is watching against their cities,
   every one who goes out of them shall be torn in
    pieces;

71

because their transgressions are many,
their apostasies are great.

7 "How can I pardon you?
Your children have forsaken me,
and have sworn by those who are no gods.
When I fed them to the full,
they committed adultery
and trooped to the houses of harlots.
8 They were well-fed lusty stallions,
each neighing for his neighbor's wife.
9 Shall I not punish them for these things?
says the **LORD**;
and shall I not avenge myself
on a nation such as this?

10 "Go up through her vine-rows and destroy,
but make not a full end;
strip away her branches,
for they are not the **LORD'S.**
11 For the house of Israel and the house of Judah
have been utterly faithless to me,
says the **LORD.**
12 They have spoken falsely of the LORD,
and have said, 'He will do nothing;
no evil will come upon us,
nor shall we see sword or famine.
13 The prophets will become wind;
the word is not in them.
Thus shall it be done to them!'"

14 Therefore thus says the LORD, the God of hosts:
"Because they *e* have spoken this word,
behold, I am making my words in your mouth a fire,

*e* Heb *you*

and this people wood, and the fire shall devour
   them.
<sup>15</sup> Behold, I am bringing upon you
   a nation from afar, O house of Israel,
                                    says the **LORD**.
It is an enduring nation,
   it is an ancient nation,
a nation whose language you do not know,
   nor can you understand what they say.
<sup>16</sup> Their quiver is like an open tomb,
   they are all mighty men.
<sup>17</sup> They shall eat up your harvest and your food;
   they shall eat up your sons and your daughters;
they shall eat up your flocks and your herds;
   they shall eat up your vines and your fig trees;
your fortified cities in which you trust
   they shall destroy with the sword."

<sup>18</sup> "But even in those days, says the **LORD**, I will
not make a full end of you. <sup>19</sup> And when your people
say, 'Why has the **LORD** our God done all these things
to us?' you shall say to them, 'As you have forsaken
me and served foreign gods in your land, so you shall
serve strangers in a land that is not yours.'"


**1-6** The young prophet Jeremiah learns a disturbing
lesson about the real character of his audience. God
had once told Abraham that if he could find 10 righteous
men in Sodom, He would spare the city (Gen. 18:32).
Now God tells Jeremiah that if he can find one righteous
person in the city, He will spare Jerusalem. The prophet
searches anxiously among the "poor" and the "great."
His discovery is frightening. There are no righteous
people — only hypocrites who use God's name "falsely"

73

(v. 2), hardened sinners who "refuse to repent" (v. 3), and rebels who act like uncontrollable beasts (v. 5). The implications of this discovery are just as frightening. The era of patient discipline ("correction" v. 3) and repentance has passed, and the hour of judgment has come. Consequently it is only a matter of time before Judah's divinely commissioned destroyer, like some wild animal, attacks and devours God's people. Forgiveness seems to be completely out of the question. Jerusalem cannot be spared.

7-11 Yet God will not let this vital issue of forgiveness rest. Through Jeremiah we can see God wrestling with this crucial problem (cf. Hos. 6:4). "How can I pardon you?" "Shall I not punish them?" God asks. The religious evils in Judah that spark this divine reflection are once more described in terms of sexual license (see the comment on 2:20 ff.), and once again the verdict is an oracle of doom and annihilation. God's people, the choice vine Yahweh had tenderly planted (2:21; Is. 5:1-7), is to be stripped bare. Judah is no longer the chosen people of God. They do not belong to Yahweh any more (v. 10; Hos. 1:9). This assertion means that the old covenant with God's people has been terminated. Judah's history as God's people has come to an end. This verdict, moreover, applies equally to the "faithless" houses Israel and Judah, a concern that suggests the same historical period as that reflected in 3:6-11.

12-14 Verses 12-14 complete the oracle of judgment announced in v. 10. The reaction of God's people to Jeremiah's message of an "evil" from the north (4:6 and 5:15-17) was one not of sobriety but of scorn. The people had frivolously rejected his pronouncements as just so much empty "wind" rather than the authoritative "word" from God. The Hebrew word for "wind" is *ruach,* but it can also mean "the spirit" of God that moved the true prophets. The false prophets who claimed "the spirit" were really nothing but "windbags." "No evil will come upon us," the people retorted. This passage, in the context of this chapter, illustrates the truth that when God's people refuse to recognize the discipline, blessing, and serious word of God, this God brings disaster to make His presence felt. Jeremiah's word was to be the agent of this disaster in Israel (cf. 1:10). Ultimately his message would be more than "hot air." It would be a devouring "fire" from his mouth.

**15-17** The burning wrath of God's merciless judgment takes a concrete form in the ravenous foe from the north who will "devour" (RSV "eat") everything in sight. He even has the capacity to destroy fortified cities (v. 17). This feature of Jeremiah's characterization of the formidable ancient nation from the north is more appropriate for Babylon than for the marauding Scythians, who were not interested in siegeworks.

**18-19** In v. 19 we are confronted by a new element in the preaching of Jeremiah: punishment by exile. The message itself probably stems from a later period when Jeremiah discussed this subject at some length (e. g., Ch. 25). Elsewhere in Chs. 4 – 6 the oracles are all punishment by destruction. When the day of wrath comes, however, the punishment will fit the crime. For serving pagan gods Judah must serve pagan peoples! For the tempering message of v. 18 see the note on 4:27.

## GOD MUST PUNISH HIS REBELLIOUS PEOPLE 5:20-31

[20] Declare this in the house of Jacob,
  proclaim it in Judah:

75

21 "Hear this, O foolish and senseless people,
    who have eyes, but see not,
    who have ears, but hear not.
22 Do you not fear me? says the LORD;
    Do you not tremble before me?
I placed the sand as the bound for the sea,
    a perpetual barrier which it cannot pass;
though the waves toss, they cannot prevail,
    though they roar, they cannot pass over it.
23 But this people has a stubborn and rebellious
      heart;
    they have turned aside and gone away.
24 They do not say in their hearts,
    'Let us fear the LORD our God,
who gives the rain in its season,
    the autumn rain and the spring rain,
and keeps for us
    the weeks appointed for the harvest.'
25 Your iniquities have turned these away,
    and your sins have kept good from you.
26 For wicked men are found among my people;
    they lurk like fowlers lying in wait.[f]
They set a trap;
    they catch men.
27 Like a basket full of birds,
    their houses are full of treachery;
therefore they have become great and rich,
28     they have grown fat and sleek.
They know no bounds in deeds of wickedness;
    they judge not with justice
the cause of the fatherless, to make it prosper,
    and they do not defend the rights of the needy.

[f] Heb uncertain

²⁹ Shall I not punish them for these things?
                                                    says the LORD,
    and shall I not avenge myself
    on a nation such as this?"

³⁰ An appalling and horrible thing
    has happened in the land:
³¹ the prophets prophesy falsely,
    and the priests rule at their direction;
  my people love to have it so,
    but what will you do when the end comes?


20-25    The Biblical prophets utilized numerous
techniques to convey their divine messages. Although
he is addressed as a messenger in v. 20, Jeremiah's
oracle against the guilt of Israel is couched in the forms
used by a wisdom teacher. Like the wisdom teachers
of Proverbs, for example, he appeals to the analogy
of the laws of nature to make his point. He argues from
the laws of creation to the lawlessness of his people
(cf. comment on 8:4-7). If the chaotic and turbulent sea
obeys the decrees of Yahweh, how much more rebellious and chaotic must the house of Jacob be (v. 22)?
If the annual rains refuse to fall, it must be due to
Judah's astonishing sinfulness (v. 24 f.). Judah is therefore addressed with the derogatory title of "this people" instead of the covenant title of "my people." They
are convicted of being spiritually insensitive, blind and
deaf. Worse than that, they are accused of having
a "stubborn and rebellious" nature. According to ancient Israelite clan laws (Deut. 21:18-21) a "stubborn
and rebellious" son was to be stoned. In this accusation, therefore, a sentence of death is implied for God's
"firstborn son" Israel. Judah's disgusting indifference

77

to the reform of Josiah may also have occasioned this oracle.

**26-29** The accusations of guilt continue in vv. 26-29 and 30-31. The wicked of Judah are described as wily trappers and fowlers who scheme to catch other men and prosper handsomely from their downfall. A lively daily concern for justice on behalf of the underdog, such as the fatherless and the poor, was a basic criterion of righteousness both in the sight of Yahweh and of many peoples of that day (Deut. 24:17-22; 10:17-19). This was a universal law of the wisdom teachers of ancient times (Prov. 31:9). Could the rejection of this basic principle of faith and life in Israel remain unpunished by God?

**30-31** The guilt of Jacob, however, was not confined to the rank and file or to a wicked segment of the community. For it was, above all, the religious leaders entrusted with the moral and spiritual guidance of God's household who had abused their faith. The prophets were hypocrites, the priests were worthless puppets, and the people applauded willingly (cf. 8:10-11). There is always something appalling and sad about the situation when this happens, for it means the beginning of "the end." When the end comes, Judah will stand helpless before the overwhelming condemnation it deserves.

## GOD WILL FIGHT AGAINST
JERUSALEM                                          6:1-8

¹ Flee for safety, O people of Benjamin,
   from the midst of Jerusalem!
 Blow the trumpet in Teko'a,
   and raise a signal on Beth-hac-che'rem;

for evil looms out of the north,
and great destruction.
² The comely and delicately bred I will destroy,
the daughter of Zion.
³ Shepherds with their flocks shall come against her;
they shall pitch their tents around her,
they shall pasture, each in his place.
⁴ "Prepare war against her;
up, and let us attack at noon!"
"Woe to us, for the day declines,
for the shadows of evening lengthen!"
⁵ "Up, and let us attack by night,
and destroy her palaces!"

⁶ For thus says the LORD of hosts:
"Hew down her trees;
cast up a siege mound against Jerusalem.
This is the city which must be punished;
there is nothing but oppression within her.
⁷ As a well keeps its water fresh,
so she keeps fresh her wickedness;
violence and destruction are heard within her;
sickness and wounds are ever before me.
⁸ Be warned, O Jerusalem,
lest I be alienated from you;
lest I make you a desolation,
an uninhabited land."

This warfare oracle consists of four distinct parts (cf. 4:6-20): an appeal to flight (vv. 1-2), a characterization of the enemy (vv. 3-5), military orders for the foe (vv. 6-7), and a final warning for Jerusalem (v. 8). Jeremiah's countrymen, the Benjaminite refugees from the north, are urged to seek refuge in the southern

fortress cities such as Tekoa (2 Chron. 11:6). Fire sig-
nals will aid their flight. God, the Watchman of Jerusalem, is calling. He is awaiting the enemy He has
summoned to crush Zion in all her religious splendor.
Once again it is the enemy from the north. He invades
the environs of Jerusalem like a mass of nomadic shepherds about to strip a field bare of its pasture. His advent portends the certainty of Zion's doom. Although
this enemy wastes the daylight hours in preparation
(perhaps with sacred rites) for the holy war against
Zion, they can be certain of victory even if they attack
at night. For Yahweh is on their side; He is fighting
a holy war against His own people. It is He who delivers the military order to construct the siegeworks
in defiance of His own timber regulations for Israel's
holy wars (Deut. 20:19-20). This would not be a long
siege. The Warrior God of Israel even explains the
reason for the attack. This army is to execute divine
vengeance and rid the earth of an intolerable abomination. The city in question has become like a polluted
well. Its people savored wickedness and thrived on it.
The Watchman closes with one final warning to Zion:
surrender to Yahweh or perish!

## GOD WILL STRETCH OUT HIS HAND
## OVER HIS PEOPLE 6:9-15

⁹ Thus says the LORD of hosts:
   "Glean *ᵍ* thoroughly as a vine
      the remnant of Israel;
   like a grape-gatherer pass your hand again
      over its branches."
¹⁰ To whom shall I speak and give warning﹐

*ᵍ* Cn: Heb *they shall glean*

80

that they may hear?
Behold, their ears are closed,[h]
  they cannot listen;
behold, the word of the LORD is to them an object
    of scorn,
  they take no pleasure in it.
[11] Therefore I am full of the wrath of the LORD;
  I am weary of holding it in.
"Pour it out upon the children in the street,
  and upon the gatherings of young men, also;
both husband and wife shall be taken,
  the old folk and the very aged.
[12] Their houses shall be turned over to others,
  their fields and wives together;
for I will stretch out my hand
  against the inhabitants of the land,"
                              says the LORD.

[13] "For from the least to the greatest of them,
  every one is greedy for unjust gain;
and from prophet to priest,
  every one deals falsely.
[14] They have healed the wound of my people lightly,
  saying, 'Peace, peace,'
  when there is no peace.
[15] Were they ashamed when they committed abom-
    ination?
  No, they were not at all ashamed;
  they did not know how to blush.
Therefore they shall fall among those who fall;
  at the time that I punish them, they shall be
    overthrown,"
                              says the LORD.

[h] Heb uncircumcised

81

The unenviable task of preaching inevitable doom soon became frustrating for the young prophet. In 6:9-15 we are given a brief insight into personal conflicts of this prophet as he recapitulates the messages he has recently delivered (in Ch. 5), ponders the disturbing truths he has learned about his own people, and hears anew the divine imperative to announce Israel's doom. Jeremiah had previously foretold the destruction of Yahweh's own vineyard (5:10). Now he is urged to renew his trying search for good grapes on the remaining vine of God's people. Perhaps there is one righteous man whom he has overlooked (cf. 5:1). God is persistent; a prophet must learn his lessons the hard way! In return Jeremiah reaffirms the lesson he had learned about the religious character of his people (in 5:1-5, 11). Preaching is pointless; these people have "uncircumcised" ears (RSV note). Like the uninitiated, they simply cannot comprehend the things of God. They had laughed at his words, nay rather, at Yahweh's Word (as in 5:12-13). The end result for Jeremiah was an uncontrollable urge to preach condemnation. The burning fire of God's anger had become a part of him. The fire on his lips (5:14) had penetrated his soul (cf. 15:17). Without warning this anger erupts afresh over all God's people, even the helpless children and aged. The outstretched hand and arm of Yahweh, which had once been the symbol of Israel's salvation (Ex. 7:5; Deut. 4:34), is now to be the symbol of its condemnation. Israel's exodus experience was being reversed. Jeremiah asserts afresh that the great and the poor (5:4-5), as well as the prophet and the priest (5:31), deal "falsely." The term "falsely" (v. 13; cf. 5:2, 12) is a key religious concept in Jeremiah. Dealing "falsely" is tantamount to acting with conscious and hardened hypocrisy. The superficial healing of God's people with external reforms (3:10) or promises of peace and well-being (4:10) illustrate the character of this hypocrisy. In short, hypocrisy has become second nature to God's people; they have no conscience or sense of shame. National catastrophe is the inevitable consequence of this degradation.

## GOD WILL SET STUMBLING BLOCKS BEFORE HIS PEOPLE 6:16-21

16 Thus says the LORD:
  "Stand by the roads, and look,
    and ask for the ancient paths,
  where the good way is; and walk in it,
    and find rest for your souls.
  But they said, 'We will not walk in it.'
17 I set watchmen over you, saying,
    'Give heed to the sound of the trumpet!'
  But they said, 'We will not give heed.'
18 Therefore hear, O nations,
    and know, O congregation, what will happen
    to them.
19 Hear, O earth; behold, I am bringing evil upon
    this people,
  the fruit of their devices,
  because they have not given heed to my words;
    and as for my law, they have rejected it.
20 To what purpose does frankincense come to me
    from Sheba,
  or sweet cane from a distant land?
  Your burnt offerings are not acceptable,
    nor your sacrifices pleasing to me.
21 Therefore thus says the LORD:

'Behold, I will lay before this people
  stumbling blocks against which they shall
    stumble;
fathers and sons together,
  neighbor and friend shall perish.'"

God could hardly be accused of making hasty decisions. The fatal stumbling blocks He was ready to set in the path of His people (v. 21) had first been created by Israel's own devious schemes (v. 19) to avoid her obligations to Yahweh. Nevertheless, judgment is not automatic. Yahweh reminds His people how often He had recalled them to the genuine path of obedience outlined in His covenants with the forefathers. If they returned, they could have "rest for their souls," that is, security in the face of danger. The true prophets, God's "watchmen" (cf. Ezek. 3:17), had repeatedly warned Zion of the inevitable result of unfaithfulness (cf. Matt. 23:37). But the people refused to obey. Consequently their own actions were bringing down double destruction upon their heads. Not only had they sinned flagrantly, but they had totally rejected the call to repentance as well as the "law" which they had previously accepted as part of their covenant commitment (cf. 2 Kings 23:3). Admittedly some had diligently supported the cultic reforms of King Josiah with an abundance of rich offerings and sacrifices (v. 20). But these actions had not removed the cause of the corruption. The "ancient path" and the "good way" for God's people was to be sought not primarily through ritual and sacrifice but through obedience and righteousness (cf. 7:21-26). Thus God announces to all nations and all nature (vv. 18-19) that His people will find no rest but will stumble, fall, and perish.

## GOD HAS REJECTED HIS PEOPLE       6:22-30

²² Thus says the LORD:
   "Behold, a people is coming from the north country,
      a great nation is stirring from the farthest parts
         of the earth.
²³ They lay hold on bow and spear,
      they are cruel and have no mercy,
      the sound of them is like the roaring sea;
   they ride upon horses,
      set in array as a man for battle,
      against you, O daughter of Zion!"
²⁴ We have heard the report of it,
      our hands fall helpless;
   anguish has taken hold of us,
      pain as of a woman in travail.
²⁵ Go not forth into the field,
      nor walk on the road;
   for the enemy has a sword,
      terror is on every side.
²⁶ O daughter of my people, gird on sackcloth,
      and roll in ashes;
   make mourning as for an only son,
      most bitter lamentation;
   for suddenly the destroyer
      will come upon us.

²⁷ "I have made you an assayer and tester among
         my people,
      that you may know and assay their ways.
²⁸ They are all stubbornly rebellious,
      going about with slanders;
   they are bronze and iron,
      all of them act corruptly.

85

²⁹ The bellows blow fiercely,
    the lead is consumed by the fire;
  in vain the refining goes on,
    for the wicked are not removed.
³⁰ Refuse silver they are called,
    for the LORD has rejected them."


22-26 The early collection of doom oracles in 4:5 to 6:30 concludes with a renewed warning concerning the foe from the north (vv. 22-26) and a reaffirmation of Jeremiah's role as the agent of God's burning anger (vv. 27-30). The people are reminded of the monstrous cruelty and the military efficiency of the foe they must face. Jeremiah even anticipates the unbearable agony that will result from the enemy's onslaughts (cf. 4:31). In a final desperate appeal he pleads with Zion to repent in sackcloth and ashes. Only the deepest remorse, like a woman's sorrow for her only son, is appropriate now. When swift destruction strikes, it will be too late.

27-30 Despite this appeal, Jeremiah's task remains unchanged. His first job is to "break down" Israel with his word (1:10). He is the mouthpiece of God's wrath (5:14; 6:11). This function of the prophet is now portrayed in terms of the smelting process (cf. Is. 1:24-26). Jeremiah is not expected to extract good ore from his people, but he is to prove through "testing" and "assaying" that they are nothing but slag, worthless refuse silver. The oxidizing activity of the "lead" would prove ineffective. Israel could no longer be purified! Jeremiah's preaching would publicly demonstrate this fact and reveal conclusively that Yahweh had actually rejected Israel.

The message of this corpus of sermons (4:5 – 6:30)

is clear. Israel had terminated her covenant relationship with Yahweh. God's people had broken their covenant with Yahweh by relentless and flagrant rejection of Yahweh, their God. In judgment Yahweh would expose them for what they were and demonstrate that He was their covenant Overlord, whose will could not be flouted. Accordingly Jeremiah's message of doom was unequivocal. Like the other prophets, he pulled no punches. The message of God's judgment could not be softened. Total doom was the necessary prolog to Jeremiah's later word of God's free grace for the destroyed people of God. In Jeremiah's personal anguish we already have a foretaste of Yahweh's love reaching out to heal His people under judgment.

# Selected Sermons on Worship

## Jeremiah 7:1−8:3

Worship played a central role in the life of God's people. The character of Israel's religion was frequently dependent on the interest of the political ruler or rulers. Thus the reform of Josiah discussed above involved both political independence and religious reform. A false sense of religious security and prosperity often attended such reforms (cf. 6:14, 20). Should a prophet dare to attack this official worship life and the traditions that justified it, or even to oppose the "necessary political evils" of lesser deities, his actions were tantamount to treason. His words would strike at the very heart of Israelite society and politics popularly understood. The collection of prose sermons on worship embrace several such attacks. The first (7:1-15) was delivered at the beginning of the reign of Jehoiakim and exposes the overbearing religious pride and self-satisfaction the reform of Josiah had unintentionally engendered. Three of the others (7:16-20, 29-34; 8:1-3) attack the worship of Ishtar, the practice of child sacrifice, and the worship of celestial objects respectively. These aberrations

JEREMIAH 7:1-15

had been reinstated during the reign of Jehoiakim, despite their official condemnation under the Josiah reform (2 Kings 23). These sermons, therefore, were probably delivered some time during Jehoiakim's reign (609–598 B. C.). The remaining sermon in 7:21-28 is even more severe and questions the very tradition and validity of a popular attitude toward sacrifice as the vital part of a salutary relation between Judah and Yahweh. This address would have been appropriate even before the idolatry of the regime of Jehoiakim.

## JEREMIAH PREDICTS THE FALL OF THE TEMPLE 7:1-15

[1] The word that came to Jeremiah from the LORD: [2] "Stand in the gate of the LORD'S house, and proclaim there this word, and say, Hear the word of the LORD, all you men of Judah who enter these gates to worship the LORD. [3] Thus says the LORD of hosts, the God of Israel, Amend your ways and your doings, and I will let you dwell in this place. [4] Do not trust in these deceptive words: 'This is the temple of the LORD, the temple of the LORD, the temple of the LORD.'

[5] "For if you truly amend your ways and your doings, if you truly execute justice one with another, [6] if you do not oppress the alien, the fatherless or the widow, or shed innocent blood in this place, and if you do not go after other gods to your own hurt, [7] then I will let you dwell in this place, in the land that I gave of old to your fathers for ever.

[8] "Behold, you trust in deceptive words to no avail. [9] Will you steal, murder, commit adultery,

89

swear falsely, burn incense to Ba'al, and go after other gods that you have not known, [10] and then come and stand before me in this house, which is called by my name, and say, 'We are delivered!' — only to go on doing all these abominations? [11] Has this house, which is called by my name, become a den of robbers in your eyes? Behold, I myself have seen it, says the LORD. [12] Go now to my place that was in Shiloh, where I made my name dwell at first, and see what I did to it for the wickedness of my people Israel. [13] And now, because you have done all these things, says the LORD, and when I spoke to you persistently you did not listen, and when I called you, you did not answer, [14] therefore I will do to the house which is called by my name, and in which you trust, and to the place which I gave to you and to your fathers, as I did to Shiloh. [15] And I will cast you out of my sight, as I cast out all your kinsmen, all the offspring of E'phraim.

According to the parallel account in Jer. 26, this famous temple address was delivered early in the reign of Jehoiakim, perhaps at the time of his coronation or a covenant renewal festival. Whatever the occasion, the people of Judah had apparently assembled in Jerusalem, the central shrine for all of Judah. The reform of Josiah in 621 B. C., eliminating all other centers of worship, had been based on the injunctions of Deuteronomy (e. g., Deut. 12:5-14). Apart from the contagious feeling of optimism that attended the advent of a new king, the people had succumbed to the perennial disease of religious smugness, self-satisfaction, and self-righteousness. The imposing presence of the temple, which bore the very name of Yahweh Himself, was considered an unconditional guarantee of God's presence, protection, and good pleasure. To such an audience the sermon of Jeremiah sounded like sheer heresy and religious treason. Avowedly the people had come to glorify Yahweh (v. 2), but the glibly repeated assurance that "this is the temple of the Lord" had become nothing but a huge lie (v. 4). Jeremiah insists that the temple is no longer a symbol of victory and protection. The fall of Shiloh provides an uncomfortable precedent to show what Yahweh can and will do to Jerusalem as well, because this self-willed and grossly misguided people were trusting in the beautiful temple itself instead of in the God who deigned to confront His people there. Formal worship can never be a substitute for a living faith; means are no substitute for the grace they are designed to convey. Go to Shiloh and see for yourself what can happen, concludes Jeremiah. The destruction of Shiloh, implied in 1 Samuel 4, has been dated by excavations to about 1050 B. C.

## JEREMIAH LEARNS THE SERIOUSNESS
## OF THE SITUATION                                       7:16-20

<sup>16</sup> "As for you, do not pray for this people, or lift up cry or prayer for them, and do not intercede with me, for I do not hear you. <sup>17</sup> Do you not see what they are doing in the cities of Judah and in the streets of Jerusalem? <sup>18</sup> The children gather wood, the fathers kindle fire, and the women knead dough, to make cakes for the queen of heaven; and they pour out drink offerings to other gods, to provoke me to anger. <sup>19</sup> Is it I whom they provoke? says the LORD. Is it not themselves, to their own confusion? <sup>20</sup> Therefore thus says the Lord GOD: Behold, my anger and my wrath will be poured out on this place, upon man and

beast, upon the trees of the field and the fruit of the ground; it will burn and not be quenched."

Breach of covenant faithfulness was normally followed by intercession for the people by the covenant mediator. The action of Samuel is a case in point (1 Sam. 12:19 ff.; cf. Jer. 15:1-4). But Jeremiah was told that he should not follow suit; prayer had become pointless (cf. 11:14; Mark 3:29). As at other times, God made him realize what was happening before his very eyes. In addition to the hypocritical worship in Zion (7:1-15) there had arisen a frantic and unabashed performance of pagan rites addressed to the "queen of heaven" (the fertility goddess Ishtar of Babylon). Whole families were preoccupied with cooking cultic cakes bearing her image (cf. 44:9). The consequences of these actions could not be avoided; an irrevocable covenant curse would soon fall on man and beast, vegetation and fertility just as the first curse of disobedience had affected all life. (Gen. 3:14-19)

## JEREMIAH GIVES GOD'S VERDICT ON SACRIFICES 7:21-28

²¹ Thus says the LORD of hosts, the God of Israel: "Add your burnt offerings to your sacrifices, and eat the flesh. ²² For in the day that I brought them out of the land of Egypt, I did not speak to your fathers or command them concerning burnt offerings and sacrifices. ²³ But this command I gave them, 'Obey my voice, and I will be your God, and you shall be my people; and walk in all the way that I command you, that it may be well with you.' ²⁴ But they did not obey or incline their ear, but walked in their own

counsels and the stubbornness of their evil hearts, and went backward and not forward. [25] From the day that your fathers came out of the land of Egypt to this day, I have persistently sent all my servants the prophets to them, day after day; [26] yet they did not listen to me, or incline their ear, but stiffened their neck. They did worse than their fathers.

[27] "So you shall speak all these words to them, but they will not listen to you. You shall call to them, but they will not answer you. [28] And you shall say to them, 'This is the nation that did not obey the voice of the LORD their God, and did not accept discipline; truth has perished; it is cut off from their lips.

Many early prophets were critical of Israel's sacrificial practices (Amos 5:4-6, 21-25; Hos. 5:6; 6:6; Is. 1:11-15). This antagonism was not only the result of flagrant abuses of accepted rites. A few prophets seemed to question the validity of the tradition that Yahweh had made sacrifice a mandatory part of Israel's religious life. Sacrifice, moreover, was a common heritage of numerous peoples. Jeremiah even goes so far as to assert in Yahweh's name, "I did not speak to your fathers or command them concerning burnt offerings and sacrifices" (v. 22; cf. Amos 5:21-27). The essence of God's command was obedience, not sacrifice. This basic covenant obligation had been reaffirmed through the words of Deuteronomy in the Josiah reform. Hence Jeremiah can sarcastically advise the worshipers to sacrifice as much as they wish. But God is not condemning them on that score. Their downfall is due to an incessant and unremitting disobedience, exhibited from the time of the first promise of covenant obedience given immediately after the exodus (Ex. 19:8). Yet the more the people had been warned of their fate, the worse their defiant reaction became (vv. 25 f.). In a different context Jeremiah could speak favorably about those years following the exodus (cf. comment on 2:1-3). In the present context we meet two favorite expressions of Jeremiah in juxtaposition. The "stubbornness of heart" in each generation counteracted the remedial work of God in "persistently" sending (v. 25) or speaking (v. 13) or warning (11:7) the rebellious sons whom he loved. Jeremiah is compelled to speak his message of woe to these people despite the futility of such a sermon (v. 27). The terrible truth remains: persistent disobedience and persistent rejection of Yahweh's discipline meant that any "truth" or redeeming faithfulness that could bind God's people to Yahweh had been lost forever. (V. 28)

## JEREMIAH DENOUNCES REVIVED
## RELIGIOUS EVILS                                    7:29 – 8:3

²⁹ Cut off your hair and cast it away,
   raise a lamentation on the bare heights,
for the LORD has rejected and forsaken
   the generation of his wrath.'
   ³⁰ "For the sons of Judah have done evil in my sight, says the LORD; they have set their abominations in the house which is called by my name, to defile it. ³¹ And they have built the high place ⁱ of Topheth, which is in the valley of the son of Hinnom, to burn their sons and their daughters in the fire; which I did not command, nor did it come into my mind. ³² Therefore, behold, the days are coming, says

ⁱ Gk Tg: Heb *high places*

the LORD, when it will no more be called Topheth, or the valley of the son of Hinnom, but the valley of Slaughter: for they will bury in Topheth, because there is no room elsewhere. [33] And the dead bodies of this people will be food for the birds of the air, and for the beasts of the earth; and none will frighten them away. [34] And I will make to cease from the cities of Judah and from the streets of Jerusalem the voice of mirth and the voice of gladness, the voice of the bridegroom and the voice of the bride; for the land shall become a waste.

[1] "At that time, says the LORD, the bones of the kings of Judah, the bones of its princes, the bones of the priests, the bones of the prophets, and the bones of the inhabitants of Jerusalem shall be brought out of their tombs; [2] and they shall be spread before the sun and the moon and all the host of heaven, which they have loved and served, which they have gone after, and which they have sought and worshiped; and they shall not be gathered or buried; they shall be as dung on the surface of the ground. [3] Death shall be preferred to life by all the remnant that remains of this evil family in all the places where I have driven them, says the LORD of hosts.

The diverse background of the sermons from this selection (7:1 – 8:3) is further illustrated by the fact that part of the final address was delivered elsewhere to the kings of Judah and the inhabitants of Jerusalem (compare 19:5-7 with 7:31-33). The sermon is directed against the restored abominations of idolatry in the temple and the reinstated high places in the valley of Topheth. These shrines had been torn down by Josiah during his

95

reform (2 Kings 23:10; cf. 2 Kings 21:6). The revival of child sacrifice to Molech (an Ammonite deity) in this valley outside Jerusalem inevitably meant desecration for God's people and land. The land would be cursed with unburied dead left for carrion. Death and gloom were imminent (vv. 30-34). Accordingly Jeremiah prefaces his sermon on the doom of Judah with a fitting lament for the death of a nation. (V. 29)

A similar, almost unthinkable, punishment calling for the desecration of Judah's dead is also predicted. The reason is the revived worship of heavenly bodies (cf. 2 Kings 21:1-6; 23:4 f.). To return to the dust was the inevitable lot of man, but to lie as dung above the earth meant unconditional rejection of man as nothing but an animal. To be unearthed from the tomb for such a fate adds a sadistic element to this rejection. Nevertheless, concludes the prophet, such a fate will be preferable to the intolerable "living hell" of exile.

# A Collection of Poignant
# Questions and Answers

## Jeremiah 8:4 – 9:26

The provocative question provides a unifying element
in this miscellaneous collection of materials. The ancient technique of asking questions and/or suggesting
analogies from nature or human experience to impart
a general truth was also practiced by the wise men of
Israel (cf. Prov. 6:27-30). Jeremiah is apparently using
this appropriate methodology against these wise men
(whom he mentions specifically in 8:8-9; 9:12, 23) and
against the people educated by the wise men. Inter-
spersed among these questions are divine accusations
and personal reactions that reflect the constant theme of
Judah's intolerable guilt and Yahweh's insufferable
verdict. Throughout the mood is one of pessimism and
despair suggesting the general attitude characteristic
of Jeremiah's preaching during the reign of Jehoiakim.

"IF ONE TURNS AWAY, DOES HE
NOT RETURN?"                                              8:4-7

4 "You shall say to them, Thus says the LORD:
When men fall, do they not rise again?

97

If one turns away, does he not return?
5 Why then has this people turned away
in perpetual backsliding?
They hold fast to deceit,
they refuse to return.
6 I have given heed and listened,
but they have not spoken aright;
no man repents of his wickedness,
saying, 'What have I done?'
Every one turns to his own course,
like a horse plunging headlong into battle.
7 Even the stork in the heavens
knows her times;
and the turtledove, swallow, and crane *j*
keep the time of their coming;
but my people know not
the ordinance of the LORD.

*j* The meaning of the Hebrew word is uncertain

From the observation of human experience and the laws of nature certain courses of action are recognized as natural and normal. If someone falls, he gets up again. If someone makes a detour, he returns to his former route. In season migratory birds follow their natural instincts. But God's own people, by contrast, invariably act in an unnatural and abnormal manner (cf. 18:14-19). They refuse to follow even the normal laws of human religious experience. Repentance and the quest for a knowledge of God's ordained will ("ordinance") have become alien to their nature. Like headstrong horses, they are bent on plunging to their ruin (cf. 5:22-23). And these unbelievable facts, insists Jeremiah (in v. 6), are things which he, like a truly sensitive wise man, has verified by personal observation.

98

# "How Can You Say, 'We Are Wise?'"    8:8-13

8 "How can you say, 'We are wise,
  and the law of the LORD is with us'?
But, behold, the false pen of the scribes
  has made it into a lie.
9 The wise men shall be put to shame,
  they shall be dismayed and taken;
lo, they have rejected the word of the LORD,
  and what wisdom is in them?
10 Therefore I will give their wives to others
  and their fields to conquerors,
because from the least to the greatest
  every one is greedy for unjust gain;
from prophet to priest
  every one deals falsely.
11 They have healed the wound of my people lightly,
  saying, 'Peace, peace,'
  when there is no peace.
12 Were they ashamed when they committed abomi-
    nation?
  No, they were not at all ashamed;
  they did not know how to blush.
Therefore they shall fall among the fallen;
  when I punish them, they shall be overthrown,
                              says the LORD.

13 When I would gather them, says the LORD,
  there are no grapes on the vine,
  nor figs on the fig tree;
even the leaves are withered,
  and what I gave them has passed away from
    them." *k*

  *k* Heb uncertain

Two pointed questions of the prophet provoke additional oracles of doom. Where is your common sense (v. 8)? Where is your conscience (v. 12)? Rather than acting like intelligent religious people, the masses had become sheer fools, deluded by the perverted wise men and recognized religious leaders of their generation (vv. 8-9). God's people had been hypnotized by the comfortable and profitable doctrine of peace and prosperity. They had thereby become blind to the mortal nature of their malady (v. 11). The end of such folly could only mean bereavement, war, and humiliating exposure at the hand of God Himself (vv. 10 and 12). Appropriately enough, an agonizing cry of divine despair over the worthlessness of God's family, the beloved vineyard of God, is appended to these oracles. (V. 13; cf. 5:10-11)

## "Why Do We Sit Still?"      8:14-17

14 Why do we sit still?
  Gather together, let us go into the fortified cities
    and perish there;
  for the LORD our God has doomed us to perish.
    and has given us poisoned water to drink,
    because we have sinned against the LORD.
15 We looked for peace, but no good came,
    for a time of healing, but behold, terror.

16 "The snorting of their horses is heard from Dan;
    at the sound of the neighing of their stallions
    the whole land quakes.
  They come and devour the land and all that fills it,
    the city and those who dwell in it.
17 For behold, I am sending among you serpents,

100

adders which cannot be charmed,
and they shall bite you,"

says the LORD.

The vivid portrait of Judah's onrushing foe in 4:5-8, 14-18 is envisioned again with a new display of bold imagery. Once again the petrified inhabitants flee to the fortified cities although they realize the futility of their action. Once more the overwhelming power of the enemy cavalry descends from Dan. Even a frantic confession of sins comes too late to avert national disaster. A new dimension seems to be given to this oracle, however, by making veiled allusions to past evils in Israel. The fate of God's people will be analogous to that of their forefathers in the wilderness, whose punishment was to drink water polluted with the ashes of the golden calf (cf. 9:15; Ex. 32:20) and who were bitten by poisonous serpents sent by Yahweh (Num. 21:4-9). Because Yahweh was the real foe behind these new historical enemies, no charm could ward off the clutches of death.

## "Is There No Balm in Gilead?"    8:18 – 9:9

18 My grief is beyond healing,[l]
  my heart is sick within me.
19 Hark, the cry of the daughter of my people
  from the length and breadth of the land:
 "Is the LORD not in Zion?
  Is her King not in her?"
 "Why have they provoked me to anger with their
    graven images,
  and with their foreign idols?"

[l] Cn Compare Gk: Heb uncertain

20 "The harvest is past, the summer is ended,
    and we are not saved."
21 For the wound of the daughter of my people is my
    heart wounded,
    I mourn, and dismay has taken hold on me.

22 Is there no balm in Gilead?
    Is there no physician there?
    Why then has the health of the daughter of my
    people
    not been restored?


1 [m] O that my head were waters,
    and my eyes a fountain of tears,
    that I might weep day and night
    for the slain of the daughter of my people!
2 [n] O that I had in the desert
    a wayfarers' lodging place,
    that I might leave my people
    and go away from them!
    For they are all adulterers,
    a company of treacherous men.
3 They bend their tongue like a bow;
    falsehood and not truth has grown strong [o] in
    the land;
    for they proceed from evil to evil,
    and they do not know me, says the LORD.

4 Let every one beware of his neighbor,
    and put no trust in any brother;
    for every brother is a supplanter,
    and every neighbor goes about as a slanderer.
5 Every one deceives his neighbor,

[m] Ch 8. 23 in Heb      [n] Ch 9. 1 in Heb
[o] Gk: Heb *and not for truth they have grown strong*

and no one speaks the truth;
they have taught their tongue to speak lies;
   they commit iniquity and are too weary to repent.ᵖ
⁶ Heaping oppression upon oppression, and deceit
    upon deceit,
   they refuse to know me, says the LORD.

⁷ Therefore thus says the LORD of hosts:
"Behold, I will refine them and test them,
   for what else can I do, because of my people?
⁸ Their tongue is a deadly arrow;
   it speaks deceitfully;
with his mouth each speaks peaceably to his
    neighbor,
   but in his heart he plans an ambush for him.
⁹ Shall I not punish them for these things? says the
    LORD;
   and shall I not avenge myself
   on a nation such as this?

ᵖ Cn Compare Gk: Heb *your dwelling*

18-20 The vehement outcry of 8:18—9:3 further underscores the prophet's emotional involvement in his fateful message. (See the comment on 4:19-22.) His heart and mind are torn by a bitter struggle. Crucial questions that concern the very life of his people vie within him. In his soul he overhears the desperate outburst of his own doomed people. "Is Yahweh not in Zion?" "Has the God who promised undying faithfulness now deserted us?" In the same instant, however, he senses the tearful pleading of a righteous but loving God. "Why did they provoke me with idols" (with "objects worth nothing" according to the Hebrew)? Once more the screams of the people rise heavenward:

103

"We are not saved!" After the harvest and the desolate summer they expected God's perennial intervention with the new year. But nothing happened.

**21-22** The sad plight of this people also belongs to Jeremiah. In a new fit of anguish, therefore, the prophet flings Judah's case before Yahweh. Is there no hope, no cure, no doctor, no celebrated medication like the balm made from the resin of trees in Gilead (cf. 46:11; 51:8)? The answer is obvious. Yahweh, the Physician, is no longer willing to heal in the usual way.

**9:1-3** Two courses of action seem desirable to Jeremiah. Either he can attempt to change God's heart by a flood of sympathetic tears, or he can try to escape the whole pathetic situation by isolating himself in the desert far away from his hypocritical brethren.

**4-9** In actual fact, however, the prophet must take a third course. He resumes his role as an assayer and refiner (see 6:27; cf. 9:7). In so doing he breaks forth into a tirade of divine accusations against the flagrant duplicity and vicious deceit of his people. He knows from personal experience what their slander means (11:19; 12:6; 20:10). Every brother was a Jacob ("supplanter") in the original sense of that name. God's people refused to know Yahweh and thereby acknowledge His will in their lives. Their hearts had been poisoned by hypocrisy. No healing balm would avail — only the refining fire of the divine smelter to eliminate everything vile. In these questions of Yahweh (vv. 7 and 9) we sense a strong kinship between the agonizing love of the prophet and the underlying pain of God. Perhaps we can speak here of the frustration of God's love, which outlasts the lovelessness of His people. Consider these cries again! "What else can I do?" "Must I not punish you?"

104

## "WHY IS THE LAND RUINED?" 9:12-16

**12 Who is the man so wise that he can under-
stand this? To whom has the mouth of the LORD
spoken, that he may declare it? Why is the land ruined
and laid waste like a wilderness, so that no one passes
through? 13 And the LORD says: "Because they have
forsaken my law which I set before them, and have
not obeyed my voice, or walked in accord with it,
14 but have stubbornly followed their own hearts and
have gone after the Ba'als, as their fathers taught
them. 15 Therefore thus says the LORD of hosts, the
God of Israel: Behold, I will feed this people with
wormwood, and give them poisonous water to drink.
16 I will scatter them among the nations whom neither
they nor their fathers have known; and I will send
the sword after them, until I have consumed them."**

When the cruel punishment of Yahweh was actually experienced during the first captivity of Jerusalem in March 597 B. C. (and later with its fall in 587 B. C.), even the celebrated wise men were compelled to ask why. "Why this wilderness?" The drastic answer of Yahweh summarizes the reasons so often given (e. g., 7:24; 11:8) and reaffirms the totality of the impending disaster of exile and massacre already foretold (e. g., 8:14; 13:24; 23:15). In short, God's people were still suffering beneath the curse of the covenant they had persistently violated. (Cf. Deut. 28:64)

## "FOR DEATH HAS COME INTO OUR WINDOWS!" 9:10-11, 17-22

**10 "Take up [q] weeping and wailing for the mountains,**

[q] Gk Syr: Heb *I will take up*

and a lamentation for the pastures of the wilderness,
because they are laid waste so that no one passes
through,
and the lowing of cattle is not heard;
both the birds of the air and the beasts
have fled and are gone.
[11] I will make Jerusalem a heap of ruins,
a lair of jackals;
and I will make the cities of Judah a desolation,
without inhabitant."

[17] Thus says the LORD of hosts:
"Consider, and call for the mourning women to
come;
send for the skilful women to come;
[18] let them make haste and raise a wailing over us,
that our eyes may run down with tears,
and our eyelids gush with water.
[19] For a sound of wailing is heard from Zion:
'How we are ruined!
We are utterly shamed,
because we have left the land,
because they have cast down our dwellings.'"

[20] Hear, O women, the word of the LORD,
and let your ear receive the word of his mouth;
teach to your daughters a lament,
and each to her neighbor a dirge.
[21] For death has come up into our windows,
it has entered our palaces,
cutting off the children from the streets
and the young men from the squares.
[22] Speak, "Thus says the LORD:

'The dead bodies of men shall fall
   like dung upon the open field,
like sheaves after the reaper,
   and none shall gather them.' "

The preceding prose summary of 9:12-16 interrupts
a threefold poetic summons to lament the gloomy scenes
of desolation projected for Jerusalem. Each summons
offers a frantic appeal based on an urgent "because."
The first (vv. 10-11) is a general call to wail because of
the widespread agony of nature accompanying the
future desecration of Zion. The second (vv. 17-19) pleads
for immediate professional mourning in sympathy with
the forthcoming excruciating travail of the people of
Zion. The third (vv. 20-22) advocates emergency guidance in the art of lamentation inasmuch as death has
already entered the inner sanctuary of their homes.
In that hour the words of the final gruesome eulogy
on Death, the Reaper, will surely be fitting. (V. 22)

## "LET HIM WHO GLORIES, GLORY IN THIS . . . !" 9:23-26

23 Thus says the LORD: "Let not the wise man
glory in his wisdom, let not the mighty man glory
in his might, let not the rich man glory in his riches;
24 but let him who glories glory in this, that he understands and knows me, that I am the LORD who
practice steadfast love, justice, and righteousness
in the earth; for in these things I delight, says the
LORD."
25 "Behold, the days are coming, says the LORD,
when I will punish all those who are circumcised
but yet uncircumcised — 26 Egypt, Judah, Edom, the

107

sons of Ammon, Moab, and all who dwell in the desert that cut the corners of their hair; for all these nations are uncircumcised, and all the house of Israel is uncircumcised in heart."

23-24 The first of the two final messages in this collection again reverts to language of the wise men. "To glory" and "to find understanding" were of concern to these men (cf. Prov. 27:1-2; 1:2-4). Jeremiah asserts that man's boast can never be measured by cultural (wisdom), technical (might), or material (wealth) advancements but only by his efforts to understand God's scale of values. For God delights in a lasting bond of faithfulness, an unwavering desire for just action, and a generous concern for the rights of those in need.

25-26 The history of God's ancient people, however, was not characterized by such an attitude of inner devotion. The closing proclamation of doom is therefore in place. Israel was apparently inclined to claim exemption from punishment by virtue of its circumcision, the coveted rite of initiation into the covenant with God. Their way of life, however, had long since demonstrated that in reality they were uncircumcised in heart (cf. 4:4), that is, they were pagan in their attitude to life, as pagan as those neighbors who dared to shave their temples (cf. Lev. 19:27 and Jer. 25:23, where Arab tribes are mentioned). Their fate would therefore be identical with that of the uncircumcised nations. No religious rite could protect them from divine retribution.

# A Brief Selection of Relevant Oracles

## Jeremiah 10:1-25

ORACLES IN PRAISE OF GOD'S
ETERNAL POWER                          10:1-16

¹ Hear the word which the **LORD** speaks to you,
O house of Israel. ² Thus says the **LORD**:
"Learn not the way of the nations,
   nor be dismayed at the signs of the heavens
   because the nations are dismayed at them,
³ for the customs of the peoples are false.
A tree from the forest is cut down,
   and worked with an axe by the hands of a crafts-
      man.
⁴ Men deck it with silver and gold;
   they fasten it with hammer and nails
   so that it cannot move.
⁵ Their idols ʳ are like scarecrows in a cucumber field,
   and they cannot speak;
they have to be carried,
   for they cannot walk.

ʳ Heb *They*

Be not afraid of them,
    for they cannot do evil,
    neither is it in them to do good."

6 There is none like thee, O LORD;
    thou art great, and thy name is great in might.
7 Who would not fear thee, O King of the nations?
    For this is thy due;
for among all the wise ones of the nations
    and in all their kingdoms
    there is none like thee.
8 They are both stupid and foolish;
    the instruction of idols is but wood!
9 Beaten silver is brought from Tarshish,
    and gold from Uphaz.
They are the work of the craftsman and of the
    hands of the goldsmith;
    their clothing is violet and purple;
    they are all the work of skilled men.
10 But the LORD is the true God;
    he is the living God and the everlasting King.
At his wrath the earth quakes,
    and the nations cannot endure his indignation.

11 Thus shall you say to them: "The gods who
did not make the heavens and the earth shall perish
from the earth and from under the heavens." [s]

12 It is he who made the earth by his power,
    who established the world by his wisdom,
    and by his understanding stretched out the
    heavens.
13 When he utters his voice there is a tumult of waters
    in the heavens,

[s] This verse is in Aramaic

and he makes the mist rise from the ends of the
earth.
He makes lightnings for the rain,
and he brings forth the wind from his storehouses.
¹⁴ Every man is stupid and without knowledge;
every goldsmith is put to shame by his idols;
for his images are false,
and there is no breath in them.
¹⁵ They are worthless, a work of delusion;
at the time of their punishment they shall perish.
¹⁶ Not like these is he who is the portion of Jacob,
for he is the one who formed all things,
and Israel is the tribe of his inheritance;
the LORD of hosts is his name.


A close study of passages such as Is. 40:19-20;
41:7, 29; 44:9-20; 46:5-7 reveals a much closer similarity
of the materials in Jer. 10:1-16 to Is. 40 – 46, often dated
about 540 B. C., than to the preaching of Jeremiah in
general. This marked affinity has led many to assign
this section of the book of Jeremiah to a later author.
Verses 12-16, moreover, are included in Jer. 51 (vv. 15-
19), which is generally regarded as an appendix to the
works of Jeremiah.

The historical situation presupposed seems to be
that of the exile. The house of Israel is surrounded by
idols. The people have been impressed by astrological
signs. The prophet urgently warns the people against
succumbing to the charm of idolatry. "Do not be afraid
of them, for they cannot do evil!" he exclaims. Such
an expression hardly fits among those who cheerfully
followed pagan gods prior to the exile. The gods in this
chapter are the gods of Israel's conquerors. Accordingly

111

the author employs a biting satire to expose the idols in question as lifeless, worthless, and ludicrous scarecrows.

The God of Israel, by contrast, is incomparable in every way. He is also the "King" of those victorious nations who are infatuated with idol worship (vv. 6-7). He alone is a genuine God, a living, active, divine being, who has always existed. He is not restricted by the confines of form, time, or space (v. 10-11). His eternal wisdom alone created the forms of the universe (cf. Prov. 8:22-31), and His sovereign power sustains the existing forces of nature (vv. 12-13). Above all, this God is "the portion of Jacob," that is, the One who personally committed Himself to espouse the cause of His people Israel. Israel, in turn, becomes His "inheritance," a people with a preferred status in His eyes. In short, Yahweh is *still* the covenant God of Israel (v. 16). Hence Israel need not be terrified on the day of international retribution, when all pagan idols will vanish. (Vv. 10-11)

## CRIES OF ANGUISH FROM GOD'S PEOPLE 10:17-22

<sup></sup>17 Gather up your bundle from the ground,
  O you who dwell under siege!
18 For thus says the LORD:
  "Behold, I am slinging out the inhabitants of the land
    at this time,
  and I will bring distress on them,
    that they may feel it."

19 Woe is me because of my hurt!
  My wound is grievous.

But I said, "Truly this is an affliction,
and I must bear it."
<sup>20</sup> My tent is destroyed,
and all my cords are broken;
my children have gone from me,
and they are not;
there is no one to spread my tent again,
and to set up my curtains.
<sup>21</sup> For the shepherds are stupid,
and do not inquire of the LORD;
therefore they have not prospered,
and all their flock is scattered.

<sup>22</sup> Hark, a rumor! Behold, it comes! —
a great commotion out of the north country
to make the cities of Judah a desolation,
a lair of jackals.

The dialog of this unit falls into three parts: vv. 17-18, an appeal; vv. 19-21, an outcry; and v. 22, a report. (Some feel these verses belong after 9:22.) The language of the dialog reflects the personal anguish experienced by Jeremiah on other occasions (cf. 8:18 and 4:20). The city of Jerusalem is under siege. The date is probably 597 B. C. or 588 B. C., prior to the total destruction of the city. Jeremiah pleads with Jerusalem to pack her bags in preparation for the worst. The worst he describes as Yahweh "slinging" her inhabitants abroad into captivity. Jerusalem's response is a cry from the depths of her intolerable affliction. Her home is virtually a shambles, much of her family is already scattered, and her rulers ("shepherds") are helpless, irreligious dolts. Jeremiah's answer takes the form of a watchman's

113

report. The final predicted devastation at the hands of the cruel enemy from the north (cf. 4:6, 15; 6:1) is now in progress. Behold, "It has come!"

## PLEAS FOR MERCY AND JUSTICE
## FROM GOD'S HAND                                    10:23-25

²³ I know, O LORD, that the way of man is not in
himself,
that it is not in man who walks to direct his steps.
²⁴ Correct me, O LORD, but in just measure;
not in thy anger, lest thou bring me to nothing.

²⁵ Pour out thy wrath upon the nations that know
thee not,
and upon the peoples that call not on thy name;
for they have devoured Jacob;
they have devoured him and consumed him,
and have laid waste his habitation.

Jeremiah's preaching reveals a deep sensitivity to the impotence of the human will. The perverted heart of Judah was a living illustration of this truth (cf. 2:22, 25; 17:1, 9; 13:23). Jeremiah's private confessions attest to his consciousness of Yahweh as the One who exposes the deep recesses of the human self (12:3; 20:12). Yet in the same breath Jeremiah could demand vengeance on his venomous foes (12:3; 15:15; 17:14-18). All of this personal experience is brought together in the present word of intercession on Judah's behalf. He appeals for aid on the basis of man's weak will, for discipline tempered with mercy, and for retribution on the unbelieving nations who have dared to injure God's chosen covenant people. Surely God could not

114

ignore such a plea. The years that followed the humiliation of 597 B. C. seem appropriate for this message.
(In the light of the context it seems preferable in v. 24
to follow the alternate reading provided by the Greek
translation [Septuagint] and read "correct *us*" and
"bring *us*.")

# Crises and Critical Sermons
# in the Life of Jeremiah

## Jeremiah 11:1 – 20:18

The large corpus of materials grouped in Chs. 11 to 20 is disparate in form, historical orientation, and content. Yet a number of prominent features serve to characterize this selection of Jeremiah's sayings as a whole. First of all, we are no longer dealing only with a collection of divine oracles or sermons about God's people. Judah is directly involved, to be sure, but narrative and autobiographical elements now become prominent as well. Jeremiah preaches an itinerant sermon (11:1-17), buries a waistcloth (13:1-11), visits a potter's shop (18:1-12), breaks a flask and clashes with a priest (19:1 – 20:6). These activities disclose Jeremiah's close contact with the public and his deep involvement in the message his audience found so distasteful. Jeremiah himself found his own words hard to swallow. It is noteworthy, therefore, that the framework of this collection consists of the intimate confessions of Jeremiah as he faces the personal crises of his faith (11:18 – 12:6; 15:10-21; 17:14-18; 18:18-23; and 20:7-18). These passages are termed confessions in the sense that they are the frank and personal cries of anguish from the heart of a man of faith at odds with his God. At first glance these confessions read like entries in a private diary that was never intended for publication. Such confessions underscore the living personal involvement of the prophet in crises and messages of his day and give a new dimension of meaning to the work and life of Jeremiah. This prophet is a spokesman chosen to repeat the oral messages of God. But something more is involved. His whole life is affected. His emotions, his faith, his feelings, his experiences are recorded. They are messages too. In this sense the prophet becomes virtually identified with the dynamic word he must speak. He becomes a living word.

Closely related to the confessions is that prohibition which apparently helped to precipitate these outbursts of despair and doubt (16:1-13). The confessions as a whole are difficult to date. Persecution was the lot of the prophet throughout the reigns of Jehoiakim and Zedekiah and perhaps even earlier. The era of terror under Jehoiakim, however, seems a likely setting for some of these confessions at least (cf. 26:20-23; 36:5, 19). Included within the framework of the personal materials are two smaller selections of brief oracles (14:1—15:9 and 17:1-18). Several of the prose sermons of this corpus have definite affinities to the language of Deuteronomy and are frequently considered the work of a later editor other than Jeremiah (11:1-8; 17:19-27). A few of the smaller units of material reflect a plausible historical background. 12:7-13 seems to be concerned with the uprisings of 601 B. C.; 13:1-11 and 18:1-12 presumably relate to the problem of Judah's first captivity in 597 B. C.; and 13:15-27 apparently revolves around the dilemma posed by the regime of Jehoiachin and Nehushta.

117

## SERMONS ON THE COVENANT CURSE        11:1-17

¹ The word that came to Jeremiah from the LORD: ² "Hear the words of this covenant, and speak to the men of Judah and the inhabitants of Jerusalem. ³ You shall say to them, Thus says the LORD, the God of Israel: Cursed be the man who does not heed the words of this covenant ⁴ which I commanded your fathers when I brought them out of the land of Egypt, from the iron furnace, saying, Listen to my voice, and do all that I command you. So shall you be my people, and I will be your God, ⁵ that I may perform the oath which I swore to your fathers, to give them a land flowing with milk and honey, as at this day." Then I answered, "So be it, LORD."

⁶ And the LORD said to me, "Proclaim all these words in the cities of Judah, and in the streets of Jerusalem: Hear the words of this covenant and do them. ⁷ For I solemnly warned your fathers when I brought them up out of the land of Egypt, warning them persistently, even to this day, saying, Obey my voice. ⁸ Yet they did not obey or incline their ear, but every one walked in the stubbornness of his evil heart. Therefore I brought upon them all the words of this covenant, which I commanded them to do, but they did not."

⁹ Again the LORD said to me, "There is revolt among the men of Judah and the inhabitants of Jerusalem. ¹⁰ They have turned back to the iniquities of their forefathers, who refused to hear my words; they have gone after other gods to serve them; the house of Israel and the house of Judah have broken my covenant which I made with their fathers. ¹¹ Therefore, thus says the LORD, Behold, I am

118

bringing evil upon them which they cannot escape; though they cry to me, I will not listen to them. [12] Then the cities of Judah and the inhabitants of Jerusalem will go and cry to the gods to whom they burn incense, but they cannot save them in the time of their trouble. [13] For your gods have become as many as your cities, O Judah; and as many as the streets of Jerusalem are the altars you have set up to shame, altars to burn incense to Ba'al.

[14] "Therefore do not pray for this people, or lift up a cry or prayer on their behalf, for I will not listen when they call to me in the time of their trouble. [15] What right has my beloved in my house, when she has done vile deeds? Can vows ' and sacrificial flesh avert your doom? Can you then exult? [16] The LORD once called you, 'A green olive tree, fair with goodly fruit'; but with the roar of a great tempest he will set fire to it, and its branches will be consumed. [17] The LORD of hosts, who planted you, has pronounced evil against you, because of the evil which the house of Israel and the house of Judah have done, provoking me to anger by burning incense to Ba'al."

' Gk: Heb *many*

The reform of Josiah was based on the "book of the law" discovered in the temple by Hilkiah (2 Kings 22:8-20). This book seems to be closely related to the Book of Deuteronomy and may have been identical with part or all of Deuteronomy. In general the reform of Josiah was a reaffirmation of the ancient covenant with Yahweh in a manner similar to the terms spelled out in Deuteronomy (2 Kings 23:2-3; cf. Deut. 12). Was Jeremiah an active participant in this reform, at least

119

in its early stages? The sermon of Jer. 11:1-8 has been cited in favor of this position. Jeremiah was commanded by God to advocate a return to the covenant by proclaiming its binding words throughout the cities of Judah and the streets of Jerusalem (v. 6; cf. Deut. 31:10-11). Significantly the language of Jeremiah's sermon is taken largely from Deuteronomy. He speaks of "the words of this covenant" (cf. Deut. 29:1, 9, 14, 21), the curse of the covenant (Deut. 27), the iron furnace of Egypt (Deut. 4:20), the oath sworn to the patriarchs (cf. Deut. 8:18; 9:5), and similar related concepts in a manner closely resembling that of Deuteronomy. In Jeremiah, however, the emphasis lies on inner covenant obedience rather than on Jerusalem as the only place of worship, a feature that was apparently prominent in the Josiah reform. The gist of the sermon in vv. 1-8 is that despite the undeserved election of Israel as God's chosen people and the repeated promise of a land of plenty, the evil hearts of the forefathers of Israel had persistently led them astray. Their vile ways had evoked the curses of the covenant apparent in the past history of God's people. In vv. 9-13 the prophet insists that the blatant actions of the current generation in worshiping Baal throughout the cities of Judah represent a covenant atrocity as vile as any perpetrated by the forefathers. For this generation, therefore, the covenant curse was irrevocable and inescapable. God would not heed its cry for salvation the way He had once heard the Israelite slaves in Egypt (Ex. 3:7). Judah's prayers to false gods would soon be exposed as futile. The reference to Baal worship throughout the cities of Judah suggests that this sermon was either delivered at the beginning of the reform of Josiah or during the reign of Jehoiakim, when the effect of the reform of Josiah had worn off.

Appended to this sermon are two brief notes. The first (v. 14) is a repetition of the restriction imposed on Jeremiah (7:16) not to pray for the people any longer. The command is appropriate at this point also, for it underscores the terrible certainty that God will not hear the intercessions or cries of His people in its present condition (cf. v. 11). The second note (v. 15) further emphasizes the futility of Judah's efforts to avert the oncoming disaster at God's hand. Rich sacrifices can no longer atone for His people's burdensome guilt. God cannot tolerate Baal worship. The burning of incense meant total commitment to a false god. God's wrath, in turn, would burn His people, His chosen olive tree. In anguish God would devour what once He had tenderly planted.

## THE FIRST PERSONAL CRISIS
### FOR JEREMIAH                                        11:18—12:6

<sup>18</sup> The **LORD** made it known to me and I knew;
   then thou didst show me their evil deeds.
<sup>19</sup> But I was like a gentle lamb
   led to the slaughter.
 I did not know it was against me
   they devised schemes, saying,
 "Let us destroy the tree with its fruit,
   let us cut him off from the land of the living,
   that his name be remembered no more."
<sup>20</sup> But, O **LORD** of hosts, who judgest righteously,
   who triest the heart and the mind,
 let me see thy vengeance upon them,
   for to thee have I committed my cause.
   <sup>21</sup> Therefore thus says the **LORD** concerning
 the men of An'athoth, who seek your life, and say,

121

"Do not prophesy in the name of the LORD, or you will die by our hand" — [22] therefore thus says the LORD of hosts: "Behold, I will punish them; the young men shall die by the sword; their sons and their daughters shall die by famine; [23] and none of them shall be left. For I will bring evil upon the men of An'athoth, the year of their punishment."

[1] Righteous art thou, O LORD, when I complain
    to thee;
  yet I would plead my case before thee.
 Why does the way of the wicked prosper?
 Why do all who are treacherous thrive?
[2] Thou plantest them, and they take root;
  they grow and bring forth fruit;
 thou art near in their mouth
  and far from their heart.
[3] But thou, O LORD, knowest me;
  thou seest me, and triest my mind toward thee.
 Pull them out like sheep for the slaughter,
  and set them apart for the day of slaughter.
[4] How long will the land mourn,
  and the grass of every field wither?
 For the wickedness of those who dwell in it
  the beasts and the birds are swept away,
  because men said, "He will not see our latter
    end."

[5] "If you have raced with men on foot, and they have
    wearied you,
  how will you compete with horses?
 And if in a safe land you fall down,
  how will you do in the jungle of the Jordan?
[6] For even your brothers and the house of your
    father,

even they have dealt treacherously with you;
they are in full cry after you;
believe them not,
though they speak fair words to you."

**18-20** The first major personal crisis for Jeremiah
that is recorded arose from an insidious plan of his
relatives to take his life. At first Jeremiah was ignorant
of this plan. In the words of the Hebrew text, God
"caused" him to see (11:18) that his own family was
plotting his downfall (12:6). Similar revelations about
matters of a personal nature are relatively uncommon
in the Old Testament. Persecution and rejection by
one's own household is doubly vicious and disturbing.
The innocent, helpless, and distraught character of the
prophet is underscored by the select Hebrew terms
for "gentle" and "lamb" as well as by the biting dialog
placed in the mouth of those friends (v. 19) who are
later designated "sheep destined for slaughter" (12:3).
Jeremiah's name has become a disgrace to his family
and must therefore be erased from history. Consequently Jeremiah pleads for divine aid and vengeance —
God's vengeance, not his own! His cause (Hebrew:
"case at court") is now in God's hands, for God's own
word and name are at stake according to v. 21. To
avenge the prophet meant to vindicate the prophet's
message and publicly demonstrate the righteousness
of Yahweh.

**21-23** The precise historical occasion for this persecution is not immediately evident. Perhaps Jeremiah's
activities were related to the ancient feud between
the ostracized priests of Anathoth (cf. 1:1; 1 Kings
2:26-27) and the legitimate priests of Jerusalem. If
Jeremiah had supported the reform of Josiah (11:6),

123

he would have indirectly sided with the priests of Jerusalem against his own family (cf. 2 Kings 23:4-20). In any case, Yahweh pronounces a verdict of annihilation upon Jeremiah's household in terms comparable to the verdict upon Jerusalem. For Jeremiah this total commitment brought dire consequences (cf. Luke 14:26) and recurring inner turmoil.

**12:1-4** God, however, apparently delayed the enforcement of His verdict. Jeremiah therefore reopens his "case" and demands another hearing. He is distressed because God has been planting (cf. 1:10) and nourishing those He has condemned. Where, then, is the righteousness of God? (Cf. Ps. 73; Job 21.) How long will God wait? Jeremiah reminds God of his own tested sincerity and of his persecutors' exposed hypocrisy. With tense bitterness the prophet describes how all of nature is being affected by God's apparent hesitancy. He flinches beneath the popular cry that God is really blind to the fate of His people.

**5-6** This time, however, God's reply is an unexpected rebuff. It presents a challenge rather than an answer. "If you can't keep up with men on foot, how will you fare against men on horseback?" For the prophet there were worse trials to come. To sit and sulk about the righteousness of God was pointless. A mammoth task lay ahead, and courage was called for!

## THE DEEP COMPASSION OF GOD
## FOR HIS PEOPLE                                      12:7-13

⁷ "I have forsaken my house,
  I have abandoned my heritage;

I have given the beloved of my soul
   into the hands of her enemies.
8 My heritage has become to me
   like a lion in the forest,
she has lifted up her voice against me;
   therefore I hate her.
9 Is my heritage to me like a speckled bird of prey?
   Are the birds of prey against her round about?
Go, assemble all the wild beasts;
   bring them to devour.
10 Many shepherds have destroyed my vineyard,
   they have trampled down my portion,
they have made my pleasant portion
   a desolate wilderness.
11 They have made it a desolation;
   desolate, it mourns to me.
The whole land is made desolate,
   but no man lays it to heart.
12 Upon all the bare heights in the desert
   destroyers have come;
for the sword of the LORD devours
   from one end of the land to the other;
   no flesh has peace.
13 They have sown wheat and have reaped thorns,
   they have tired themselves out but profit nothing.
They shall be ashamed of their ᵘ harvests
   because of the fierce anger of the LORD."

ᵘ Heb *your*

In juxtaposition with the preceding portrait of Jeremiah's inner anguish stands a stark portrait of that suffering of God which the prophet has partially mirrored in his own life. The tension between God's justice and God's compassion is viewed from God's own vantage point (cf. 31:20). Throughout this section God speaks of "my house," "my heritage," "the beloved of my soul," and "my pleasant portion." In these expressions we see God looking back to His tender choice of Israel as a bride and to the years of undeserved love He had showered upon her (cf. 2:2-3). But like a traitor He must abandon His people and like an unfaithful husband desert His bride. He must "hate" His own, that is, He must reject His bride (cf. Mal. 1:3) because she has become dangerous like a lion (v. 8). God Himself is now being attacked. Nevertheless, beneath this rejection lies a burning compassion. God suffers when He sees His people being devoured. In His eyes these people are like a beautiful bird attacked by greedy birds of prey whose cries summon the wild beasts. The birds, beasts, and shepherds are the destroyers from across the deserts to the east (v. 12) who ravage the countryside at the instigation of God's wrath. When it is all over, God is melancholy. He hears the land whimpering, and He shudders to think that no one cares (v. 11). The disaster in question is probably the destructive onslaught of the hordes from the desert around 601 B. C. (Cf. 2 Kings 24:2; Jer. 35:11)

## THE ULTIMATE COMPASSION OF GOD
## FOR ISRAEL'S NEIGHBORS                    12:14-17

**14 Thus says the LORD concerning all my evil neighbors who touch the heritage which I have given my people Israel to inherit: "Behold, I will pluck them up from their land, and I will pluck up the house of Judah from among them. 15 And after I have plucked them up, I will again have compassion on them, and I will bring them again each to his heritage**

and each to his land. [16] And it shall come to pass, if they will diligently learn the ways of my people, to swear by my name, 'As the LORD lives,' even as they taught my people to swear by Ba'al, then they shall be built up in the midst of my people. [17] But if any nation will not listen, then I will utterly pluck it up and destroy it, says the LORD."

If the elect people of "Israel" are not spared God's wrath, how will its pagan neighbors fare? In this brief but poignant prose oracle those pagan nations who had been the agents of God's punishment against Judah are now condemned for having "touched" God's chosen people. These peoples, too, must be uprooted and destroyed like Judah. It is noteworthy that the deportations of Nebuchadnezzar included many of Judah's neighbors. However, God's underlying compassion extends also to these nations. They are given the option of reception into the family of God by confessing (or "swearing" publicly by) the name of Yahweh as their covenant Overlord and by renouncing their former allegiances (cf. Joshua 24:19-24). They, too, can be "built" into the temple of God's people (cf. 1 Peter 2:5). Through this missionary outreach Jeremiah filled his role as a prophet to the nations who must "pluck up" and "build." (1:10)

## THE PARABLE OF THE WAISTCLOTH    13:1-11

[1] Thus said the LORD to me, "Go and buy a linen waistcloth, and put it on your loins, and do not dip it in water." [2] So I bought a waistcloth according to the word of the LORD, and put it on my loins. [3] And

127

the word of the LORD came to me a second time,
⁴ "Take the waistcloth which you have bought, which
is upon your loins, and arise, go to the Eu-phra'tes,
and hide it there in a cleft of the rock." ⁵ So I went,
and hid it by the Eu-phra'tes, as the LORD commanded me. ⁶ And after many days the LORD said
to me, "Arise, go to the Eu-phra'tes, and take from
there the waistcloth which I commanded you to hide
there." ⁷ Then I went to the Eu-phra'tes, and dug,
and I took the waistcloth from the place where I had
hidden it. And behold, the waistcloth was spoiled,
it was good for nothing.

⁸ Then the word of the LORD came to me: ⁹ "Thus
says the LORD: Even so will I spoil the pride of
Judah and the great pride of Jerusalem. ¹⁰ This evil
people, who refuse to hear my words, who stubbornly
follow their own heart and have gone after other
gods to serve them and worship them, shall be like
this waistcloth, which is good for nothing. ¹¹ For as
the waistcloth clings to the loins of a man, so I made
the whole house of Israel and the whole house of
Judah cling to me, says the LORD, that they might
be for me a people, a name, a praise, and a glory,
but they would not listen.

Chapter 13 presents an unusual parable in which
the prophet enacts his message. The divine word is
translated into action. Symbolic actions of other prophets (e. g., Ezek. 4) allow the possibility that token jour-
neys are here involved rather than two long trips to
the River Euphrates, although the latter is not unlikely
when one considers the fanatical character of the pro-

phetic activity. A vision seems to be excluded by the commission of v. 1. The River Euphrates provides the key to the background of this parable. At the Battle of Carchemish on the Euphrates (605 B. C.) Babylon defeated Egypt for the supremacy of the Near East. The parable can be interpreted in relation to the meaning of this event for Judah. By 597 B. C., however, a segment of Judah had been deported beyond the Euphrates by the victorious army of Babylon. Even more pressing was the subsequent question of the fate of the subjugated men of Judah in the hands of this mighty tyrant. The answer of the parable is unequivocal.

Whether the linen waistcloth was an undergarment or an ornamental waistband (such as the girdle of the priest in Ex. 28:39) is debated. In either case it cost money. Israel, the people of God, was "bought" with a price; she was "created" by God (as in Deut. 32:6, where the same verb is used). The waistcloth, therefore, reflected the peculiar status of Israel as God's elect nation and represented the covenant by which Yahweh as a magnanimous overlord bound Israel to Himself as a vassal people (v. 11; cf. 2:32). Being unwashed it also characterized Israel as a people saturated with sin. The action of hiding the waistcloth in the River Euphrates suggests Judah's captivity by Babylon in 597 B. C. When Jeremiah returned to the Euphrates, he no doubt hoped to receive a favorable message. Would God's people soon be released from captivity as some expected (cf. 28:3; 29:8)? The answer was clear. The waistcloth was spoiled and worthless. At that time Judah's captivity meant full punishment and destruction of her great pride because of her constant allegiance to other gods (cf. 2:18). No immediate return seemed possible in God's dispensation.

129

## THE PARABLE OF THE WINE JARS          13:12-14

12 "You shall speak to them this word: 'Thus says the LORD, the God of Israel, "Every jar shall be filled with wine."' And they will say to you, 'Do we not indeed know that every jar will be filled with wine?' 13 Then you shall say to them, 'Thus says the LORD: Behold, I will fill with drunkenness all the inhabitants of this land: the kings who sit on David's throne, the priests, the prophets, and all the inhabitants of Jerusalem. 14 And I will dash them one against another, fathers and sons together, says the LORD. I will not pity or spare or have compassion, that I should not destroy them.'"

The theme of Judah's harsh destruction persists in the second parable (v. 14). Here the royal house, the prophets, and the priests are singled out for special condemnation and the doom pronounced on God's household is given in absolute terms typical of these judgment oracles. A drinking scene provides the opportunity for this divine "joke." Jeremiah greets the crowd with the popular cry of prosperity: "Every jar will be filled with wine." The prophet is then heckled by the crowd with the reply, "Sure! We know that every jar will be filled." They hadn't grasped the pun. *They* were the jars and they would soon be filled with the wine of God's wrath (cf. 25:15; 49:12; 51:7; Ps. 60:3). Their imminent self-destruction would ultimately be God's means of effecting retribution upon this presumptuous nation. They were drinking themselves to death.

130

## Pleading with the Doomed
## Flock of God                                    13:15-27

¹⁵ Hear and give ear; be not proud,
   for the **LORD** has spoken.
¹⁶ Give glory to the **LORD** your God
   before he brings darkness,
  before your feet stumble
   on the twilight mountains,
  and while you look for light
   he turns it into gloom
   and makes it deep darkness.
¹⁷ But if you will not listen,
   my soul will weep in secret for your pride;
  my eyes will weep bitterly and run down with
      tears,
   because the **LORD'S** flock has been taken captive.

¹⁸ Say to the king and the queen mother:
   "Take a lowly seat,
  for your beautiful crown
   has come down from your head." *v*
¹⁹ The cities of the Negeb are shut up,
   with none to open them;
  all Judah is taken into exile,
   wholly taken into exile.

²⁰ "Lift up your eyes and see
   those who come from the north.
  Where is the flock that was given you,
   your beautiful flock?
²¹ What will you say when they set as head over you
   those whom you yourself have taught
   to be friends to you?

   *v* Gk Syr Vg: Heb obscure

Will not pangs take hold of you,
  like those of a woman in travail?
22 And if you say in your heart,
  'Why have these things come upon me?'
  it is for the greatness of your iniquity
  that your skirts are lifted up,
  and you suffer violence.
23 Can the Ethiopian change his skin
  or the leopard his spots?
Then also you can do good
  who are accustomed to do evil.
24 I will scatter you *w* like chaff
  driven by the wind from the desert
25 This is your lot,
  the portion I have measured out to you, says
    the LORD,
because you have forgotten me
  and trusted in lies.
26 I myself will lift up your skirts over your face,
  and your shame will be seen.
27 I have seen your abominations,
  your adulteries and neighings, your lewd har-
    lotries,
  on the hills in the field.
Woe to you, O Jerusalem!
  How long will it be
  before you are made clean?"

*w* Heb *them*


Despite the assertion of most scholars that the
oracles of this section stem from divers historical occasions, it is nevertheless possible to relate them all to
one confined period. In v. 18 young King Jehoiachin
and his mother, Nehushta, seem to be addressed (cf.

2 Kings 24:8 f.). By the time Jehoiachin ascended the throne, the first downfall of Jerusalem (597 B. C.) was imminent. The situation was pathetic and desperate. The darkness of captivity had almost overtaken Jerusalem (v. 16). The flock of God's people, which had been Jerusalem's responsibility, had been almost demolished (vv. 17, 20). The cities of the Negeb to the south were already in enemy hands (v. 19). The destroyer was none other than Babylon, that fierce enemy from the north whom Jeremiah had long predicted (v. 20; cf. 4:6; 6:22) and with whom Judah had tried to make friends by political alliances (v. 21). Jerusalem's captivity was a foregone conclusion (v. 25). She was the defiled shepherdess who had to be exposed and humiliated before the pagan world like a disreputable woman of the streets. (Vv. 22, 26)

These pronouncements during Jerusalem's 11th hour are also characterized by a tone of desperate pleading. Harsh judgments are tempered by heart-rending cries and questions. Reflecting the attitude of Yahweh Himself (cf. 12:7-11), the prophet expresses his own uncontrollable grief over the fate of God's flock (v. 17). Surely Judah would listen now. He urges the king and the queen mother to humble themselves in the light of recent developments (v. 18). Where is your beautiful flock now? Where are your "friends"? What are these pains (vv. 20-22)? These cries reach a bitter climax with the words, "How long will it be before you are made clean (v. 27)?" Alas, Judah could not even recognize her own filth and guilt. To do evil had become second nature to her. It was a part of her like the skin of an Ethiopian or the spots of a leopard. Her will was bound (v. 23). But God pleads to the very end. (V. 27)

## LAMENTS FOR THE DOOMED
## PEOPLE OF GOD                              14:1 — 15:9

[1] The word of the LORD which came to Jeremiah
concerning the drought:
[2] "Judah mourns
  and her gates languish;
 her people lament on the ground,
  and the cry of Jerusalem goes up.
[3] Her nobles send their servants for water;
  they come to the cisterns,
 they find no water,
  they return with their vessels empty;
 they are ashamed and confounded
  and cover their heads.
[4] Because of the ground which is dismayed,
  since there is no rain on the land,
 the farmers are ashamed,
  they cover their heads.
[5] Even the hind in the field forsakes her newborn
    calf
  because there is no grass.
[6] The wild asses stand on the bare heights,
  they pant for air like jackals;
 their eyes fail
  because there is no herbage.

[7] "Though our iniquities testify against us,
  act, O LORD, for thy name's sake;
 for our backslidings are many,
  we have sinned against thee.
[8] O thou hope of Israel,
  its savior in time of trouble,
 why shouldst thou be like a stranger in the land,

like a wayfarer who turns aside to tarry for
a night?
9 Why shouldst thou be like a man confused,
like a mighty man who cannot save?
Yet thou, O LORD, art in the midst of us,
and we are called by thy name;
leave us not."

10 Thus says the LORD concerning this people:
"They have loved to wander thus,
they have not restrained their feet;
therefore the LORD does not accept them,
now he will remember their iniquity
and punish their sins."

11 The LORD said to me: "Do not pray for the
welfare of this people. 12 Though they fast, I will
not hear their cry, and though they offer burnt offering and cereal offering, I will not accept them; but
I will consume them by the sword, by famine, and
by pestilence."

13 Then I said: "Ah, Lord GOD, behold, the
prophets say to them, 'You shall not see the sword,
nor shall you have famine, but I will give you assured
peace in this place.'" 14 And the LORD said to me:
"The prophets are prophesying lies in my name;
I did not send them nor did I command them or speak
to them. They are prophesying to you a lying vision,
worthless divination, and the deceit of their own
minds. 15 Therefore thus says the LORD concerning
the prophets who prophesy in my name although
I did not send them, and who say, 'Sword and famine
shall not come on this land': By sword and famine
those prophets shall be consumed. 16 And the people
to whom they prophesy shall be cast out in the streets

135

of Jerusalem, victims of famine and sword, with none
to bury them—them, their wives, their sons, and
their daughters. For I will pour out their wickedness
upon them.

¹⁷ "You shall say to them this word:
  'Let my eyes run down with tears night and day,
      and let them not cease,
  for the virgin daughter of my people is smitten
      with a great wound,
      with a very grievous blow.
¹⁸ If I go out into the field,
      behold, those slain by the sword!
  And if I enter the city,
      behold, the diseases of famine!
  For both prophet and priest ply their trade through
      the land,
      and have no knowledge.'"

¹⁹ Hast thou utterly rejected Judah?
      Does thy soul loathe Zion?
  Why hast thou smitten us
      so that there is no healing for us?
  We looked for peace, but no good came;
      for a time of healing, but behold, terror.
²⁰ We acknowledge our wickedness, O LORD,
      and the iniquity of our fathers,
      for we have sinned against thee.
²¹ Do not spurn us, for thy name's sake;
      do not dishonor thy glorious throne;
      remember and do not break thy covenant with us.
²² Are there any among the false gods of the nations
      that can bring rain?
  Or can the heavens give showers?              .
  Art thou not he, O LORD our God?

We set our hope on thee,
for thou doest all these things.

[1] Then the LORD said to me, "Though Moses and Samuel stood before me, yet my heart would not turn toward this people. Send them out of my sight, and let them go! [2] And when they ask you, 'Where shall we go?' you shall say to them, 'Thus says the LORD:
"Those who are for pestilence, to pestilence,
    and those who are for the sword, to the sword;
those who are for famine, to famine,
    and those who are for captivity, to captivity."'
[3] "I will appoint over them four kinds of destroyers, says the LORD: the sword to slay, the dogs to tear, and the birds of the air and the beasts of the earth to devour and destroy. [4] And I will make them a horror to all the kingdoms of the earth because of what Manas'seh the son of Hezeki'ah, king of Judah, did in Jerusalem.

[5] "Who will have pity on you, O Jerusalem,
    or who will bemoan you?
Who will turn aside
    to ask about your welfare?
[6] You have rejected me, says the LORD,
    you keep going backward;
so I have stretched out my hand against you and
        destroyed you; —
    I am weary of relenting.
[7] I have winnowed them with a winnowing fork
    in the gates of the land;
I have bereaved them, I have destroyed my people;
    they did not turn from their ways.

137

⁸ I have made their widows more in number
  than the sand of the seas;
 I have brought against the mothers of young men
  a destroyer at noonday;
 I have made anguish and terror
  fall upon them suddenly.
⁹ She who bore seven has languished;
  she has swooned away;
 her sun went down while it was yet day;
  she has been shamed and disgraced.
 And the rest of them I will give to the sword
  before their enemies,

                              says the **LORD**."

Intercession was an important aspect of the prophet's task (cf. 1 Sam. 7:8; 12:19). Here Jeremiah exercises this function as prophetic mediator. In the process he learns several harsh lessons. Jeremiah offers two formal laments. He apparently uses the plural form of address to speak in the name of the community of God's people. The first lament is evoked by a severe drought (14:2-9) and the second by a critical war (14:17-22). Each lament is similar to community laments found elsewhere in the Old Testament (Pss. 44 and 60). The famine theme reappears in the second lament (v. 22). This fact probably accounts for the juxtaposition of these two laments and for the superscription (14:1) "concerning droughts" (RSV reads "drought" in the singular). Each lament or prayer is followed by a corresponding divine assertion that intercession is futile to help God's people (14:10-12; 15:1-4). These assertions, in turn, are linked with cruel words of total doom for those prophetic intercessors who had rejected God's Word (14:13-16) and the people of Judah who had rejected God Himself (15:5-9). Thus despite the apparent disparate date of the various sections they form a meaningful sequence and unit.

**1-9** The Old Testament prophets never viewed a drought or famine as a chance event. Natural catastrophes were related to Israel's sin and part of God's righteous plan. To evoke God's sympathy and pity during a certain drought, probably quite early in the prophet's career, Jeremiah first portrays the pathetic scene of desolation. The sad state of affairs is illustrated by the lot of the noble and the farmer (vv. 3-4) as well as by two examples from nature (vv. 5-6). The ensuing prayer includes a confession of sins and a cultic cry for divine aid (v. 7), a bold challenge to arouse God to action and a closing affirmation of faith (vv. 8-9). The drought is considered confirming evidence of Judah's defection from God's side (cf. Hos. 4:1-3; Jer. 12:4), while the name of God dwelling in Jerusalem is the acknowledged basis for any hope of forgiveness (cf. Ps. 25:11). For that name, Yahweh, means "God with us" or "Savior in time of trouble" (cf. Ex. 3:1-17). And that is the name which Judah inevitably bears as part of God's chosen people (v. 9). Because this is true, Jeremiah can fling at God's feet the bold challenges of vv. 8 and 9. His questions are sharp and typical (cf. Lam. 5:20-22). If God is the everpresent Savior, why should He act like a disinterested transient or a confused and cowardly warrior, retorts the prophet.

**10-12** God's answer in vv. 10-12 offers a threefold lesson. This reply, however, was not the usual word of comfort and peace pronounced on the temple worshipers who offered such a lament but a cold rebuff. Jeremiah's lament on behalf of his people was to no avail. First, the unrestrained sin of God's people could no longer

139

be tolerated. Formal lament had become useless (v. 10). Second, Jeremiah's own intercession on behalf of his people was also pointless. He was obliged to desist (cf. 11:14-15). Finally, no fasts or rituals of any kind could avert the total disaster of which the previous drought was an unsavory foretaste. (V. 12)

**13-16** This verdict was apparently difficult for Jeremiah to accept. He knew that the other prophets were promising peace and salvation. God seemed to be contradicting Himself. Jeremiah was quick to bring this disturbing fact to God's attention (v. 13). Then Jeremiah learned the true character of the professional prophets. They were false prophets who used God's ominous name for their selfish ends. These prophets will therefore suffer the same violent fate as the rest of God's family — sword and famine from God's own hand (vv. 14-16). Later Jeremiah was fully aware of the hypocritical nature of the professional prophets and denounced them even more severely (23:9-32). It seems plausible, therefore, that this lesson also stems from an early period of Jeremiah's ministry.

**17-22** The lament of 14:17-22 parallels the lament of 14:2-9 at many points. The date and historical situation, however, are different: Judah, viewed from the vantage point of God's elective love as His virgin daughter, is now crushed by wars as well as famine. The day of Babylon's conquest of Judah in 597 B.C. seems the most plausible historical occasion. The initial personal reactions of the sensitive prophet serve to confront God with the prevailing crisis. Conditions in the field, in the city, and among the religious leaders illustrate the seriousness of the situation (vv. 17-18). Provocative questions similar to those of 14:8-9 are again intended to arouse God's jealousy for His people. A confession

140

of sins, an urgent plea for help on account of His name, and a forceful affirmation of hope are likewise repeated. This confession connects Judah's damning sin with that of the forefathers (such as Manasseh in 15:4). The ground of her appeal for deliverance here is not only the name that God caused to dwell in Jerusalem (Deut. 12:5) but also the ark of the covenant in the temple and the eternal bond of covenant relationship itself. The ark is here portrayed as the glorious throne from which Yahweh rules with justice and mercy (cf. 3:12). In Yahweh there is always hope, for He is not bound by the limitations of other gods but reigns as the sovereign Creator, who provides for the daily needs of all mankind. (Vv. 19-22)

15:1-4 Again the prophet's plea is futile and the formal lament worthless. Even Moses and Samuel, two of the greatest intercessors and mediators of Israel's past, could no longer have influenced God's course of action. His rejection of His people was absolutely final. Four violent destroyers will be appointed to accompany the impending fourfold destruction. The atrocities of Manasseh (2 Kings 21:1-18) marked the beginning of this terrible end for God's people.

5-9 This passage offers a dramatic conclusion to this collection of messages. Jeremiah had now learned the bitter lesson that no laments, no intercessions, no heroes of faith from the past could avert the final sentence of condemnation. Jerusalem would fall with none to give her a second thought. In the midst of this scene of utter despair the prophet hears Yahweh's own song of desolation. In a sense it was God's own lament (cf. 12:7-11). God's people had repeatedly spurned God, and God, in turn, had repeatedly restrained His destructive wrath. But God's magnanimous patience had apparently reached its limit. He would no longer "relent," that is, change His mind (vv. 5-6). With righteous nostalgia, therefore, He reviews His destructive acts of judgment until He reaches a final decision. "Those who are left I will deliver to the sword." (Vv. 7-9)

## THE SECOND PERSONAL CRISIS
### FOR JEREMIAH                                    15:10-21

[10] Woe is me, my mother, that you bore me, a man of strife and contention to the whole land! I have not lent, nor have I borrowed, yet all of them curse me. [11] So let it be, O LORD, [x] if I have not entreated [y] thee for their good, if I have not pleaded with thee on behalf of the enemy in the time of trouble and in the time of distress! [12] Can one break iron, iron from the north, and bronze?

[13] "Your wealth and your treasures I will give as spoil, without price, for all your sins, throughout all your territory. [14] I will make you serve your enemies in a land which you do not know, for in my anger a fire is kindled which shall burn for ever."

[15] O LORD, thou knowest;
 remember me and visit me,
 and take vengeance for me on my persecutors.
In thy forbearance take me not away;
 know that for thy sake I bear reproach.
[16] Thy words were found, and I ate them,
 and thy words became to me a joy
 and the delight of my heart;
for I am called by thy name,
 O LORD, God of hosts.
[17] I did not sit in the company of merrymakers,

---

[x] Gk Old Latin: Heb *the* LORD *said*   [y] Cn: Heb obscure

nor did I rejoice;
I sat alone, because thy hand was upon me,
   for thou hadst filled me with indignation.
[18] Why is my pain unceasing,
   my wound incurable,
   refusing to be healed?
Wilt thou be to me like a deceitful brook,
   like waters that fail?

[19] Therefore thus says the LORD:
   "If you return, I will restore you,
   and you shall stand before me.
If you utter what is precious, and not what is worthless,
   you shall be as my mouth.
They shall turn to you,
   but you shall not turn to them.
[20] And I will make you to this people
   a fortified wall of bronze;
they will fight against you,
   but they shall not prevail over you,
for I am with you
   to save you and deliver you,
                              says the LORD.
[21] I will deliver you out of the hand of the wicked,
   and redeem you from the grasp of the ruthless."


10-12 The confession of Jeremiah's first personal
crisis appeared in 11:18–12:6. The present intimate expression of anguish taken from the diary of Jeremiah's
private life before God is similar and probably arose in
a similar period. It begins with a forceful ejaculation
of despair (vv. 10-11) and frustration (v. 12). The prophet
regrets his birth because life has become unbearable.

Even his intercessions on behalf of his persecutors had proved fruitless (cf. Is. 53:12). He has become a man of sorrows with no good reason to exist (cf. Is. 53:3). He could not do the impossible; he could not break "iron from the north." Would he perhaps take the advice of Job's wife to "curse God and die"? (Job 2:9)

**13-18** In the midst of his confession he repeats an oracle of doom and deportation that God had elsewhere forced him to pronounce on those who had become his enemies (vv. 13-14; cf. 17:3 f., where the same verses appear). But again, God delayed the execution of His word. (Compare the comment on 12:1.) Suddenly the prophet turns from self-pity to anger and demands justice at God's hands. He cries for God's condescending concern "to remember and visit" him in his extremity (cf. Ps. 8:4; 106:4, where the same Hebrew terms are used). He claims to have borne intolerable insults on God's behalf. He has become God's whipping boy, and God should do something about it (v. 15)! With a measure of nostalgia he recollects the initial excitement of his call (Ch. 1). He recalls how he first discovered that God's word had possessed him, that he was actually speaking God's words, and that he really belonged to God (cf. Ezek. 2:8 – 3:3). He had become identified with God's word and God's mysterious name. And he remembers how he had been forced by the same compelling hand of God (cf. 1 Kings 18:46; 2 Kings 3:15) to live alone, alienated from his people (cf. 16:1-9). In the end he had become identified with God's wrath, a man "filled" with God's wrath (vv. 16-17). Such a life was nothing but an intolerable sickness. God had promised His formidable protection (1:8, 17-19) and personal vengeance (11:21-23). Neither seemed to be forthcoming. In his final outburst Jeremiah almost curses God. Is God as

144

unreliable as a mirage or a dry wadi, as "waters that fail?" (V. 18)

19-21 Jeremiah had gone too far. God therefore called him to repentance and renewed his call (cf. 1:9). He could continue as God's spokesman only if he uttered God's message and dismissed his own concerns. Then he would receive all the protection he really needed.

## THE PERSONAL LONELINESS OF JEREMIAH                          16:1-9

[1] The word of the LORD came to me: [2] "You shall not take a wife, nor shall you have sons or daughters in this place. [3] For thus says the LORD concerning the sons and daughters who are born in this place, and concerning the mothers who bore them and the fathers who begot them in this land: [4] They shall die of deadly diseases. They shall not be lamented, nor shall they be buried; they shall be as dung on the surface of the ground. They shall perish by the sword and by famine, and their dead bodies shall be food for the birds of the air and for the beasts of the earth.

[5] "For thus says the LORD: Do not enter the house of mourning, or go to lament, or bemoan them; for I have taken away my peace from this people, says the LORD, my steadfast love and mercy. [6] Both great and small shall die in this land; they shall not be buried, and no one shall lament for them or cut himself or make himself bald for them. [7] No one shall break bread for the mourner, to comfort him for the dead; nor shall any one give him the cup of consolation to drink for his father or his mother. [8] You shall not go into the house of feasting to sit with them, to eat and drink. [9] For thus says the LORD of hosts, the

145

God of Israel: Behold, I will make to cease from this place, before your eyes and in your days, the voice of mirth and the voice of gladness, the voice of the bridegroom and the voice of the bride.

**1-4** In the previous confession Jeremiah had reminded God of his painful loneliness. He was forced to live the unpleasant role of God's alienated prophet (15:7). Jer. 16:1-9 presents the specific details of certain phases of that solitary life as Yahweh had outlined it relatively early in the prophet's ministry. First of all, Jeremiah is forbidden to marry and have children, as a living memorial to the ill-fated parents and children who were about to suffer terrible disasters on the coming day of divine wrath. None would even lament their passing. Childlessness, moreover, was a cruel curse in the mind of an Israelite. For Jeremiah to suffer such a fate on behalf of a people who blatantly rejected him and his message made God's command even crueler and his own lot even more isolated.

**5-7** Jeremiah is also prohibited from expressing any outward sympathy or concern for his people by joining in their conventional mourning rituals of laceration, shaving the head, communal eating or drinking from the cup of fellowship and sympathy. In so doing the prophet anticipates God's deliberate retraction of covenant mercy and sympathy from His own people. The doom of God's people has been planned. There will be no eulogy for them.

**8-9** Similarly the prophet is prevented from participating in communal festivities as a public sign or portent that the normal joys of life would soon cease in Judah. Through these practices Jeremiah's life and activities became a continuous sermon, a visible living word. His whole life had a symbolic dimension. As the alienated prophet he visibly portrayed the complete alienation of God from Judah and the ensuing loneliness of His forsaken people. (Cf. Hos. 1–3)

## A VEHEMENT MESSAGE CONCERNING THE FATE OF GOD'S PEOPLE 16:10-21

10 "And when you tell this people all these words, and they say to you, 'Why has the LORD pronounced all this great evil against us? What is our iniquity? What is the sin that we have committed against the LORD our God?' 11 then you shall say to them: 'Because your fathers have forsaken me, says the LORD, and have gone after other gods and have served and worshiped them, and have forsaken me and have not kept my law, 12 and because you have done worse than your fathers, for behold, every one of you follows his stubborn evil will, refusing to listen to me; 13 therefore I will hurl you out of this land into a land which neither you nor your fathers have known, and there you shall serve other gods day and night, for I will show you no favor.'

14 "Therefore, behold, the days are coming, says the LORD, when it shall no longer be said, 'As the LORD lives who brought up the people of Israel out of the land of Egypt,' 15 but 'As the LORD lives who brought up the people of Israel out of the north country and out of all the countries where he had driven them.' For I will bring them back to their own land which I gave to their fathers.

16 "Behold, I am sending for many fishers, says the LORD, and they shall catch them; and afterwards I will send for many hunters, and they shall hunt

147

them from every mountain and every hill, and out of the clefts of the rocks. [17] For my eyes are upon all their ways; they are not hid from me, nor is their iniquity concealed from my eyes. [18] And [z] I will doubly recompense their iniquity and their sin, because they have polluted my land with the carcasses of their detestable idols, and have filled my inheritance with their abominations."

[19] O LORD, my strength and my stronghold,
    my refuge in the day of trouble,
to thee shall the nations come
    from the ends of the earth and say:
"Our fathers have inherited nought but lies,
    worthless things in which there is no profit.
[20] Can man make for himself gods?
    Such are no gods!"

[21] "Therefore, behold, I will make them know, this once I will make them know my power and my might, and they shall know that my name is the LORD."

[z] Gk: Heb *And first*

10-13 The symbolic activities delineated in 16:1-9 would naturally evoke quizzical comment. In answer to this comment Jeremiah summarizes his living message of doom. God's people had become entrenched in the idolatry and rebelliousness of their forefathers (cf. 14:20). A perverted and obstinate heart made the present generation even more repulsive to God (cf. 7:24-26). The will of His people had become a slave to corruption, idol worship, and disobedience (vv. 10-12). The appropriate sentence called for rejection from the polluted land (cf. v. 18; Lev. 18:24-28), slavery to the pagan gods currently worshiped, and rejection by the God whom the people had persistently rejected (v. 13; cf. 15:6). Here as elsewhere in Jeremiah the integral relationship between a sin and its corresponding punishment is demonstrated. (See 5:19; 8:1-2; 2:19)

**16-18** The execution of the sentence of exile is graphically portrayed as God summoning fishermen and hunters to capture all Israelites destined for captivity. Attempts to hide will be futile. Their sin will always give them away; it can never be hidden from God. Moreover, its crass character elicits a double measure of divine punishment (cf. Is. 40:2). The fishermen and hunters are presumably the Babylonians (cf. Hab. 1:14-17). If so, a date sometime after the Battle of Carchemish (605 B. C.) seems fitting for these words.

**14-15** Two oracles of future hope are also included among these harsh messages of unrelenting chastisement. By means of a forceful "therefore" introducing v. 14 the author takes immediate cognizance of the full execution of God's punitive justice prior to the day of restoration. The sentence is not modified. The day of hope will be a new beginning, a completely new era in Yahweh's plan of salvation. The previous epoch had begun with the dramatic exodus from Egypt. With this saving deed the name of Yahweh had been linked confessionally (cf. Ex. 19:4; 20:2; Deut. 26:8; Jer. 2:6). With the forthcoming exodus from captivity in Babylon a new era and a corresponding new confession would be initiated. These verses are repeated in 23:7-8.

**19-21** New universal features will also characterize this era (cf. 3:17; 4:2). The ancient covenant promise to Abraham will be fulfilled thereby (Gen. 12:3). Foreign nations will worship Yahweh as God. Their confession

149

of faith will include a renunciation of false gods according to the practice of the old covenant liturgy (cf. Joshua 24:19-24). In that day the name of Yahweh will be completely vindicated (cf. Ezek. 36:23; Is. 59:18-19). The full import of this hope can be seen only in the cosmic and universal dimensions of the resurrection of Christ (Phil. 2:9-11). In Him the name of Yahweh was fully vindicated.

## A SELECTION OF TYPICAL SAYINGS    17:1-18

¹ "The sin of Judah is written with a pen of iron; with a point of diamond it is engraved on the tablet of their heart, and on the horns of their altars, ² while their children remember their altars and their Ashe'-rim, beside every green tree, and on the high hills, ³ on the mountains in the open country. Your wealth and all your treasures I will give for spoil as the price of your sin *a* throughout all your territory. ⁴ You shall loosen your hand *b* from your heritage which I gave to you, and I will make you serve your enemies in a land which you do not know, for in my anger a fire is kindled which shall burn for ever."

⁵ Thus says the LORD:
"Cursed is the man who trusts in man
    and makes flesh his arm,
    whose heart turns away from the LORD.
⁶ He is like a shrub in the desert,
    and shall not see any good come.
He shall dwell in the parched places
        of the wilderness,
    in an uninhabited salt land.

⁷ "Blessed is the man who trusts in

*a* Cn: Heb *your high places for sin*    *b* Cn: Heb *and in you*

the LORD,
whose trust is the LORD.

⁸ He is like a tree planted by water,
that sends out its roots by the stream,
and does not fear when heat comes,
for its leaves remain green,
and is not anxious in the year of drought,
for it does not cease to bear fruit."

⁹ The heart is deceitful above all things,
and desperately corrupt;
who can understand it?
¹⁰ "I the LORD search the mind
and try the heart,
to give to every man according to his ways,
according to the fruit of his doings."

¹¹ Like the partridge that gathers a brood which she
did not hatch,
so is he who gets riches but not by right;
in the midst of his days they will leave him,
and at his end he will be a fool.

¹² A glorious throne set on high from the beginning
is the place of our sanctuary.
¹³ O LORD, the hope of Israel,
all who forsake thee shall be put to shame;
those who turn away from thee ᶜ shall be written in
the earth,
for they have forsaken the LORD, the fountain of
living water.

¹⁴ Heal me, O LORD, and I shall be healed;
save me, and I shall be saved;
for thou art my praise.

ᶜ Heb *me*

¹⁵ Behold, they say to me,
  "Where is the word of the LORD?
  Let it come!"
¹⁶ I have not pressed thee to send evil,
  nor have I desired the day of disaster,
  thou knowest;
  that which came out of my lips
  was before thy face.
¹⁷ Be not a terror to me;
  thou art my refuge in the day of evil.
¹⁸ Let those be put to shame who persecute me,
  but let me not be put to shame;
  let them be dismayed,
  but let me not be dismayed;
  bring upon them the day of evil;
  destroy them with double destruction!

This corpus consists of a selection of miscellaneous observations and sayings. In most cases no obvious historical date is discernible. The selection incorporates a new pronouncement concerning Judah's irremovable guilt (vv. 1-4), a brief psalm (vv. 5-8), two proverbs (vv. 9-11), an invocation of praise (vv. 12-13), and a sharp prayer for vengeance (vv. 14-18). In general these sayings reflect Jeremiah's repeated preoccupation with the inner corruption of his people.

1-4 The message of Jer. 17:1-4 is closely related to that of 16:10-13. The total perversion of Judah is reaffirmed through the use of pointed imagery from the engraving profession. In Jeremiah the heart is the seat of religious and spiritual life. The heart determines man's motives and decisions. Like a stone tablet, Judah's heart has been deeply engraved with her sins. They cannot be erased; the people cannot repent. Rebellion has become the driving force of life. Even the horns of the altar, where the atoning blood was periodically sprinkled (cf. Lev. 4:7), were likewise engraved. Mere ritual blood, therefore, could no longer cover Judah's engraven guilt. Judah's sin was too deep to be eradicated. The mind of the younger generation would also be indelibly marked by the memory of vile fertility shrines. A sin of such magnitude and depth meant surrender of wealth, forfeit of heritage, and loss of freedom. It meant the full exposure of Yahweh's jealous wrath. Against this Judah had no defense.

**5-8** The psalm of Jer. 17:5-8, which bears a marked similarity to Psalm 1, contrasts the foolish man who relies on human ingenuity and strength with the man who trusts fervently in Yahweh as his strength (cf. Is. 31:3). This contrast is reinforced by comparing the struggling desert bramble with the prosperous tree on the river bank. The man of faith is blessed and prosperous. There were times, however, when Jeremiah's own experiences seemed to challenge this truth. (Cf. 12:1-3)

**9-11** The proverb of the hypocritical heart reflects a fundamental concern of Jeremiah's preaching (cf. vv. 1-4 above). He insists that man's inner self exhibits an incomprehensible duplicity. It is characterized by self-deception and spiritual sickness. Jeremiah had observed this truth among his people (17:1) as well as within himself (15:18-19). Although this reality may have appeared a mystery for man, it does not negate the righteousness of God. He can and does analyze the motives of man's will or "mind" (the RSV rendering of the Hebrew word for heart) and understand the emotions of man's "heart" (the RSV rendering of the Hebrew word for kidneys). On this basis God takes appropriate action.

The second proverb (v. 11) is apparently dependent on a popular belief that a partridge that hatches the eggs of other birds is deserted by her young. Similarly ill-gotten gain affords a precarious security. The proverb is applicable to many of the rulers and people of Jeremiah's day. (Cf. Jer. 22:13-19)

**12-13** Reflecting the worship language of the temple, the invocation of vv. 12-13 provides a fitting prelude to the ensuing cry for vindication. Jeremiah calls upon Yahweh as the God who descends from His heavenly throne to rule His people in His earthly sanctuary and place of refuge (cf. Is. 6). His rule, moreover, is just. Those who forsake Him will find their names written in the dust of the earth rather than in the heavenly book of life (cf. Ex. 32:32). How different is Jeremiah's cry to the false trust in the eternal character of the earthly temple fostered by the religious leaders of that day. (Cf. Jer. 7:4 ff.)

**14-18** Jeremiah thereupon urges God to demonstrate this just rule in his own life. His prayer (17:14-18) is another blunt and frank confession. The prophet is rent by a dilemma from which he requests God to save him. He was possessed by the Word of God and compelled to preach it. His misguided adversaries laughed him to scorn because his word, that is, his prediction of doom, had not yet come to pass. This mockery was doubly sharp because Jeremiah had previously interceded before God that He refrain from executing the sentence of doom pronounced upon these people. God's sympathetic prophet could endure it no longer. He now pleaded for full vindication of his word. He saw his own adversaries as God's enemies. For the sake of his own name as well as of God's he demanded justice. Should his message prove untrue, he would be disgraced and

God's word scorned (cf. Deut. 18:19 ff.). With tortured soul he therefore cries for excessive vengeance. (Cf. 15:10-18)

## A SERMON ON THE SABBATH                    17:19-27

<sup>19</sup> Thus said the LORD to me: "Go and stand in the Benjamin <sup>d</sup> Gate, by which the kings of Judah enter and by which they go out, and in all the gates of Jerusalem, <sup>20</sup> and say: 'Hear the word of the LORD, you kings of Judah, and all Judah, and all the inhabitants of Jerusalem, who enter by these gates. <sup>21</sup> Thus says the LORD: Take heed for the sake of your lives, and do not bear a burden on the sabbath day or bring it in by the gates of Jerusalem. <sup>22</sup> And do not carry a burden out of your houses on the sabbath or do any work, but keep the sabbath day holy, as I commanded your fathers. <sup>23</sup> Yet they did not listen or incline their ear, but stiffened their neck, that they might not hear and receive instruction.

<sup>24</sup> "'But if you listen to me, says the LORD, and bring in no burden by the gates of this city on the sabbath day, but keep the sabbath day holy and do no work on it, <sup>25</sup> then there shall enter by the gates of this city kings <sup>e</sup> who sit on the throne of David, riding in chariots and on horses, they and their princes, the men of Judah and the inhabitants of Jerusalem; and this city shall be inhabited for ever. <sup>26</sup> And people shall come from the cities of Judah and the places round about Jerusalem, from the land of Benjamin, from the Shephe'lah, from the hill country, and from the Negeb, bringing burnt offerings and sacrifices, cereal offerings and frankincense, and bringing thank

<sup>d</sup> Cn: Heb *sons of people*    <sup>e</sup> Cn: Heb *kings and princes*

155

offerings to the house of the LORD. [27] But if you do not listen to me, to keep the sabbath day holy, and not to bear a burden and enter by the gates of Jerusalem on the sabbath day, then I will kindle a fire in its gates, and it shall devour the palaces of Jerusalem and shall not be quenched.'"

How can a prophet who repeatedly insists that God is far greater than the means of worship and the institutions he has established preach a sermon such as this? How can Jeremiah, who had vigorously affirmed that Jerusalem, the ark, the temple, the sacrifices, and all the temple rites could not guarantee the safety of God's people (3:16; 7:14, 21-22; 14:12, etc.), in the same breath assert that if the future kings and people of Judah and Jerusalem keep the Sabbath day holy by refraining from transporting their wares into Jerusalem, they will be blessed? Many consider this sermon the work of a later scribe from the postexilic period, when the restoration of the Sabbath laws was a major concern (Neh. 10:31; 13:15-22). It is conceivable, however, that Jeremiah placed the Sabbath law in a different category from that of the institutions of the temple and its sacrifices and that this sermon reflects the heart of his message. The sanctification of the Sabbath was an integral part of the Decalog, basic to God's covenant relations with His people. The Decalog was the touchstone for Israel's obedient response to God's covenant. Regulations of the Decalog were employed in a similar manner in a temple sermon of Jeremiah (7:9). Moreover, the covenant language from Deuteronomy is obvious in the present sermon. The occasion for the sermon is apparently a certain festival event (v. 20). The prophet concentrates on the abuse of the Sabbath (v. 21) and

156

advocates its sanctification according to the ancient covenant law (v. 22) lest the fate of the fathers befall Judah (v. 23; cf. Deut. 8). He demands abstinence from work and from transportation of wares on the Sabbath (v. 24). In return, he promises an unbroken dynasty, a perpetual habitation, and abundant expressions of worship. (Vv. 25-27)

## JEREMIAH LEARNS THE LESSON OF THE POTTER AT WORK 18:1-12

¹ The word that came to Jeremiah from the LORD: ² "Arise, and go down to the potter's house, and there I will let you hear my words." ³ So I went down to the potter's house, and there he was working at his wheel. ⁴ And the vessel he was making of clay was spoiled in the potter's hand, and he reworked it into another vessel, as it seemed good to the potter to do.

⁵ Then the word of the LORD came to me: ⁶ "O house of Israel, can I not do with you as this potter has done? says the LORD. Behold, like the clay in the potter's hand, so are you in my hand, O house of Israel. ⁷ If at any time I declare concerning a nation or a kingdom, that I will pluck up and break down and destroy it, ⁸ and if that nation, concerning which I have spoken, turns from its evil, I will repent of the evil that I intended to do to it. ⁹ And if at any time I declare concerning a nation or a kingdom that I will build and plant it, ¹⁰ and if it does evil in my sight, not listening to my voice, then I will repent of the good which I had intended to do to it. ¹¹ Now, therefore, say to the men of Judah and the inhabitants of Jerusalem: 'Thus says the LORD, Behold, I am shaping

157

evil against you and devising a plan against you. Return, every one from his evil way, and amend your ways and your doings.'

¹² "But they say, 'That is in vain! We will follow our own plans, and will every one act according to the stubbornness of his evil heart.'

God often uses commonplace objects and experiences to teach an important lesson of faith. The sign of the almond rod was one case in point (1:11-12). The case of the potter at work is another. After years of preaching the harsh message of doom, this lesson was apropos. At God's direction, Jeremiah the prophet observes a potter molding his clay. He had watched the process many times. On this occasion the vessel is badly spoiled on the potter's wheel. Using the marred pieces of clay, the potter creates a new vessel to his liking. The parable of this experience was quite clear. God, the divine Potter, who had "formed" man (Gen. 2:7) and Jeremiah (1:5), now holds His people in His creative hands. Regardless of appearances, God has everything under control. Two messages are derived from this truth, one for Jeremiah and one for the rebellious people. The personal dimension of the first message is underscored by the repetition of language taken from the account of Jeremiah's call (1:4-10). The prophet must learn that God's work is not merely to destroy. He is not capricious and mechanical. His sovereignty and goodness guarantee the remaking of His people if they repent. He had bound Himself to them in the covenant, but they had spurned His covenant love and refused to listen. Repentance is a possible goal of preaching severe words of doom year after year. Accordingly the second message of the parable of the potter (v. 11) is another vehement oracle of doom for God's people. The divine Potter is "forming" a plan of "evil," that is, disaster for His people. Alas, the reaction of the people sounds the familiar refrain, "It's hopeless." They are not penitent; the plan of doom must go into effect.

## THE THIRD PERSONAL CRISIS
## FOR JEREMIAH                                    18:13-23

13 "Therefore thus says the LORD:
   Ask among the nations,
     who has heard the like of this?
   The virgin Israel
     has done a very horrible thing.
14 Does the snow of Lebanon leave
     the crags of Sirion?[f]
   Do the mountain[g] waters run dry,[h]
     the cold flowing streams?
15 But my people have forgotten me,
     they burn incense to false gods;
   they have stumbled[i] in their ways,
     in the ancient roads,
   and have gone into bypaths,
     not the highway,
16 making their land a horror,
     a thing to be hissed at for ever.
   Every one who passes by it is horrified
     and shakes his head.
17 Like the east wind I will scatter them
     before the enemy.
   I will show them my back, not my face,
     in the day of their calamity."

[f] Cn: Heb *the field*   [g] Cn: Heb *foreign*
[h] Cn: Heb *Are . . . plucked up?*
[i] Gk Syr Vg: Heb *they made them stumble*

159

¹⁸ Then they said, "Come, let us make plots against Jeremiah, for the law shall not perish from the priest, nor counsel from the wise, nor the word from the prophet. Come, let us smite him with the tongue, and let us not heed any of his words."

¹⁹ Give heed to me, O LORD,
    and hearken to my plea.ʲ
²⁰ Is evil a recompense for good?
    Yet they have dug a pit for my life.
  Remember how I stood before thee
    to speak good for them,
    to turn away thy wrath from them.
²¹ Therefore deliver up their children to famine;
    give them over to the power of the sword,
  let their wives become childless and widowed.
    May their men meet death by pestilence,
    their youths be slain by the sword in battle.
²² May a cry be heard from their houses,
    when thou bringest the marauder suddenly upon
      them!
  For they have dug a pit to take me,
    and laid snares for my feet.
²³ Yet, thou, O LORD, knowest
    all their plotting to slay me.
  Forgive not their iniquity,
    nor blot out their sin from thy sight.
  Let them be overthrown before thee;
    deal with them in the time of thine anger.

    ʲ Gk Compare Syr Tg: Heb *my adversaries*

13-17  The oracle of Jer. 18:13-17 provides a fitting prelude to the third major confession of Jeremiah in 18:18-23. (The first two appeared in 11:8 – 12:6 and 15: 10-21.) The essential thoughts of this oracle have been encountered earlier. The setting is probably the age of Jehoiakim, when the adoration of false gods was rampant (v. 15). Jeremiah's public exposure of this public disgrace may have sparked the plots on the prophet's life that follow (v. 18). Jeremiah reiterates the charge that the "virgin" Israel, God's elect people, has committed the twofold atrocity of deserting Yahweh and "stumbling" after the usual false gods (v. 15, cf. 2:11). Nature does not forsake its natural order. There is always snow on Lebanon and Sirion (v. 14; Sirion offers the best rendering of the Hebrew text as in Ps. 29:6). But Israel's behavior is quite the opposite; it is unnatural and without parallel on the world scene (v. 13, cf. 2:10). Its activities have polluted the land to such an extent that a violent appearance of Yahweh's anger seems inevitable. God would finally turn His back on those who had repeatedly turned their back on Him.

**18** The third lengthy text from Jeremiah's personal diary of confessions was evoked by specific intrigues to "smite Jeremiah with the tongue," that is, to promulgate a public slander about him. Earlier Jeremiah's own family had instigated plots against him (11:21-23). Now his enemies seem to belong to the upper echelon of Israelite society. They would permit no one to disturb or threaten the established order of society in which the official priests pronounced the authoritative interpretation of God's law, the wise men gave appropriate counsel for social, moral, and political issues, and the professional prophet gave official oracles to popular requests for valid answers from God.

**19-23** Once more Jeremiah reminds his God of his good will and of his sincere intercessions on behalf of these persecutors (cf. 17:16). He had repeatedly prayed for salvation from the impending day of doom (cf. 14:11;

161

Amos 7:1-6). Jeremiah had indeed been a faithful prophet in this respect (see the comment on 14:1 – 15:9). But his recent total rejection by the leaders of Judah had changed the situation. Vengeance was the only solution he could envision to demonstrate the validity of his messages. The language of this passionate outcry for revenge sounds crude and bloodthirsty to our ears (vv. 21-23). These expressions, however, are typical of those psalms which cry for vengeance against the enemies of God (cf. Ps. 109:1-20). The closing cry to "forgive not their iniquity" seems to be a vindictive prayer for God to strike down the persecutors in their sins (cf. Lev. 10:2). Had Jeremiah gone too far? This time God does not answer. Is His silence a judgment on the prophet? (Compare the answer of God in Jer. 15:11 and the threat of Amos 8:11-12.)

## JEREMIAH BREAKS THE POTTER'S FLASK AND SUFFERS IN THE STOCKS 19:1 – 20:6

¹ Thus said the **LORD**, "Go, buy a potter's earthen flask, and take some of the elders of the people and some of the senior priests, ² and go out to the valley of the son of Hinnom at the entry of the Potsherd Gate, and proclaim there the words that I tell you. ³ You shall say, 'Hear the word of the LORD, O kings of Judah and inhabitants of Jerusalem. Thus says the **LORD** of hosts, the God of Israel, Behold, I am bringing such evil upon this place that the ears of every one who hears of it will tingle. ⁴ Because the people have forsaken me, and have profaned this place by burning incense in it to other gods whom neither they nor their fathers nor the kings of Judah have known;

162

and because they have filled this place with the blood of innocents, ⁵ and have built the high places of Ba'al to burn their sons in the fire as burnt offerings to Ba'al, which I did not command or decree, nor did it come into my mind; ⁶ therefore, behold, days are coming, says the LORD, when this place shall no more be called Topheth, or the valley of the son of Hinnom, but the valley of Slaughter. ⁷ And in this place I will make void the plans of Judah and Jerusalem, and will cause their people to fall by the sword before their enemies, and by the hand of those who seek their life. I will give their dead bodies for food to the birds of the air and to the beasts of the earth. ⁸ And I will make this city a horror, a thing to be hissed at; every one who passes by it will be horrified and will hiss because of all its disasters. ⁹ And I will make them eat the flesh of their sons and their daughters, and every one shall eat the flesh of his neighbor in the siege and in the distress, with which their enemies and those who seek their life afflict them.'

¹⁰ "Then you shall break the flask in the sight of the men who go with you, ¹¹ and shall say to them, 'Thus says the LORD of hosts: So will I break this people and this city, as one breaks a potter's vessel, so that it can never be mended. Men shall bury in Topheth because there will be no place else to bury. ¹² Thus will I do to this place, says the LORD, and to its inhabitants, making this city like Topheth. ¹³ The houses of Jerusalem and the houses of the kings of Judah — all the houses upon whose roofs incense has been burned to all the host of heaven, and drink offerings have been poured out to other gods — shall be defiled like the place of Topheth.'"

¹⁴ Then Jeremiah came from Topheth, where the

163

LORD had sent him to prophesy, and he stood in the court of the LORD'S house, and said to all the people: ¹⁵ "Thus says the LORD of hosts, the God of Israel, Behold, I am bringing upon this city and upon all its towns all the evil that I have pronounced against it, because they have stiffened their neck, refusing to hear my words."

¹ Now Pashhur the priest, the son of Immer, who was chief officer in the house of the LORD, heard Jeremiah prophesying these things. ² Then Pashhur beat Jeremiah the prophet, and put him in the stocks that were in the upper Benjamin Gate of the house of the LORD. ³ On the morrow, when Pashhur released Jeremiah from the stocks, Jeremiah said to him, "The LORD does not call your name Pashhur, but Terror on every side. ⁴ For thus says the LORD: Behold, I will make you a terror to yourself and to all your friends. They shall fall by the sword of their enemies while you look on. And I will give all Judah into the hand of the king of Babylon; he shall carry them captive to Babylon, and shall slay them with the sword. ⁵ Moreover, I will give all the wealth of the city, all its gains, all its prized belongings, and all the treasures of the kings of Judah into the hand of their enemies, who shall plunder them, and seize them, and carry them to Babylon. ⁶ And you, Pashhur, and all who dwell in your house, shall go into captivity; to Babylon you shall go; and there you shall die, and there you shall be buried, you and all your friends, to whom you have prophesied falsely."

Jer. 19:1 — 20:6 relates three separate incidents from the life of Jeremiah. The first is an ominous action out-

164

side the Potsherd Gate of the city. This act is similar
to the burying of the waistcloth (Ch. 13), but it presumably stems from an earlier period during the days
of Jehoiakim (19:1-2a, 10-11a). The second activity is a
sermon against the evils of the valley of Topheth, rampant under Jehoiakim (19:2b-9, 11b-13). The third event
involves Jeremiah's misfortunes at the hands of Pashhur
(19:14 — 20:6). These incidents are reported in the third
person, apparently written by Baruch. Jeremiah's
personal accounts of similar symbolic actions, for example, are related in the first person. (See 13:1; 18:3; 28:1)

**19:1-2a, 10-11a** In Ch. 18 Jeremiah relates how he
learned that although God could remold His people if
they repented (vv. 6-10), it was still the prophet's task
to preach the destruction of God's chosen vessel (v. 11).
In the first report of Jer. 19 Baruch relates how at one
time Jeremiah translated this message into action. The
people of God, His chosen vessel, are symbolized as
a costly, artistic decanter *(baqbuq)*, whose narrow neck
could not be repaired once broken. This figurative action
is performed before the responsible leaders of Judah as
witnesses. God's Word cannot be hidden (cf. 32:12).
The act of breaking this flask in the public square before
a city gate was accompanied by a clear interpretation.
Judah's precious character was no guarantee that her
destruction at the hands of Yahweh would not be beyond
repair (v. 11a). This symbolic act probably had hidden
associations not obvious to us today. The breaking of
vessels, for example, was a common feature of some
Near Eastern funeral rites.

**2b-9, 11b-13** The subsequent sermon repeats the
theme of Yahweh's projected "evil," that is, the violent
catastrophe impending for Judah (see 18:11). This evil is
so grotesque that it will make "the ears tingle," or as we

165

would say, "send shivers down one's spine" (19:3). The depth of Judah's degradation is illustrated by the presence of child sacrifice at Jerusalem. Jeremiah had denounced the practice on an earlier occasion (see 7:27-34 and the comment). The nature of God's evil on Judah would be, first of all, to "make void" its own glorious plans (19:7). The verb "to make void" *(baqaq)* suggests a harsh pun on the term for decanter *(baqbuq)* used above. When Judah's plan is nullified, God's plan goes into effect. His plan involves warfare, intrigue, the disgrace of no burial (v. 7), public humiliation (v. 8), and starvation during siege (v. 9). Once again the punishment would be linked with the crime. The Topheth valley, where God's people had worshiped in such a vile manner, would soon become the local dump for human corpses. Topheth would be exposed for what it really was, "A Valley of Murder" (v. 6). In addition, every part of the holy city where idolatrous worship had been practiced would likewise be defiled with dead bodies. (V. 13)

**19:14—20:6** After the events near the Potsherd Gate facing Topheth, Jeremiah repeated his message of "evil" in the Jerusalem temple courtyard (vv. 14-15). These activities seem to have aroused considerable opposition. At that time Pashhur, the priest or overseer in charge of law and order in the temple, was also responsible for any prophetic incidents. In his opinion, the disruptive influence of Jeremiah could not be tolerated. Jeremiah was therefore thrown into the stocks to suffer public humiliation for a day and a night, with the hope of deterring him from further outbursts. This situation could plausibly have given rise to the very confession of anguish that follows in Jer. 20:7-18.

When Jeremiah was released (20:3-6), he imposed

166

on Pashhur the curse-name "Terror on Every Side," just as he had done to Topheth (19:6). Pashhur had terrorized Jeremiah; now Pashhur would experience the same terror and anguish of heart. The curse would become evident through the ravaging of Jerusalem by the Babylonian armies. Pashhur would personally experience the agony of captivity because of his false prophecies. There is no reason to assume that this Pashhur is identical with the figure in 21:1 and 38:1.

## THE FOURTH PERSONAL CRISIS
### FOR JEREMIAH 20:7-18

7 O LORD, thou hast deceived me,
 and I was deceived;
thou art stronger than I,
 and thou hast prevailed.
I have become a laughingstock all the day;
 every one mocks me.
8 For whenever I speak, I cry out,
 I shout, "Violence and destruction!"
For the word of the LORD has become for me
 a reproach and derision all day long.
9 If I say, "I will not mention him,
 or speak any more in his name,"
there is in my heart as it were a burning fire
 shut up in my bones,
and I am weary with holding it in,
 and I cannot.
10 For I hear many whispering.
 Terror is on every side!
"Denounce him! Let us denounce him!"
 say all my familiar friends,
 watching for my fall.

167

> "Perhaps he will be deceived,
>> then we can overcome him,
>> and take our revenge on him."

11 But the LORD is with me as a dread warrior;
>> therefore my persecutors will stumble,
>> they will not overcome me.
> They will be greatly shamed,
>> for they will not succeed.
> Their eternal dishonor
>> will never be forgotten.

12 O LORD of hosts, who triest the righteous,
>> who seest the heart and the mind,
> let me see thy vengeance upon them,
>> for to thee have I committed my cause.

13 Sing to the LORD;
>> praise the LORD!
> For he has delivered the life of the needy
>> from the hand of evildoers.

14 Cursed be the day
>> on which I was born!
> The day when my mother bore me,
>> let it not be blessed!

15 Cursed be the man
>> who brought the news to my father,
> "A son is born to you,"
>> making him very glad.

16 Let that man be like the cities
>> which the LORD overthrew without pity;
> let him hear a cry in the morning
>> and an alarm at noon,

17 because he did not kill me in the womb;
>> so my mother would have been my grave,
>> and her womb for ever great.

[18] Why did I come forth from the womb
to see toil and sorrow,
and spend my days in shame?

This outburst is the most vehement of all Jeremiah's confessions. The text consists of three major divisions: the prophet's presentation of his case before God (vv. 7-12), a brief hymn of praise (v. 13), and a self-portrait of the prophet's pathetic condition. (Vv. 14-18)

7-12 Jeremiah opens his case by accusing God of deception. The language he employs has a strong sexual connotation. He asserts that God has "seduced" (RSV "deceived") and "overpowered" (RSV "prevailed") him (cf. Ex. 22:16 and Deut. 22:25). He does not deny his prophetic call but charges God with having made a mockery out of it. Jeremiah feels like a persecuted puppet of God. In vv. 8-9 he relates his own version of the situation. Impelled by the inescapable power of the word that God had set in his mouth (1:9; cf. 15:16), he acts like some watchman who is always crying danger, or more specifically, "violence and destruction from God." If he tries to keep silent and disassociate himself from the message, the words build up inside him like an unbearable fire. Once more the Word of God has become a stumbling block for the prophet as well as for his hearers. Before God as his Judge, Jeremiah thereupon testifies to the malicious attitude and words of his persecutors. They brand Jeremiah as a "terrorizer" (cf. 20:3) and plan for revenge. Their caustic speech includes the same terms for "seduce" and "overpower," or "rape," used in Jeremiah's complaint above. In other words, Jeremiah had accused God (in v. 7) of doing what his persecutors were planning. God had apparently become his enemy. Despite this fact, the

169

prophet is driven in vv. 11-12 to appeal to God as his Defender (cf. 1:18-19) and as the Creator who judges human hearts (cf. Ps. 33:15). He hopes to close his case (RSV "cause") before God and see the execution of vengeance. The verdict of damnation for which he pleaded was a name of eternal shame comparable to that of Pontius Pilate.

**13** A short hymn of praise interrupts the prophet's cries of spiritual torment. Like Ps. 117, this verse consists of an opening invitation to hymnic praise and song. coupled with the reason for such praise, namely, God's saving intervention in the life of those in distress. The hymn anticipates the happy outcome of Jeremiah's dilemma.

**14-18** In a manner similar to that of Job (Ch. 3), Jeremiah paints his pathetic lot in the language of a miserable plaintiff. His broken cries, it would seem, are designed to evoke the sympathy of God. For Jeremiah the ideal escape from the torture of living was never to have been born. By cursing his birthday and everything associated with it, he called into question his very existence as one of God's servants. His birthday became his enemy and his own being something worthless. He became "nothing" before God, nothing but a huge question mark. "Why?" he screamed! His "toil" unto death seemed a fruitless waste (cf. Is. 53:11), and his suffering for others a lifelong shame that really benefited no one.

# Sermons and Oracles Pertaining
# to the Leaders of God's People

## Jeremiah 21–23

This division of the Book of Jeremiah consists of three major sections, the first (21:1-10) stemming from the last days of Jerusalem and directed to Zedekiah. Why this prose narrative is located at this point in the book remains a riddle. All subsequent oracles of this division are earlier. The second section (21:11–23:8) consists of a series of messages directed to the house of David. The essentials of kingship are set up as a norm, and each of the kings of Judah (from Josiah to Jehoiachin) is judged accordingly. The oracles probably stem from the reign of the respective kings. The final hope of an ideal Messianic ruler (23:5-6) probably comes from the day of Zedekiah, who does not come in for a direct oracle of evaluation here. The third major section (23:9-40) has the prophet and his task as the unifying theme even though many units were probably delivered separately.

## A SERMON ADDRESSED
## TO ZEDEKIAH                                      21:1-10

¹ This is the word which came to Jeremiah from the LORD, when King Zedeki'ah sent to him Pashhur

the son of Malchi'ah and Zephani'ah the priest, the son of Ma-asei'ah, saying, ² "Inquire of the LORD for us, for Nebuchadrez'zar king of Babylon is making war against us; perhaps the LORD will deal with us according to all his wonderful deeds, and will make him withdraw from us."

³ Then Jeremiah said to them: ⁴ "Thus you shall say to Zedeki'ah, 'Thus says the LORD, the God of Israel: Behold, I will turn back the weapons of war which are in your hands and with which you are fighting against the king of Babylon and against the Chalde'ans who are beseiging you outside the walls; and I will bring them together into the midst of this city. ⁵ I myself will fight against you with outstretched hand and strong arm, in anger, and in fury, and in great wrath. ⁶ And I will smite the inhabitants of this city, both man and beast; they shall die of a great pestilence. ⁷ Afterward, says the LORD, I will give Zedeki'ah king of Judah, and his servants, and the people in this city who survive the pestilence, sword, and famine, into the hand of Nebuchadrez'zar king of Babylon and into the hand of their enemies, into the hand of those who seek their lives. He shall smite them with the edge of the sword; he shall not pity them, or spare them, or have compassion.'

⁸ "And to this people you shall say: 'Thus says the LORD: Behold, I set before you the way of life and the way of death. ⁹ He who stays in this city shall die by the sword, by famine, and by pestilence; but he who goes out and surrenders to the Chalde'ans who are besieging you shall live and shall have his life as a prize of war. ¹⁰ For I have set my face against this city for evil and not for good, says the

**LORD**: it shall be given into the hand of the king of Babylon, and he shall burn it with fire.'

**1-7** Chapters 21 – 45 differ considerably from those that precede. In these chapters there are considerable references to specific times, people, and places. The first individual we meet is Zedekiah, the last king of Judah, whom Nebuchadnezzar had placed on the throne as his vassal ruler (2 Kings 24:17). Zedekiah was young, weak, and dominated by the princes. He later rebelled against Nebuchadnezzar, who thereupon laid siege to the city of Jerusalem (2 Kings 25:1-2). Early in this siege Zedekiah sent Pashhur (cf. 20:1, where a different Pashhur is mentioned) and Zephaniah (cf. 29:25) to obtain an oracle from the old prophet Jeremiah. The expression "to inquire of the Lord" is a technical idiom for requesting an oracle from a professional prophet. The king, like Hezekiah before him (Is. 37:1-7), hoped to receive a message of spectacular salvation and appealed to Yahweh's past "wonderful deeds" of redemption. The past saving deeds of God were, however, no guarantee of grace. The oracle of doom could not be repudiated; God had begun His strange work as the enemy of His people, and He would complete it. The vacillating Zedekiah had dug his own grave. Yahweh would fight with ferocity against His own people as He had once done with "outstretched hand and strong arm" on behalf of Israel in the exodus (see Deut. 4:34; 5:15). The army of Nebuchadnezzar was the visible extension of God's arm. Those who escaped the destruction of Jerusalem would be taken captive by Nebuchadnezzar. The people were to prepare themselves for a merciless massacre. They would see the exodus in reverse.

**8-10** Jeremiah delivered an oracle for the public

173

to supplement the oracle solicited by Zedekiah. If Nebuchadnezzar was God's agent, then to resist him was to resist God. The option was clear for every man of Judah; to fight meant death, to surrender meant life. To the man on the street of Jerusalem Jeremiah must have sounded like a traitor and his words like blasphemy. Jeremiah had taken the sacred words of covenant commitment, "the way of life and the way of death" (see Deut. 30:15-20), and advised commitment into the hands of a pagan enemy. "The way of life" was not the fullness of blessing but a chance for the people of Judah to save their skins. Their lives would be an unexpected "prize of war." To survive that ordeal was grace in abundance. For Zedekiah there was no excuse inasmuch as Jeremiah had given this same advice at the beginning of that king's reign (27:1-15), when he was still a vassal to Nebuchadnezzar.

## ORACLES ADDRESSED
## TO THE HOUSE OF DAVID                    21:11 — 22:9

11 "And to the house of the king of Judah say, 'Hear the word of the LORD, 12 O house of David! Thus says the LORD:

" 'Execute justice in the morning,
and deliver from the hand of the oppressor
him who has been robbed,
lest my wrath go forth like fire,
and burn with none to quench it,
because of your evil doings.' "

13 "Behold, I am against you, O inhabitant of the
valley,
O rock of the plain,
says the LORD;

you who say, 'Who shall come down against us,
  or who shall enter our habitations?'
[14] I will punish you according to the fruit of your
    doings,
                        says the LORD;
  I will kindle a fire in her forest,
  and it shall devour all that is round about her.' "


[1] Thus says the LORD: "Go down to the house
of the king of Judah, and speak there this word,
[2] and say, 'Hear the word of the LORD, O King of
Judah, who sit on the throne of David, you, and your
servants, and your people who enter these gates.
[3] Thus says the LORD: Do justice and righteousness,
and deliver from the hand of the oppressor him who
has been robbed. And do no wrong or violence to the
alien, the fatherless, and the widow, nor shed innocent blood in this place. [4] For if you will indeed
obey this word, then there shall enter the gates of
this house kings who sit on the throne of David,
riding in chariots and on horses, they, and their
servants, and their people. [5] But if you will not heed
these words, I swear by myself, says the LORD, that
this house shall become a desolation. [6] For thus says
the LORD concerning the house of the king of Judah:
  " 'You are as Gilead to me,
    as the summit of Lebanon,
  yet surely I will make you a desert,
    an uninhabited city.[k]
[7] I will prepare destroyers against you,
    each with his weapons;
  and they shall cut down your choicest cedars,
    and cast them into the fire.

  [k] Cn: Heb cities

175

⁸ " 'And many nations will pass by this city, and every man will say to his neighbor, "Why has the LORD dealt thus with this great city?" ⁹ And they will answer, "Because they forsook the covenant of the LORD their God, and worshiped other gods and served them." ' "

**21:11-14** Jer. 21:11 — 23:8 embraces a series of oracles concerning the kings of Judah with whom Jeremiah had personal contact. The original setting of these oracles is not given, although each of them probably arose from specific historical situations, and they were later collected together with Jer. 21:11-14 as a general introductory exhortation for an indictment of the Davidic dynasty. The royal house is exhorted to "execute justice" and espouse the cause of the oppressed. These demands were basic for all kingship in the ancient Near East. If the chosen kings of Judah could not keep the elementary rules of kingship, God would surely punish them for their apathy and negligence. A moral sensitivity was essential for a stable regime. The threat of 21:13-14 is rather obscure but seems to be directed against the smug sense of security that many leaders fostered by promulgating the teaching that Jerusalem was invincible (cf. Micah 3:9-12) and that the divine election of the Davidic dynasty, promised in the covenant with David (2 Sam. 7:12-16), guaranteed its eternal character despite the evils of the monarchy (see the note on 22:6-7 below).

**22:1-5** In the prose interlude of 22:1-5 the prophet confronts the king with an unsolicited oracle, as Nathan had done (compare 21:1-2), reminding the royal family and his subjects that the original election of David naturally involved faithful allegiance to Yahweh on the part of David and his descendants.

176

Moral justice and righteousness befitting a Near Eastern monarch was demanded (see 21:12; 23:5; Ps. 72:2; Is. 9:7); injustice and immoral action meant divine retribution (see 2 Sam. 7:14). For an unbroken line of kings "to sit on the throne of David" henceforward, a new obedience to the will of Yahweh was urgently needed.

**6-9** The thought of 21:13-14 seems to be continued in 22:6-7, where the Davidic household is designated a "forest" of "choicest cedars" that Yahweh will soon cut down and burn with fire. This disaster is imminent despite the fact that the Davidic dynasty, by virtue of its divine election, is, in the eyes of Yahweh, like the glorious "summit of Lebanon," where the best cedars crown the mountains. The cedar forest may have been used as an image for the Davidic household because of the extensive use of cedar by Jehoiakim in his building operations (see 22:13-14 and compare 1 Kings 7:2-5). The brief prose lines of 22:8-9 are an apparently unrelated appendix that speaks of the disgrace of Jerusalem in the eyes of other nations after her destruction (compare Deut. 29:24-26). The reason given is a broken covenant and in the light of the context the references seem to be to the covenant with David. (2 Sam. 7)

## AN ORACLE CONCERNING JEHOAHAZ    22:10-12

[10] Weep not for him who is dead,
  nor bemoan him;
 but weep bitterly for him who goes away,
  for he shall return no more
  to see his native land.
  [11] For thus says the **LORD** concerning Shallum the son of Josi'ah, king of Judah, who reigned instead

177

of Josi'ah his father, and who went away from this place: "He shall return here no more, ¹²but in the place where they have carried him captive, there shall he die, and he shall never see this land again."

The poem in memory of Shallum was probably delivered while the people were still mourning the death of the beloved Josiah. The prose oracle of vv. 11-12 explains the import of the poem. Shallum, whose throne name was Jehoahaz, became king in 609 B. C., after the death of his father Josiah at the hands of the Egyptians. Three months later Jehoahaz was deported to Egypt, where he died in disgrace. The Egyptians placed Jehoiakim, a political opportunist, on the throne as their vassal. Jeremiah's point is that it is futile to weep for Josiah; the sad story is the exile of Jehoahaz while Jehoiakim rules according to his own whims. (See v. 13)

## AN ORACLE CONCERNING JEHOIAKIM    22:13-19

¹³ "Woe to him who builds his house by unrighteous-
     ness,
     and his upper rooms by injustice;
   who makes his neighbor serve him for nothing,
     and does not give him his wages;
¹⁴ who says, 'I will build myself a great house
     with spacious upper rooms,'
   and cuts out windows for it,
     paneling it with cedar,
     and painting it with vermilion.
¹⁵ Do you think you are a king
     because you compete in cedar?
   Did not your father eat and drink
     and do justice and righteousness?
     Then it was well with him.

<sup>16</sup> He judged the cause of the poor and needy;
   then it was well.
 Is not this to know me?
   says the LORD.
<sup>17</sup> But you have eyes and heart
   only for your dishonest gain,
 for shedding innocent blood,
   and for practicing oppression and violence."
<sup>18</sup> Therefore thus says the LORD concerning
Jehoi'akim the son of Josi'ah, king of Judah:
 "They shall not lament for him, saying,
   'Ah my brother!' or 'Ah sister!'
 They shall not lament for him, saying,
   'Ah lord!' or 'Ah his majesty!'
<sup>19</sup> With the burial of an ass he shall be buried,
   dragged and cast forth beyond the gates of Jerusalem."

13-15a Jehoiakim, whose private name was Eliakim,
was a violent and undesirable ruler who had no interest
in righteousness, that is, he showed no concern for the
covenant rights of the underprivileged and no love for
"his neighbor." His selfishness and ambitious pride
were exhibited by his pretentious building program,
in which he constructed a gaudy and luxurious palace
(a "great house"), using the forced labor of Israelite
citizens to accomplish the task. With appropriate sar-
casm Jeremiah asks whether great achievements in
carpentry are the mark of a true king.

15b-17 In comparison to that of Jehoiakim, the life
of Josiah was a model of justice and righteousness
(cf. 2 Kings 23:25). He had been personally concerned
about the rights of the "poor and needy" and had
thereby followed the covenant ideal. In this he found

179

enjoyment ("it was well with him"), and through this he expressed his knowledge of God (cf. Hos. 4:1; 6:6). Nevertheless he could "eat and drink" the blessings of God like any other king. The regime of Jehoiakim, by contrast, was marked by brutality, dishonesty, and the exploitation of the innocent citizen.

**18-19** All of Jeremiah's relations with Jehoiakim were unpleasant and objectionable. But did Jeremiah therefore enjoy delivering this unsavory woe upon this hated king? No one would cry when he died. The usual lament rites in which the mourners addressed each other as "my brother" and "my sister" would be disregarded. The anointed king would be left like a worthless animal to lie exposed for birds of prey outside the city walls. No greater dishonor could be imagined. The evidence of 2 Kings 24:6, however, may suggest a peaceful end for Jehoiakim. (On prophecy and fulfillment see pages 24–26 above.)

## A CRY OF DOOM FOR JUDAH'S LEADERS                                  22:20-23

20 "Go up to Lebanon, and cry out,
    and lift up your voice in Bashan;
cry from Ab'arim,
    for all your lovers are destroyed.
21 I spoke to you in your prosperity,
    but you said, 'I will not listen.'
This has been your way from your youth,
    that you have not obeyed my voice.
22 The wind shall shepherd all your shepherds,
    and your lovers shall go into captivity;
then you will be ashamed and confounded
    because of all your wickedness.

²³ O inhabitant of Lebanon,
  nested among the cedars,
how you will groan ¹ when pangs come upon you,
  pain as of a woman in travail!"

¹ Gk Vg Syr: Heb be pitied

This rather enigmatic cry of doom repeats the
theme of 21:14; 22:7; and 22:14 concerning the Davidic
household "nested among the cedars" as though taking
refuge in a forest (v. 23). Here an anonymous messenger
is summoned to go to the famed heights of Lebanon,
Bashan, and Abarim (Num. 27:12) and there announce
to all the world the failure of Judah's allies (her "lovers"),
the downfall of her leaders ("shepherds"), and the future
anguish she will experience once her false security has
been exposed. After all, Judah had received fair warning
when things were going well ("in your prosperity").
Persistent disobedience now spelled disaster. The
shepherds of Judah will soon be "shepherded" by the
wind of a gathering storm from God.

AN ORACLE CONCERNING
JEHOIACHIN                                    22:24-30

²⁴ "As I live, says the LORD, though Coni'ah
the son of Jehoi'akim, king of Judah, were the signet
ring on my right hand, yet I would tear you off ²⁵ and
give you into the hand of those who seek your life,
into the hand of those of whom you are afraid, even
into the hand of Nebuchadrez'zar king of Babylon
and into the hand of the Chalde'ans. ²⁶ I will hurl
you and the mother who bore you into another country, where you were not born, and there you shall
die. ²⁷ But to the land to which they will long to return, there they shall not return."

²⁸ Is this man Coni'ah a despised, broken pot,
  a vessel no one cares for?
Why are he and his children hurled and cast
  into a land which they do not know?
²⁹ O land, land, land,
  hear the word of the LORD!
³⁰ Thus says the LORD:
"Write this man down as childless,
  a man who shall not succeed in his days;
for none of his offspring shall succeed
  in sitting on the throne of David,
  and ruling again in Judah."

Jehoiachin, who is here called Coniah, inherited the onslaughts of Nebuchadnezzar (597 B. C.) that his father Jehoiakim had brought upon his people. Consequently Jehoiachin ruled only three months before he and his mother (Nehushta) were taken captive to Babylon, where he remained until he died (2 Kings 24:8-17; 25:27-30). This course of events had been announced to the king previously by Jeremiah, who insisted that despite Jehoiachin's Davidic heritage, which made him like a "signet ring" on God's right hand, he was still the leader of God's people and must therefore bear the dreadful burden of their fate. His lot was like that of a useless pot. People would wonder why; but the Word of God against the land was final! "Land, land, land, hear the word," the prophet cries. The legitimate Davidic line had come to an end, it seemed. Was the promise to David (2 Sam. 7:12-16) thereby revoked? Although Jehoiachin's grandson Zerubbabel returned from exile and was ruler in Jerusalem for a time, none of Jehoiachin's progeny actually "succeeded in sitting on the throne of David." When Haggai (2:23) designates

Zerubbabel as Yahweh's "signet ring," he is apparently recalling a Messianic term (see again Jer. 22:24) and expressing the hope that Zerubbabel would become the destined Messiah.

## THE PROMISE OF AN IDEAL RULER          23:1-8

[1] "Woe to the shepherds who destroy and scatter the sheep of my pasture!" says the LORD. [2] Therefore thus says the LORD, the God of Israel, concerning the shepherds who care for my people: "You have scattered my flock, and have driven them away, and you have not attended to them. Behold, I will attend to you for your evil doings, says the LORD. [3] Then I will gather the remnant of my flock out of all the countries where I have driven them, and I will bring them back to their fold, and they shall be fruitful and multiply. [4] I will set shepherds over them who will care for them, and they shall fear no more, nor be dismayed, neither shall any be missing, says the LORD.

[5] "Behold, the days are coming, says the LORD, when I will raise up for David a righteous Branch, and he shall reign as king and deal wisely, and shall execute justice and righteousness in the land. [6] In his days Judah will be saved, and Israel will dwell securely. And this is the name by which he will be called: 'The LORD is our righteousness.'

[7] "Therefore, behold, the days are coming, says the LORD, when men shall no longer say, 'As the LORD lives who brought up the people of Israel out of the land of Egypt,' [8] but 'As the LORD lives who brought up and led the descendants of the house of Israel out of the north country and out of all the

183

countries where he *m* had driven them.' Then they
shall dwell in their own land."

*m* Gk: Heb *I*

**1-4** Jeremiah's promise of a faithful ruler forms the
climax of this series of oracles in 21:11 – 23:8. The
promise is preceded by an oracle of woe against all the
faithless shepherds who have scattered the flock of
God's people instead of keeping them safely together.
The kings mentioned in the preceding oracles are the
faithless shepherds. Zedekiah, although not explicitly
mentioned, is probably included in the prophet's mind.
The kings were held responsible for the welfare of
God's people. Now the people were scattered in exile.
God's grace comes to the rescue. He promises that He
will round up what is left ("the remnant") of His flock
and provide new shepherds who will be so diligent in
their care that no sheep will ever be lost.

**5-6** In addition to the promise of faithful rulers,
there is the promise of one king from the Davidic line
who is designated a "righteous Branch," or "Sprout."
He is a "shoot" from the dying family tree of David. The
same idea, but a different term, is found in Is. 11:1. As
in Is. 11:1-9; 9:6-7; and elsewhere, the rule of this figure
is given in terms of the ideal Davidic ruler. That is, the
reign of this chosen ruler will be God's work and hence
free from the deficiencies of past rulers. The glories
and good features of David's reign often color this
portrait of the ideal ruler. Thus this new king will execute the demands of the Davidic covenant perfectly
(see the note on 22:1-5 above); his rule will be characterized by wisdom, justice, and righteousness. As a result his people will be safe from their enemies and dwell
"securely," that is, in peace and prosperity under

God's blessing. The oracle was probably delivered during the reign of Mattaniah, who chose the throne name Zedekiah, which means "The Lord (Yahweh) is my righteousness." But the rule of Zedekiah proved pathetically weak, and Jeremiah hoped for the day when a king would arise who truly lived up to the name "The Lord (Yahweh) is our righteousness," that is, a Messianic ruler who would espouse the cause of the downtrodden and helpless completely in accordance with Yahweh's will. Thus the "righteous" Branch from David's family tree will depend on Yahweh to effect "righteousness" or "salvation" in the land. Although this prophecy is not explicitly quoted in the New Testament, the confession is frequently made that Jesus Christ was that chosen figure through whom God's righteousness was fully revealed (Matt. 3:15; Rom. 5:18-20; 1 Cor. 1:30-31). For a later amplification of this oracle see Jer. 33:14-26. On 23:7-8 see the comment for 16:14-15 above.

## A Series of Oracles Concerning
## the False Prophets                                   23:9-32

⁹ Concerning the prophets:
  My heart is broken within me,
    all my bones shake;
  I am like a drunken man,
    like a man overcome by wine,
  because of the LORD
    and because of his holy words.
¹⁰ For the land is full of adulterers;
    because of the curse the land mourns,
    and the pastures of the wilderness are dried up.
  Their course is evil,
    and their might is not right.

185

¹¹ "Both prophet and priest are ungodly;
    even in my house I have found their wickedness,
                says the LORD.
¹² Therefore their way shall be to them
    like slippery paths in the darkness,
    into which they shall be driven and fall;
  for I will bring evil upon them
    in the year of their punishment,
                says the LORD.

¹³ In the prophets of Samar'ia
    I saw an unsavory thing:
  they prophesied by Ba'al
    and led my people Israel astray.
¹⁴ But in the prophets of Jerusalem
    I have seen a horrible thing:
  they commit adultery and walk in lies;
    they strengthen the hands of evildoers,
    so that no one turns from his wickedness;
  all of them have become like Sodom to me,
    and its inhabitants like Gomor'rah."
¹⁵ Therefore thus says the LORD of hosts concerning
the prophets:
  "Behold, I will feed them with wormwood,
    and give them poisoned water to drink;
  for from the prophets of Jerusalem
    ungodliness has gone forth into all the land."

¹⁶ Thus says the LORD of hosts: "Do not listen
to the words of the prophets who prophesy to you,
filling you with vain hopes; they speak visions of their
own minds, not from the mouth of the LORD. ¹⁷ They
say continually to those who despise the word of the
LORD, 'It shall be well with you'; and to every one

who stubbornly follows his own heart, they say, 'No evil shall come upon you.'"

18 For who among them has stood in the council of the LORD
to perceive and to hear his word,
or who has given heed to his word and listened?
19 Behold, the storm of the LORD!
Wrath has gone forth,
a whirling tempest;
it will burst upon the head of the wicked.
20 The anger of the LORD will not turn back
until he has executed and accomplished
the intents of his mind.
In the latter days you will understand it clearly.

21 "I did not send the prophets,
yet they ran;
I did not speak to them,
yet they prophesied.
22 But if they had stood in my council,
then they would have proclaimed my words to
my people,
and they would have turned them from their evil
way,
and from the evil of their doings.

23 "Am I a God at hand, says the LORD, and not a God afar off? 24 Can a man hide himself in secret places so that I cannot see him? says the LORD. Do I not fill heaven and earth? says the LORD. 25 I have heard what the prophets have said who prophesy lies in my name, saying, 'I have dreamed, I have dreamed!' 26 How long shall there be lies[n] in the

---

[n] Cn Compare Syr: Heb obscure

heart of the prophets who prophesy lies, and who prophesy the deceit of their own heart, [27] who think to make my people forget my name by their dreams which they tell one another, even as their fathers forgot my name for Ba'al? [28] Let the prophet who has a dream tell the dream, but let him who has my word speak my word faithfully. What has straw in common with wheat? says the LORD. [29] Is not my word like fire, says the LORD, and like a hammer which breaks the rock in pieces? [30] Therefore, behold, I am against the prophets, says the LORD, who steal my words from one another. [31] Behold, I am against the prophets, says the LORD, who use their tongues and say, 'Says the LORD.' [32] Behold, I am against those who prophesy lying dreams, says the LORD, and who tell them and lead my people astray by their lies and their recklessness, when I did not send them or charge them; so they do not profit this people at all, says the LORD.

9-12 One difficult task that Jeremiah had to perform was to speak God's holy words of judgment against the prophets and priests of God's house. The oracle he must preach here is so disturbing that Jeremiah reels "like a drunken man"; he feels the pain of his message. The charge against these "servants" (and the people in general) is "adultery" and "ungodliness." Both immorality and idolatry are probably involved. The inevitable consequence of such action is serious downfall; they were walking on "slippery paths in the darkness," trusting in their own authority, their "might." They were deluded hypocrites.

188

**13-15** In the second oracle (vv. 13-15) the prophets of Jerusalem are singled out for special censure. The prophets of Samaria, the capital of the former Northern Kingdom of Israel, had previously led God's people to worship Baal. An even worse state of affairs existed in Jerusalem. For although the prophets of Jerusalem profess to be Yahweh's spokesmen, they speak lies in His name and live loose licentious lives like the infamous inhabitants of Sodom. Both their preaching and their actions had led God's people astray. The curse which God will bring upon them is not fire and brimstone but wormwood and poisoned water (cf. Ex. 32:20). In short, they would taste a bitter end.

**16-22** The third unit of these oracles against the prophets deals with the very source of the prophet's message. Jeremiah claimed to stand in the line of prophets like Moses (Deut. 18:15-18), in whose mouth God set His words (Jer. 1:9). The prophets of Jeremiah's day, however, were frauds. Jeremiah could see this because they preached "peace," that is, the assurance that everything will turn out fine and that "no evil will come" (see 28:8). Such sermons were wishful thinking, "visions of their own mind." These prophets had not stood in the heavenly "council," like Micaiah (1 Kings 22:19-23), Isaiah (Is. 6), and Jeremiah. From that council or assembly of heavenly beings (cf. Ps. 89:5-8) Yahweh sent forth his messengers. But "I did not send the prophets," insists Yahweh (v. 21). If Yahweh had sent them, they would have been urging God's people to "turn," that is, to effect a complete change of heart, and desist from "the evil of their doings." Their negligence in this area was another proof that they were false prophets who had never stood in God's heavenly council, seen (rather than "perceived" in v. 18) what went on there,

189

or heard God's Word personally. Accordingly the wrath of God would rage like a storm against these prophets also; and when God refused to "turn" His anger away from them, they would finally realize how deluded they were. And Jeremiah knew that judgment was the pressing message Yahweh was speaking at that time, not the comfortable cry of the false prophets, "Don't worry."

23-32 A fourth unit, mostly prose, deals with the contrast between prophetic dreams and the direct Word of God. The opening questions are directed to those prophets who foolishly believe that they can escape God's scrutiny, as though He were a local deity with limited areas of control rather than the Lord of the heavens, whose eye can penetrate everywhere, even into the heart (cf. 17:10). These false prophets had been speaking in Yahweh's "name," that is, they claimed to represent Yahweh exactly. They maintained further that they received their communications from God by dreams (as distinct from visions seen when one is awake). Dreams are purely subjective, retorts Jeremiah. They express personal opinions, not God's direct Word. The prophet is at liberty to relate his dream if he wishes, but he has no right to pass it off as a sure Word of God. Honesty (faithfulness) not hypocrisy (deceit) must characterize a prophet. A dream is like "straw" when compared to the Word, the real "wheat." The Word is powerful and penetrating, like a hammer and like fire (cf. Heb. 4:12-13). The ludicrous hypocrisy of the false prophets is further demonstrated by the way they copy each other's sermons. They do not have the original Word from the mind of God. Thus the people are led into error and delusion. Therefore God will condemn these prophets whom He has not commissioned. Precisely when Jeremiah spoke these oracles against the false prophets we cannot determine. They would be appropriate under Zedekiah, when we know Jeremiah clashed with such prophets as Hannaniah. (28:1-17)

## THE MEANING OF THE BURDEN OF THE LORD                           23:33-40

[33] "When one of this people, or a prophet, or a priest asks you, 'What is the burden of the LORD?' you shall say to them, 'You are the burden,[o] and I will cast you off, says the LORD.' [34] And as for the prophet, priest, or one of the people who says, 'The burden of the LORD,' I will punish that man and his household. [35] Thus shall you say, every one to his neighbor and every one to his brother, 'What has the LORD answered?' or 'What has the LORD spoken?' [36] But 'the burden of the LORD' you shall mention no more, for the burden is every man's own word, and you pervert the words of the living God, the LORD of hosts, our God. [37] Thus you shall say to the prophet, 'What has the LORD answered you?' or 'What has the LORD spoken?' [38] But if you say, 'The burden of the LORD,' thus says the LORD, 'Because you have said these words, "The burden of the LORD," when I sent to you, saying, "You shall not say, 'The burden of the LORD,'" [39] therefore, behold, I will surely lift you up and cast you away from my presence, you and the city which I gave to you and your fathers. [40] And I will bring upon you everlasting reproach and perpetual shame, which shall not be forgotten.'"

[o] Gk Vg: Heb *What burden*

191

In this supplement to the oracles against the false prophets Jeremiah develops a harsh play on the word *massa'*, which these prophets frequently used. This Hebrew word can mean both an "oracle," or word from God (Hab. 1:1), and a "burden." When God's people ask "What is the *massa'* today?" requesting an oracle, Jeremiah replies, "You are the *massa'*," the "burden" that Yahweh has borne patiently and sorrowfully long enough (Is. 46:3-4). Verses 34-40 discuss variant interpretations of this opening oracle. Verse 34 speaks of punishing those who dared to use this term. Verses 35-36 affirm that because of the abuse of this term it will fall into disuse as an objectionable expression. Other terms will take its place. Verses 37-40 state that any who did use this expression would themselves be lifted up ("borne") as a burden and thrown away from God's presence as something shameful. It is possible that behind this series of oracles there was a custom in Israel according to which people would greet each other by saying, "What's the *massa'*," in a manner similar to the American idiom "What's new?" or "What's the matter?"

# Momentous Visions of the Future

## Jeremiah 24–25

Jeremiah 24 and 25 are coupled here as a separate division not because of any obvious textual connection but because of a common concern for God's future involvement in the Babylonian exile and because these two chapters stand isolated between the preceding series of oracles against individuals in Chs. 21 and 23 and the biographical materials in Chs. 26 to 29. It seems probable that 25:13 (see the note below on that verse) was the end of the scroll or book written by Jeremiah in 605 B. C. (See Ch. 36.) Perhaps Ch. 24 was later inserted near the end of this book to soften the harsh conclusion of 25:1-13. Many of the prophetic books end with a similar message of hope. Chapter 24 was written some time after the first captivity of Judah in 597 B. C. but before the second in 587 B. C., but 25:1 is dated 605 B. C.

## THE VISION OF TWO BASKETS OF FIGS    24

¹ After Nebuchadrez'zar king of Babylon had taken into exile from Jerusalem Jeconi'ah the son

of Jehoi'akim, king of Judah, together with the princes of Judah, the craftsmen, and the smiths, and had brought them to Babylon, the LORD showed me this vision: Behold, two baskets of figs placed before the temple of the LORD. ² One basket had very good figs, like first-ripe figs, but the other basket had very bad figs, so bad that they could not be eaten. ³ And the LORD said to me, "What do you see, Jeremiah?" I said, "Figs, the good figs very good, and the bad figs very bad, so bad that they cannot be eaten."

⁴ Then the word of the LORD came to me: ⁵ "Thus says the LORD, the God of Israel: Like these good figs, so I will regard as good the exiles from Judah, whom I have sent away from this place to the land of the Chalde'ans. ⁶ I will set my eyes upon them for good, and I will bring them back to this land. I will build them up, and not tear them down; I will plant them, and not uproot them. ⁷ I will give them a heart to know that I am the LORD; and they shall be my people and I will be their God, for they shall return to me with their whole heart.

⁸ "But thus says the LORD: Like the bad figs which are so bad they cannot be eaten, so will I treat Zedeki'ah the king of Judah, his princes, the remnant of Jerusalem who remain in this land, and those who dwell in the land of Egypt. ⁹ I will make them a horror ᵖ to all the kingdoms of the earth, to be a reproach, a byword, a taunt, and a curse in all the places where I shall drive them. ¹⁰ And I will send sword, famine, and pestilence upon them, until they shall be utterly destroyed from the land which I gave to them and their fathers."

ᵖ Compare Gk: Heb *horror for evil*

This experience of Jeremiah stems from the years immediately after Nebuchadnezzar had taken King Jehoiachin ("Jeconiah"), the leading political figures, and the skilled artisans of Judah captive to Babylon in 597 B. C. (See the note on 22:24-30. Cf. 2 Kings 24: 8-17.) Some three thousand men of Judah were exiled on that campaign (according to Jer. 52:28). On this occasion Nebuchadnezzar spared the city of Jerusalem itself and placed a puppet king on the throne, the pathetic Zedekiah. Jerusalem and its inhabitants survived by the grace of Nebuchadnezzar. These fortunate citizens did not, however, appreciate their lot or take to heart the lesson of divine judgment already pronounced on the city. Some complacently assumed that they were now God's specially chosen remnant and that only those in exile were under God's direct condemnation (cf. Ezek. 11:5; 33:24). The message of Jeremiah affirms that the reverse is true.

Jeremiah says that Yahweh caused him to see "two baskets of figs placed before the temple." The word "vision" does not actually appear in the Hebrew text. Jeremiah may have seen two actual baskets near the temple, just as he may have seen the almond rod (1:11), the boiling pot (1:13), and the potter at work (18:3), although the wording of this text suggests the idea of a vision that God created for the prophet to see. The figs of these two baskets differ in character; the one lot being rotten, repulsive, and inedible, the other "like first-ripe figs." These figs represent two groups of people. The people in exile are God's chosen people. Once before God had described the election of His people as the discovery of first-ripe figs in the wilderness (Hos. 9:10). Thus a new election is implied for the exiles. The bad figs are those in Judah who must yet experience the full expression of God's wrath. Jeremiah is not saying that the people in exile are better than those in Judah but rather that the plan of Yahweh calls for special undeserved favor on those in exile. He promises them a new day, when they will leave Babylon and inherit their promised land as once before. For King Zedekiah and those left (the "remnant") in Jerusalem the opposite would happen; they would be scattered in disgrace far from their sacred land and home. This course of action was not automatic, however. God must first cause a change of heart among those in exile; God would have to re-create them and begin anew with a totally fresh approach, a new covenant in which His "people" experienced His reality as their "God" to a degree not known before (compare v. 7 with 31:31-34; 29:10-14; and Ezek. 36:26). God's choice made the exiles "good figs" in His eyes. God would now work on them to change them and make them good. At times this meant telling the self-satisfied in exile, in no uncertain terms, what He expected of them. (See 29:1-14)

## A RECAPITULATION OF JEREMIAH'S
## MESSAGE                                           25:1-12

¹ **The word that came to Jeremiah concerning all the people of Judah, in the fourth year of Jehoi'- akim the son of Josi'ah, king of Judah (that was the first year of Nebuchadrez'zar king of Babylon), ² which Jeremiah the prophet spoke to all the people of Judah and all the inhabitants of Jerusalem: ³ "For twenty-three years, from the thirteenth year of Josi'ah the son of Amon, king of Judah, to this day, the word of the LORD has come to me, and I have spoken persistently to you, but you have not listened. ⁴ You**

**have neither listened nor inclined your ears to hear,
although the LORD persistently sent to you all his
servants the prophets, [5] saying, 'Turn now, every
one of you, from his evil way and wrong doings, and
dwell upon the land which the LORD has given to
you and your fathers from of old and for ever; [6] do
not go after other gods to serve and worship them,
or provoke me to anger with the work of your hands.
Then I will do you no harm.' [7] Yet you have not
listened to me, says the LORD, that you might provoke me to anger with the work of your hands to your
own harm.**

**[8] "Therefore thus says the LORD of hosts: Be-
cause you have not obeyed my words, [9] behold, I will
send for all the tribes of the north, says the LORD,
and for Nebuchadrez'zar the king of Babylon, my
servant, and I will bring them against this land and
its inhabitants, and against all these nations round
about; I will utterly destroy them, and make them
a horror, a hissing, and an everlasting reproach.[q]
[10] Moreover, I will banish from them the voice of
mirth and the voice of gladness, the voice of the
bridegroom and the voice of the bride, the grinding
of the millstones and the light of the lamp. [11] This
whole land shall become a ruin and a waste, and
these nations shall serve the king of Babylon seventy
years. [12] Then after seventy years are completed,
I will punish the king of Babylon and that nation,
the land of the Chalde'ans, for their iniquity, says
the LORD, making the land an everlasting waste.**

[q] Gk Compare Syr: Heb *desolations*

This summary of Jeremiah commences with a reference to the ominous year 605 B. C., in which Nebuchadnezzar defeated Pharaoh Necho of Egypt at the battle of Carchemish on the Euphrates and thereby demonstrated the supremacy of Babylon throughout the ancient Near East. (See the comment on 46:2.) This is the same year in which Jeremiah collected many of his oracles to form a scroll (36:1-3). The recapitulation of Jeremiah's life and message in 25:1-7 may well represent the closing summary for that scroll. Reflecting on 23 years of ministry, Jeremiah can assert that Judah remains untouched by his preaching. Jeremiah is not alone in this dilemma. The Israelites had traditionally rejected the word of God's "servants the prophets" in the past. Their message can be summed up in the words, "turn (repent)" and "do not go after other gods." In short, Israel should return to the covenant way of life. Alas, they had repeatedly not done so. The anger of God was therefore roused as never before.

The inevitable message of doom, which had often been given in general terms in the preceding chapters, is now made very explicit in the light of Nebuchadnezzar's recent victory at Carchemish. He is called "My servant," that is, the chosen agent of Yahweh. Nebuchadnezzar is the living symbol of the tribes from the north that Jeremiah had previously envisioned (1:15-16) as the powers of destruction on God's people. Such a title for Nebuchadnezzar, the future archenemy of Judah, would have been repulsive to these people. By the hand of Nebuchadnezzar God will bring upon His elect the curses of a broken covenant (v. 10), curses that were essential to treaties in the ancient Near East and the covenant with Yahweh in Israel (Deut. 27–28). For all practical purposes, adds Jeremiah, this meant a lifetime ("70 years") of captivity in Babylon for the people of Judah and subsequently the political downfall of Babylon according to God's plan. (For later interpretations and applications of the 70 years see Zech. 1:12; 7:5; 2 Chron. 36:21; Ezra 1:1; Dan. 9:2.)

THE END OF ONE BOOK
AND THE CAPTION FOR ANOTHER        25:13-14

¹³ I will bring upon that land all the words which I have uttered against it, everything written in this book, which Jeremiah prophesied against all the nations. ¹⁴ For many nations and great kings shall make slaves even of them; and I will recompense them according to their deeds and the work of their hands."

Jer. 25:13 concludes by saying that Yahweh will bring to pass all the threats He has pronounced on "that land." It is not clear whether Babylon or Judah was originally meant. The threats alluded to, however, are those of a specific "book." The scroll or "book" of Ch. 36 is probably the book involved since it was written at the same time as the date given at the head of the summary in Jer. 25. Further evidence for the fact that this scroll ended with the words "this book" in v. 13 is provided by the Septuagint (an early Greek translation of the Hebrew), which inserts most of the oracles against the nations (found in Jer. 46–51) at precisely this point. These oracles against the nations were apparently a separate collection attached to the first scroll of Jeremiah and ending with the words "this book" in 25:13. How the present Hebrew order arose cannot be readily demonstrated. The second half of 25:13 was apparently a heading for a collection of oracles concerning the nations: "That which Jeremiah

199

prophesied against the nations." Verse 14 provides an additional note to the effect that these nations, too, will suffer captivity as their just desert. Verse 15 offers a direct oracle against the nations that begins with the words, "Thus saith Yahweh." The long collection of oracles against the nations in Jer. 46–51 may well have been located after 25:13 (as in the Septuagint) at an earlier stage of the assembling of the present Hebrew text of the Book of Jeremiah, instead of the brief summary of oracles against the nations now found in 25:15-29. The above evidence and discussion indicates something of how a prophetic book like Jeremiah came into existence. Several stages of compilation are clearly involved.

## THE VISION OF THE CUP
## OF THE WINE OF WRATH                                25:15-29

[15] Thus the LORD, the God of Israel, said to me: "Take from my hand this cup of the wine of wrath, and make all the nations to whom I send you drink it. [16] They shall drink and stagger and be crazed because of the sword which I am sending among them."

[17] So I took the cup from the LORD'S hand, and made all the nations to whom the Lord sent me drink it: [18] Jerusalem and the cities of Judah, its kings and princes, to make them a desolation and a waste, a hissing and a curse, as at this day; [19] Pharaoh king of Egypt, his servants, his princes, all his people, [20] and all the foreign folk among them; all the kings of the land of Uz and all the kings of the land of the Philistines (Ash'kelon, Gaza, Ekron, and the remnant of Ashdod); [21] Edom, Moab, and the sons of Ammon; [22] all the kings of Tyre, all the kings

of Sidon, and the kings of the coastland across the sea; [23] Dedan, Tema, Buz, and all who cut the corners of their hair; [24] all the kings of Arabia and all the kings of the mixed tribes that dwell in the desert; [25] all the kings of Zimri, all the kings of Elam, and all the kings of Media; [26] all the kings of the north, far and near, one after another, and all the kingdoms of the world which are on the face of the earth. And after them the king of Babylon [r] shall drink.

[27] "Then you shall say to them, 'Thus says the LORD of hosts, the God of Israel: Drink, be drunk and vomit, fall and rise no more, because of the sword which I am sending among you.'

[28] "And if they refuse to accept the cup from your hand to drink, then you shall say to them, 'Thus says the LORD of hosts: You must drink! [29] For behold, I begin to work evil at the city which is called by my name, and shall you go unpunished? You shall not go unpunished, for I am summoning a sword against all the inhabitants of the earth, says the LORD of hosts.'

[r] Heb *Sheshach*, a cipher for Babylon

The wrath of God, a terrible mystery, is described by a wealth of grim imagery in the prophets. In this passage the wrath of God is compared to a cup of wine; those who must bear His wrath are like people forced to drink a cup of wine (cf. 49:12; 51:7). It may be that the practices of Num. 5:23-28 or Ex. 32:20 lie behind this gruesome metaphor. Jerusalem is elsewhere portrayed as drunk with the cup of God's wrath (Is. 51: 17-22; cf. Jer. 13:12-14). In concrete terms this image means that God will send warfare ("the sword") to punish the guilty (v. 16). Jeremiah receives the cup from

"the Lord's hand" as though he were standing in the
heavenly council (cf. 23:22). The same hand had touched
his lips when he was first summoned into Yahweh's
presence at the time of his call (1:9). And the present
assignment is directly in accord with the original terms
of his call as a "prophet to the nations" (1:5). For Jeremiah must now force the nations to drink of the wine
of Yahweh's wrath. Through Jeremiah's symbolic action
and prophetic word forces will be set in motion to bring
disaster to all the nations involved (cf. 1:9-10). God's
Word changes the course of history. In addition to God's
own people, the nation of Egypt, under whom Israel
had frequently suffered, was destined for destruction.
Other nations within the historical purview of the
prophet are also included (vv. 20-25). This list of nations
covers those against whom longer messages of doom
are directed in the oracles against the nations (Jer.
46–51), plus a few minor additions (Uz, Buz, Tema,
Dedan, and Zimri). Babylon, the current agent of
wrath against God's people (25:9), will not escape her
turn. The Hebrew text reads Sheshach for Babylon
at this point. Sheshach is a cryptic name, or cipher, for
Babylon, in which each consonant of the name is re-
placed by a corresponding consonant counting from
the end of the alphabet. No nation can escape from the
great catastrophe ("evil") that Yahweh has projected.
And this strange work will begin at Jerusalem (vv. 27-29).
The same image of the cup of wrath seems to lie behind
the words of Christ in Mark 10:39 and 14:36.

## A VISION OF GOD'S UNIVERSAL
## JUDGMENT                                    25:30-38

[30] "You, therefore, shall prophesy against them
all these words, and say to them:

'The LORD will roar from on high,
  and from his holy habitation utter his voice;
he will roar mightily against his fold,
  and shout, like those who tread grapes,
  against all the inhabitants of the earth.
³¹ The clamor will resound to the ends of the earth,
  for the LORD has an indictment against the
    nations;
he is entering into judgment with all flesh,
  and the wicked he will put to the sword,
                                    says the LORD.'

³² "Thus says the LORD of hosts:
  Behold, evil is going forth
    from nation to nation,
  and a great tempest is stirring
    from the farthest parts of the earth!
³³ "And those slain by the LORD on that day
shall extend from one end of the earth to the other.
They shall not be lamented, or gathered, or buried;
they shall be dung on the surface of the ground.
³⁴ "Wail, you shepherds, and cry,
  and roll in ashes, you lords of the flock,
  for the days of your slaughter and dispersion have
    come,
  and you shall fall like choice rams. ⁸
³⁵ No refuge will remain for the shepherds,
  nor escape for the lords of the flock.
³⁶ Hark, the cry of the shepherds,
  and the wail of the lords of the flock!
For the LORD is despoiling their pasture,
³⁷   and the peaceful folds are devastated,
  because of the fierce anger of the LORD.

  ⁸ Gk: Heb a choice vessel

³⁸ Like a lion he has left his covert,
   for their land has become a waste
because of the sword of the oppressor,
   and because of his fierce anger."

The poetic oracles that conclude this chapter offer
additional imagery to delineate God's intervention in
anger. In vv. 30-31 the horrible portrait is that of Yahweh
thundering forth with mighty "voice," like the ancient
storm god Baal, from His heavenly temple to revel in
displaying His kingship (cf. Amos 1:2; Micah 1:2-4;
Joel 3:16). As the heavenly King He will pass judgment
upon "all flesh" unto "the ends of the earth." He is
sovereign over all. The scope of this indictment is more
extensive than that of the oracles against the nations
in 25:17-27. Verse 32 announces that the calamities
("evil") that will befall each nation are like a tempest
that emanates from the abode of God at the extremity
of the earth (cf. 23:19). This storm will leave dead
strewn across the face of the earth with none to bury
them honorably (v. 33). The final oracle (vv. 34-38)
portrays God as an angry lion who leaves his "covert"
in heaven to attack the peaceful "folds," that is, the
complacent peoples of the earth, and to devastate their
"pastures" or lands. None of the "shepherds" (the
leaders) of the nations will be able to avert this doom.
Their only recourse is to "wail" in agony. Warfare ("the
sword") is again the actual mode of effecting this word
of doom.

# Significant Incidents
# in the Life of Jeremiah

## Jeremiah 26 – 29

In Jer. 26 – 29 we meet a new corpus of materials in narrative prose. They are primarily biographical in nature. Most of them have been written in the third person, apparently by the scribe (Baruch?) who collected them. Several autobiographical sections have also been incorporated by this scribe (see 27:1 – 28:4). Some portions are considered by many scholars to be later additions of another scribe (see the comment on 26:20-23 and 29:16-20). The temple sermon of Ch. 26 belongs to the early days of King Jehoiakim's reign. Chapters 27 – 29 revolve around the general unrest in the fourth year of King Zedekiah (see 28:1). Plans for revolt were apparently under way at that time. False prophets fanned the hopes of a return for those taken captive to Babylon in 597 B. C. At that time King Zedekiah himself was summoned to Babylon, presumably to pledge renewed allegiance to King Nebuchadnezzar and renounce all plans for rebellion (51:59). The year was a critical one, and Judah's leaders were very vocal. The unifying theme of these four chapters is Jeremiah's running battle with the authorities. Those who oppose Jeremiah's word are condemned as rebels against God. God had appointed King Nebuchadnezzar as the sovereign agent for ruling the earth and punishing Judah. To reject that plan meant death. Those who accepted it could take comfort in the long range promise of a new exodus for God's people.

## JEREMIAH PREACHES IN THE TEMPLE    26:1-6

¹ In the beginning of the reign of Jehoi'akim the son of Josi'ah, king of Judah, this word came from the LORD, ² "Thus says the LORD: Stand in the court of the LORD'S house, and speak to all the cities of Judah which come to worship in the house of the LORD all the words that I command you to speak to them; do not hold back a word. ³ It may be they will listen, and every one turn from his evil way, that I may repent of the evil which I intend to do to them because of their evil doings. ⁴ You shall say to them, 'Thus says the LORD: If you will not listen to me, to walk in my law which I have set before you, ⁵ and to heed the words of my servants the prophets whom I send to you urgently, though you have not heeded, ⁶ then I will make this house like Shiloh, and I will make this city a curse for all the nations of the earth.'"

A more complete version of this sermon appears in Jer. 7:1-15. See the comment there. In the summary of Jer. 26:1-6 the possibility of Judah's repentance is stressed and a repeat of the Shiloh incident again threatened. At Shiloh the temple of Yahweh had been destroyed by the Philistines (about 1050 B. C.) and the ark of the covenant captured (1 Sam. 4:10-22). Two elements of this sermon are not explicitly mentioned in Jer. 7. First, God's people had not kept the *torah* (that is, the "Law"). The *torah* later became identified by the Jews with the Pentateuch. The parallel material of Jer. 7:9 suggests that Jeremiah considered the Decalog the chief teststone of God's *torah*, or will. Second, verse 6 adds the thought that the curse of Jerusalem will be an example "to all the nations of the earth." Contrast this curse with the purpose that Israel was to serve according to Gen. 12:3. Jeremiah was obliged to preach this uncomfortable sermon and "not hold back one word of it."

## JEREMIAH IS ARRESTED AND TRIED    26:7-24

7 The priests and the prophets and all the people heard Jeremiah speaking these words in the house of the LORD. 8 And when Jeremiah had finished speaking all that the LORD had commanded him to speak to all the people, then the priests and the prophets and all the people laid hold of him, saying, "You shall die! 9 Why have you prophesied in the name of the LORD, saying, 'This house shall be like Shiloh, and this city shall be desolate, without inhabitant'?" And all the people gathered about Jeremiah in the house of the LORD.

10 When the princes of Judah heard these things, they came up from the king's house to the house of the LORD and took their seat in the entry of the New Gate of the house of the LORD. 11 Then the priests and the prophets said to the princes and to all the people, "This man deserves the sentence of death,

because he has prophesied against this city, as you have heard with your own ears."

¹² Then Jeremiah spoke to all the princes and all the people, saying, "The LORD sent me to prophesy against this house and this city all the words you have heard. ¹³ Now therefore amend your ways and your doings, and obey the voice of the LORD your God, and the LORD will repent of the evil which he has pronounced against you. ¹⁴ But as for me, behold, I am in your hands. Do with me as seems good and right to you. ¹⁵ Only know for certain that if you put me to death, you will bring innocent blood upon yourselves and upon this city and its inhabitants, for in truth the LORD sent me to you to speak all these words in your ears."

¹⁶ Then the princes and all the people said to the priests and the prophets, "This man does not deserve the sentence of death, for he has spoken to us in the name of the LORD our God." ¹⁷ And certain of the elders of the land arose and spoke to all the assembled people, saying, ¹⁸ "Micah of More'sheth prophesied in the days of Hezeki'ah king of Judah, and said to all the people of Judah: 'Thus says the LORD of hosts,

Zion shall be plowed as a field;

Jerusalem shall become a heap of ruins,

and the mountain of the house a wooded height.'

¹⁹ Did Hezeki'ah king of Judah and all Judah put him to death? Did he not fear the LORD and entreat the favor of the LORD, and did not the LORD repent of the evil which he had pronounced against them? But we are about to bring great evil upon ourselves."

²⁰ There was another man who prophesied in the name of the LORD, Uri'ah the son of Shemai'ah from

Kir'iath-je'arim. He prophesied against this city and against this land in words like those of Jeremiah. ²¹ And when King Jehoi'akim, with all his warriors and all the princes, heard his words, the king sought to put him to death; but when Uri'ah heard of it, he was afraid and fled and escaped to Egypt. ²² Then King Jehoi'akim sent to Egypt certain men, Elna'than the son of Achbor and others with him, ²³ and they fetched Uri'ah from Egypt and brought him to King Jehoi'akim, who slew him with the sword and cast his dead body into the burial place of the common people.

²⁴ But the hand of Ahi'kam the son of Shaphan was with Jeremiah so that he was not given over to the people to be put to death.

7-9 Jeremiah's sermon caused quite a stir. The temple priests, the professional prophets, and the worshipers in the temple were incensed. Jeremiah was looked upon as guilty of blasphemy. To predict the destruction of the temple seemed contrary to God's promise that Jerusalem was His chosen shrine. It was therefore eternally sacred, thought the people. God would never leave His house. The reform of Josiah had reinforced that belief by stressing, among other things, the centrality of worship in Jerusalem. If Jeremiah was guilty of blasphemy or false prophecy, then the penalty was death (Ex. 22:18; Lev. 24:16; and Deut. 18:20). "You shall die," screams the hostile crowd.

10-11 The princes (court officials) were probably summoned to insure the legality of Jeremiah's trial for blasphemy. They had the power to execute the punishment. The trial took place in the open courtyard inside the New Gate. The priests and prophets reaffirmed their demand for the death penalty. They point out to the princes, who were the political leaders, that Jeremiah's words are also against "the city" (rather than God or the temple) and that he is therefore guilty of treason.

**12-15** Jeremiah is then given a chance to present his defense. He retracts nothing. In fact, he takes the offensive. He insists that Yahweh had commissioned him to speak against both the "house" (including therefore the priests) and the "city" (involving also the princes). The household of God must completely amend its wicked ways to have even a chance of averting the disaster ("evil") Yahweh had planned. For Jeremiah this message was more important than his own life; he had done his job. Now the people could do what they liked with him. But he warned them against a hasty "lynching" of an innocent man. He was sure that he was speaking God's Word. How could they be sure that he was not? But Jeremiah uses no signs or wonders to prove his claim (as Moses had done). He asserts the legitimacy of his commission and leaves it at that.

**16-19, 24** The princes and the crowd were apparently swayed by the force of Jeremiah's words. And some of the elders (the heads of leading clans), who did not have the vested interest in the temple that the prophets and priests had, pointed to a crucial precedent. Micah had once preached the same message (Micah 3:12) during the reign of Hezekiah about a century earlier, and the outcome had been beneficial. Hezekiah had repented, interceded to Yahweh, and the doom was averted (note the reforms of Hezekiah in 2 Kings 18:3-6). It was ultimately the influence of Ahikam, a prince from a leading political family (2 Kings 22:12; Jer. 29:3; 39:14), that saved Jeremiah's neck.

**20-23** Scholars debate whether 26:20-23 belongs to

210

the actual trial of Jeremiah or was added by Baruch to illustrate how Jehoiakim, who had just come to the throne (26:1), later treated prophets who dared to preach the way Jeremiah did. The case of Uriah is cited. He, unlike Jeremiah, fled when his life was at stake. But Jehoiakim hunted him down in Egypt, put him to death, and left his body to lie in shame. Jeremiah later hid from Jehoiakim also (36:19, 26). Jeremiah's trial might have been very different if Jehoiakim had been involved and if the princes (who were later dominated by Jehoiakim) had not had the courage to defend the prophet.

## JEREMIAH WARNS THE ENVOYS
## TO JERUSALEM                                    27:1-11

¹ In the beginning of the reign of Zedeki'ah ᵘ the son of Josi'ah, king of Judah, this word came to Jeremiah from the LORD. ² Thus the LORD said to me: "Make yourself thongs and yoke-bars, and put them on your neck. ³ Send word ᵛ to the king of Edom, the king of Moab, the king of the sons of Ammon, the king of Tyre, and the king of Sidon by the hand of the envoys who have come to Jerusalem to Zedeki'ah king of Judah. ⁴ Give them this charge for their masters: 'Thus says the LORD of hosts, the God of Israel: This is what you shall say to your masters: ⁵ "It is I who by my great power and my outstretched arm have made the earth, with the men and animals that are on the earth, and I give it to whomever it seems right to me. ⁶ Now I have given all these lands into the hand of Nebuchadnez'zar, the king of Babylon, my servant, and I have given him also the beasts of the field to serve him. ⁷ All the nations shall serve him and

ᵘ Another reading is *Jehoiakim*   ᵛ Cn: Heb *send them*

211

his son and his grandson, until the time of his own land comes; then many nations and great kings shall make him their slave.

8 ""But if any nation or kingdom will not serve this Nebuchadnez'zar king of Babylon, and put its neck under the yoke of the king of Babylon, I will punish that nation with the sword, with famine, and with pestilence, says the LORD, until I have consumed it by his hand. 9 So do not listen to your prophets, your diviners, your dreamers,*w* your soothsayers, or your sorcerers, who are saying to you, 'You shall not serve the king of Babylon.' 10 For it is a lie which they are prophesying to you, with the result that you will be removed far from your land, and I will drive you out, and you will perish. 11 But any nation which will bring its neck under the yoke of the king of Babylon and serve him, I will leave on its own land, to till it and dwell there, says the LORD."'"

*w* Gk Syr Vg: Heb *dreams*

1-7 Jeremiah took his call as a prophet to the nations (1:5) seriously. In the fourth year of Zedekiah (594 B. C.), as 28:1 indicates, envoys from neighboring countries assembled in Jerusalem. These countries were also vassal states of Nebuchadnezzar's empire. The purpose of their meeting was apparently to plan a revolt against Babylon. Jeremiah disrupted this top-level conference by employing some rather undiplomatic and sensational tactics. At God's direction Jeremiah wears the yoke-bars for oxen around his neck. Such bars were an obvious symbol of servitude to Babylon. Jeremiah's speech further interprets this symbolic action before each of the envoys. These envoys are to tell their masters (kings) that the God of Judah created the world and all things in it. He was not merely the local God of a small power called Judah. Because He had created the earth, He still ruled and directed its history. Hence it was ultimately His plan that Nebuchadnezzar should rule the earth . . . and its "beasts." It was futile therefore to scheme any further revolts. In God's good "time" Babylon, too, would get its just deserts, but not before. Nebuchadnezzar is again called "my servant." (See comment on 25:9.)

8-11 Nebuchadnezzar ruled by Yahweh's authority, and it was tantamount to rebellion against God if any nation refused to serve Nebuchadnezzar as a vassal state. God would use Babylon to punish such a nation. In addition to political unrest there was strong religious agitation by the professional prophets and less reputable foretellers of the future. They had predicted a successful break from Babylonian rule, the release of Judah's exiles in Babylon, and the return of sacred vessels to the temple (cf. 28:3). Jeremiah called these operators lying hypocrites. The net result of heeding them would be more destruction and exile. To submit to Babylonian rule, however, would mean security and prosperity in the long run.

## JEREMIAH WARNS AGAINST
## NATIONALISTIC PROPHETS          27:12-22

¹² To Zedeki'ah king of Judah I spoke in like manner: "Bring your necks under the yoke of the king of Babylon, and serve him and his people, and live. ¹³ Why will you and your people die by the sword, by famine, and by pestilence, as the LORD has spoken

concerning any nation which will not serve the king of Babylon? [14] Do not listen to the words of the prophets who are saying to you, 'You shall not serve the king of Babylon,' for it is a lie which they are prophesying to you. [15] I have not sent them, says the LORD, but they are prophesying falsely in my name, with the result that I will drive you out and you will perish, you and the prophets who are prophesying to you."

[16] Then I spoke to the priests and to all this people, saying, "Thus says the LORD: Do not listen to the words of your prophets who are prophesying to you, saying, 'Behold, the vessels of the LORD'S house will now shortly be brought back from Babylon,' for it is a lie which they are prophesying to you. [17] Do not listen to them; serve the king of Babylon and live. Why should this city become a desolation? [18] If they are prophets, and if the word of the LORD is with them, then let them intercede with the LORD of hosts, that the vessels which are left in the house of the LORD, in the house of the king of Judah, and in Jerusalem may not go to Babylon. [19] For thus says the LORD of hosts concerning the pillars, the sea, the stands, and the rest of the vessels which are left in this city, [20] which Nebuchadnez'zar king of Babylon did not take away, when he took into exile from Jerusalem to Babylon Jeconi'ah the son of Jehoi'akim, king of Judah, and all the nobles of Judah and Jerusalem—[21] thus says the LORD of hosts, the God of Israel, concerning the vessels which are left in the house of the LORD, in the house of the king of Judah, and in Jerusalem: [22] They shall be carried to Babylon and remain there until the day when I give attention to them, says the LORD. Then I will bring them back and restore them to this place."

214

**12-15** Jeremiah did not spare Zedekiah, who was the host for the scheming envoys. His message to the king was essentially the same as before: accept the rule ("yoke") of Babylon as God's will and ignore the appeals of the false professional prophets. (Cf. 21:1-10)

**16-20** After addressing the political leaders, Jeremiah turned to the priests and the people. He warned them not to let their hopes be raised by the other prophets. The "vessels" (including furnishings) Nebuchadnezzar had taken to Babylon in 597 B. C. would not be returned to the temple "shortly," as the prophets had led them to expect. If these prophets were fulfilling their true function as mediators, they would be interceding to save those vessels left in the temple from a similar fate. For as things stood at that time, the plan of God was to eventually destroy the whole temple and leave the remaining vessels and furnishings as booty for the Babylonians. Verse 20 seems to be an explanatory footnote of the scribe explaining how some of the vessels came to be in exile and not others. This fact was quite well known to Jeremiah's audience but may not have been clear for later readers. Hence the later explanation. Verse 22 also adds the hope that one day the vessels would finally be returned to the temple. This hope seems contrary to Jeremiah's thinking (in 3:16 or 26:9, for example) and is therefore thought by some scholars to be a later expansion. The Greek version (Septuagint) probably preserves the text of Jeremiah prior to its expansion. The Greek version of vv. 19-22 reads: "For thus says the Lord: Even the rest of the vessels, which the king of Babylon did not take away, when he took Jeconiah from Jerusalem into exile, shall be carried to Babylon, says the Lord." The expansion of the Hebrew text may illustrate how

215

God's scribes amplified the prophet's word to clarify it for their audience.

## JEREMIAH CLASHES WITH HANANIAH    28:1-17

¹ In that same year, at the beginning of the reign of Zedeki'ah king of Judah, in the fifth month of the fourth year, Hanani'ah the son of Azzur, the prophet from Gib'eon, spoke to me in the house of the LORD, in the presence of the priests and all the people, saying, ² "Thus says the LORD of hosts, the God of Israel: I have broken the yoke of the king of Babylon. ³ Within two years I will bring back to this place all the vessels of the LORD'S house, which Nebuchadnez'zar king of Babylon took away from this place and carried to Babylon. ⁴ I will also bring back to this place Jeconi'ah the son of Jehoi'akim, king of Judah, and all the exiles from Judah who went to Babylon, says the LORD, for I will break the yoke of the king of Babylon."

⁵ Then the prophet Jeremiah spoke to Hanani'ah the prophet in the presence of the priests and all the people who were standing in the house of the LORD; ⁶ and the prophet Jeremiah said, "Amen! May the LORD do so; may the LORD make the words which you have prophesied come true, and bring back to this place from Babylon the vessels of the house of the LORD, and all the exiles. ⁷ Yet hear now this word which I speak in your hearing and in the hearing of all the people. ⁸ The prophets who preceded you and me from ancient times prophesied war, famine, and pestilence against many countries and great kingdoms. ⁹ As for the prophet who prophesies peace, when the word of that prophet comes to pass, then

it will be known that the LORD has truly sent the prophet."

¹⁰ Then the prophet Hanani'ah took the yoke-bars from the neck of Jeremiah the prophet, and broke them. ¹¹ And Hanani'ah spoke in the presence of all the people, saying, "Thus says the LORD: Even so will I break the yoke of Nebuchadnez'zar king of Babylon from the neck of all the nations within two years." But Jeremiah the prophet went his way.

¹² Sometime after the prophet Hanani'ah had broken the yoke-bars from off the neck of Jeremiah the prophet, the word of the LORD came to Jeremiah: ¹³ "Go, tell Hanani'ah, 'Thus says the LORD: You have broken wooden bars, but I ˣ will make in their place bars of iron. ¹⁴ For thus says the LORD of hosts, the God of Israel: I have put upon the neck of all these nations an iron yoke of servitude to Nebuchadnez'zar king of Babylon, and they shall serve him, for I have given to him even the beasts of the field.'" ¹⁵ And Jeremiah the prophet said to the prophet Hanani'ah, "Listen, Hanani'ah, the LORD has not sent you, and you have made this people trust in a lie. ¹⁶ Therefore thus says the LORD: 'Behold, I will remove you from the face of the earth. This very year you shall die, because you have uttered rebellion against the LORD.'"

¹⁷ In that same year, in the seventh month, the prophet Hanani'ah died.

ˣ Gk: Heb *you*


**1-4, 10-11** This chapter provides us with a specific case of how Jeremiah clashed with the professional prophets mentioned in the previous chapter. The same situation is involved. It takes place "in the same year."

Hananiah, a vehement prophet of hope, predicted the release of King Jehoiachin from exile and the return of the vessels of the temple (see the comment on Ch. 27) within two years. To enforce his assertion that God had "broken the yoke ('rule') of the King of Babylon," Hananiah broke the yoke-bars Jeremiah was wearing around his neck (see 27:2-7). This action reversed the symbolic action of Jeremiah in wearing the yoke-bars. Hananiah was inspired by a sincere nationalistic zeal; Jeremiah was gripped by the unwelcome word he had received from God.

**5-9** More significant than this action, however, is the insight we gain into the character of Jeremiah as a prophet. He does not counter with a violent cry of doom. He, too, loves his people. And so he replies to Hananiah "Amen," that is, "personally I hope you are right." Jeremiah's own wishes were for an immediate return of his people from exile. But his personal wishes did not count. He knew that he had history on his side, and he reminds his audience of that fact. The onus of proof was always on the side of the prophet who, like Hananiah, was predicting peace and victory (Deut. 18:21-22). Normally God sent prophets when He needed to announce His oncoming judgments. Anyone prophesying peace could only be considered a true prophet after his words came true. Imagine the confusion of the people!

**12-14** Just as noteworthy perhaps is the fact that Jeremiah does not dare to give a substitute oracle immediately. To the amazement of the crowd he walked away. It was some time before God clarified the situation. A prophet's inspiration was not instantaneous! God in turn reinforced his former oracle of servitude to Babylon. To convey this message Jeremiah was

218

bidden to wear an iron yoke instead of a wooden yoke. Revolt against Babylon was therefore impossible; Nebuchadnezzar was destined to rule all God had given into his hands.

**15-17** The epilog of this incident is likewise provocative. The death penalty was set for prophesying falsely in God's name (Deut. 18:20). Jeremiah had been tried on that charge years before (26:1-11). Here God pronounces the sentence through His agent (cf. Deut. 13:5) and also effects the punishment. Hananiah died two months later. Jeremiah, no doubt, had no more taste for this kind of preaching than he did for continually preaching doom for Israel. But when God spoke, Jeremiah was compelled to act.

## JEREMIAH'S LETTER TO THE EXILES     29:1-23

¹ **These are the words of the letter which Jeremiah the prophet sent from Jerusalem to the elders** ᵛ **of the exiles, and to the priests, the prophets, and all the people, whom Nebuchadnez'zar had taken into exile from Jerusalem to Babylon.** ² **This was after King Jeconi'ah, and the queen mother, the eunuchs, the princes of Judah and Jerusalem, the craftsmen, and the smiths had departed from Jerusalem.** ³ **The letter was sent by the hand of Ela'sah the son of Shaphan and Gemari'ah the son of Hilki'ah, whom Zedeki'ah king of Judah sent to Babylon to Nebuchadnez'zar king of Babylon. It said:** ⁴ **"Thus says the LORD of hosts, the God of Israel, to all the exiles whom I have sent into exile from Jerusalem to Babylon:** ⁴ **Build houses and live in them; plant gardens and eat their produce.** ⁶ **Take wives and have sons**

ᵛ Gk: Heb *the rest of the elders*

and daughters; take wives for your sons, and give your daughters in marriage, that they may bear sons and daughters; multiply there, and do not decrease. [7] But seek the welfare of the city where I have sent you into exile, and pray to the LORD on its behalf, for in its welfare you will find your welfare. [8] For thus says the LORD of hosts, the God of Israel: Do not let your prophets and your diviners who are among you deceive you, and do not listen to the dreams which they dream, [z] [9] for it is a lie which they are prophesying to you in my name; I did not send them, says the LORD.

[10] "For thus says the LORD: When seventy years are completed for Babylon, I will visit you, and I will fulfil to you my promise and bring you back to this place. [11] For I know the plans I have for you, says the LORD, plans for welfare and not for evil, to give you a future and a hope. [12] Then you will call upon me and come and pray to me, and I will hear you. [13] You will seek me and find me; when you seek me with all your heart, [14] I will be found by you, says the LORD, and I will restore your fortunes and gather you from all the nations and all the places where I have driven you, says the LORD, and I will bring you back to the place from which I sent you into exile.

[15] "Because you have said, 'The LORD has raised up prophets for us in Babylon,' — [16] Thus says the LORD concerning the king who sits on the throne of David, and concerning all the people who dwell in this city, your kinsmen who did not go out with you into exile: [17] 'Thus says the LORD of hosts, Behold, I am sending on them sword, famine, and

---

[z] Cn: Heb *your dreams which you cause to dream*

pestilence, and I will make them like vile figs which are so bad they cannot be eaten. [18] I will pursue them with sword, famine, and pestilence, and will make them a horror to all the kingdoms of the earth, to be a curse, a terror, a hissing, and a reproach among all the nations where I have driven them, [19] because they did not heed my words, says the LORD, which I persistently sent to you by my servants the prophets, but you would not listen, says the LORD.' — [20] Hear the word of the LORD, all you exiles whom I sent away from Jerusalem to Babylon: [21] 'Thus says the LORD of hosts, the God of Israel, concerning Ahab the son of Kola'iah and Zedeki'ah the son of Maasei'ah, who are prophesying a lie to you in my name: Behold, I will deliver them into the hand of Nebuchadnez'zar king of Babylon, and he shall slay them before your eyes. [22] Because of them this curse shall be used by all the exiles from Judah in Babylon: "The LORD make you like Zedeki'ah and Ahab, whom the king of Babylon roasted in the fire," [23] because they have committed folly in Israel, they have committed adultery with their neighbors' wives, and they have spoken in my name lying words which I did not command them. I am the one who knows, and I am witness, says the LORD.' "


1-3 Jer. 29 reflects the same period of agitation as that of Chs. 27 and 28. Even those in exile are hoping for a speedy return to their homeland. To counteract the false expectations fostered by the false prophets (see 27:16; 28:2-4), Jeremiah wrote a letter to those people who had been taken into exile some years earlier (597 B. C.) by Nebuchadnezzar. Those taken into

221

captivity were the leaders of Judah. To them the letter is addressed. This letter is delivered by two messengers whom King Zedekiah had sent to Babylon, probably with tribute money. These preliminary details appear in vv. 1-3.

**4-9** The text of the letter is found in vv. 4-15, 21-23. Verses 16-20 appear to be a prose saying that was inserted later. This letter is both radical and important. A popular tradition had apparently arisen that Jerusalem was God's holy city and the land of Israel His private domain. To live elsewhere was to be divorced from the blessing of God's presence (cf. 1 Sam. 26:19); security lay in Jerusalem, where Yahweh had fixed His abode (Micah 3:11). But Jeremiah insists that these exiles, who are elsewhere designated "good figs" (24:5), should settle down and live a normal life in that pagan land, despite the many discomforts. God's blessing was not dependent on the environment of Palestine. Even more startling is his plea to pray for the city of Babylon, where the exiles happen to live. In so doing they will further their own interests. Prayer for one's enemies is rarely found in the Old Testament. Prayers for vengeance are much more common (18:19-23). Jeremiah's advice to the exiles is directly the opposite of what other prophets had been promoting without God's approval.

**10-14** Jeremiah repeats his assertion that the exile will last a lifetime (70 years). Thereafter God will keep His promise to rehabilitate His people in Palestine according to His plans. He would bring about the expected outcome of their hopes, or in the words of the prophet, "a hope and a future." When that plan is effected, a close rapport will exist between God and His people, an intimate conversation that stems from the heart. When Israel repents completely, "with her whole heart," He will be right there waiting. Already implied is the reality that God would have to effect that change of heart in His people (see 31:18, 33-34), since they had become spiritually impotent. Israel's transformation would be accompanied by a new exodus back to Canaan and a rich life in the promised land. But all of this would take a long time, a lifetime! Still the haunting question remains: To what extent were these people changed when the exiles returned after 538 B. C.? Or are we to look for a second way of viewing this hope, that is, for a long-range fulfillment of this plan in the New Testament age?

**15, 21-23** Jeremiah's letter concludes with a condemnation of two prophets, Ahab and Zedekiah. These prophets had been guilty not only of false prophecies but also of gross immorality. Their attempts to stimulate new hopes for a swift return were, no doubt, viewed as agitation for revolt. On this ground Nebuchadnezzar would have them executed as rebels. They would be burned alive, and reference to their ugly death would become a vicious byword for cursing others.

**16-20** Verses 16-20, not found in the Septuagint (Greek version of the Old Testament), interrupt the flow of the letter and therefore seem to have been added later. They treat of a different subject than the letter, namely, the rejection of those in Jerusalem as "vile figs." Verses 16-19 are concerned with and directed to those in Jerusalem, and v. 20 provides a transition to address the following verses to those in exile again. In short, vv. 16-19 seem to be a later amplification of the thoughts of 24:1-10.

223

## Jeremiah's Letter to Shemaiah      29:24-32

²⁴ To Shemai'ah of Nehel'am you shall say: ²⁵ "Thus says the LORD of hosts, the God of Israel: You have sent letters in your name to all the people who are in Jerusalem, and to Zephani'ah the son of Ma-asei'ah the priest, and to all the priests, saying, ²⁶ 'The LORD has made you priest instead of Jehoi'ada the priest, to have charge in the house of the LORD over every madman who prophesies, to put him in the stocks and collar. ²⁷ Now why have you not rebuked Jeremiah of An'athoth who is prophesying to you? ²⁸ For he has sent to us in Babylon, saying, "Your exile will be long; build houses and live in them, and plant gardens and eat their produce." ' "

²⁹ Zephani'ah the priest read this letter in the hearing of Jeremiah the prophet. ³⁰ Then the word of the LORD came to Jeremiah: ³¹ "Send to all the exiles, saying, 'Thus says the LORD concerning Shemai'ah of Nehel'am: Because Shemai'ah has prophesied to you when I did not send him, and has made you trust in a lie, ³² therefore thus says the LORD: Behold, I will punish Shemai'ah of Nehel'am and his descendants; he shall not have any one living among this people to see ᵃ the good that I will do to my people, says the LORD, for he has talked rebellion against the LORD.' "

ᵃ Gk: Heb *and he shall not see*

24-28 Jeremiah's letter to the exiles evoked considerable protest and unrest. Shemaiah, one of the exiles, wrote back to Zephaniah the priest, who was then officer in charge of the temple. Shemaiah rebuked Zephaniah for not disciplining Jeremiah, who was acting like a mad fanatic. For Jeremiah to preach a long stay in exile was intolerable news.

**29-32** Zephaniah, however, did not get agitated. He was not in exile! He showed Jeremiah the letter from Shemaiah but did nothing about it. But Jeremiah refused to leave the matter rest. He sent a letter off to Shemaiah with a withering curse against that prophet and his progeny. The curse of vv. 31-32 apparently continues the beginning of the address in v. 25. Shemaiah, like Hananiah (28:16-17), would suffer a similar fate because of preaching false prophecy. False prophecy was open "rebellion" against God.

# The Little Book of Comfort

## Jeremiah 30–33

Chapters 30–33 are often designated the Book of Comfort since their major theme is one of hope and consolation for the condemned people of God. 30:2-3 makes reference to just such a "book" or scroll. The structure of the book is quite simple. 30:1-3 is the introduction or caption for the book. 30:4–31:22 offers a selection of poetic oracles. In this first section short doom oracles tend to alternate with hope oracles. 31:23-40 consists primarily of a collection of prose oracles. The third section (Ch. 32) presents a symbolic action of Jeremiah that dramatizes the message of hope in the preceding oracles. Chapter 33 is an appendix of prose hope oracles that may well have been added later. Half of them (vv. 14-26) are not found in the Greek (Septuagint) version of the Old Testament. That the Book of Comfort represents a distinct collection of varied materials revolving around a common theme is obvious from the above divisions as well as from the diversity of date. Some of the oracles may have been very early and have been originally directed to the Northern Kingdom, which was under the captivity of Assyria since 722 B. C. (e. g., 31:1-6, 15-20); in the present context, however, the comfort offered is primarily for those about to be exiled in Babylon or already in Babylon. Some materials are clearly from the time of the exile (e. g., 33: 10-13). Many scholars believe there is reason to assume that some of the passages are the work of later scribes of God rather than Jeremiah himself (see the comment on 31:7-14; 32:17-23; 33:14-26). Who collected these oracles, added the heading (30:1-3), and gave the chapter its topical arrangement we do not know. 32:6-15 indicates that the editor used some of Jeremiah's materials written in the first person.

## INTRODUCTION TO THE BOOK
## OF COMFORT                                           30:1-3

¹ The word that came to Jeremiah from the LORD: ² "Thus says the LORD, the God of Israel: Write in a book all the words that I have spoken to you. ³ For behold, days are coming, says the LORD, when I will restore the fortunes of my people, Israel and Judah, says the LORD, and I will bring them back to the land which I gave to their fathers, and they shall take possession of it."

The opening verses of this chapter probably represent an introduction for the entire Book of Comfort (Chs. 30 – 33). Here Jeremiah is told expressly to write certain oracles in a "book" inasmuch as God would one day "restore the fortunes" of His people. The misfortunes of "Israel and Judah" are no doubt their respective exiles, although this expression ("to restore the fortunes") need not refer only to exile (cf. Job 42:10).

227

It is noteworthy that Jeremiah apparently expressed
messages of promise to the Northern Kingdom of Israel
as well as to Judah. In this he followed the line of Hosea
(Hos. 11:11). This superscription does not eliminate the
possibility that some of the materials in Chs. 30 – 33 that
speak of hope and comfort stem from a later scribe than
Jeremiah himself. Many believe, for example, that
33:14-26 reflects a later development of Jeremiah's theology. In general, however, the materials in this Book
of Comfort are very similar to the hope oracles scattered throughout the remainder of the Book of Jeremiah. A new exodus and a new entry into the ancient
promised land, rather than the rule of a Messiah, is the
overriding hope of God's people in exile. On the question of hope and fulfillment see also the discussion in
the Introduction.

## THE DAY OF PANIC AND THE DAY OF SALVATION 30:4-11

⁴ These are the words which the **LORD** spoke
concerning Israel and Judah:
⁵ "Thus says the **LORD**:
  We have heard a cry of panic,
    of terror, and no peace.
⁶ Ask now, and see,
    can a man bear a child?
  Why then do I see every man
    with his hands on his loins like a woman in labor?
  Why has every face turned pale?
⁷ Alas! that day is so great
    there is none like it;
  it is a time of distress for Jacob;
    yet he shall be saved out of it.

228

[8] "And it shall come to pass in that day, says the LORD of hosts, that I will break the yoke from off their [b] neck, and I will burst their [b] bonds, and strangers shall no more make servants of them.[c] [9] But they shall serve the LORD their God and David their king, whom I will raise up for them.

[10] "Then fear not, O Jacob my servant, says the
    LORD,
  nor be dismayed, O Israel;
for lo, I will save you from afar,
  and your offspring from the land of their captivity.
Jacob shall return and have quiet and ease,
  and none shall make him afraid.
[11] For I am with you to save you,

                  says the LORD;

I will make a full end of all the nations
  among whom I scattered you,
  but of you I will not make a full end.
I will chasten you in just measure,
  and I will by no means leave you unpunished.

[b] Gk Old Latin: Heb *your*   [c] Heb *make a servant of him*

In general, oracles of doom or judgment alternate with oracles of hope or salvation throughout Ch. 30. To our ears the transition from one to the other sounds harsh and abrupt. Yet this sharp transition is deliberate. The full judgment of God and the free grace of God's love stand in bold contrast. God's wrath takes its toll in full measure. But His people are incapable of change (cf. 13:23). God's salvation therefore comes solely by the grace of God, freely and undeserved. It is given!

God turns to save Israel not because they have become better but because He is God. The oracles of vv. 4-11 illustrate this sharp contrast. Verses 5-7 depict a day of unbelievable panic and anguish for God's people. It is the day when God's judgment falls heavily; it is the dreaded day of the Lord, a day of decisive reckoning (cf. Amos 5:18-20; Is. 2:12-21). The historical period of the oracle describing this day cannot be determined. In sharp juxtaposition to these verses stand the words of promise and salvation in vv. 8-11. The transition came already in v. 7. This day of judgment is without equal in severity; yet inexplicably there is fresh salvation for Jacob, God's people. Israel would be rescued from its historical crisis. In vv. 10-11 this salvation is defined as deliverance from captivity far and wide. The form of these verses follows that of the oracles of comfort pronounced by the priests. God's wrath is never weak and partial; He brings down a "full measure" of punishment (which is what Jeremiah means by "chasten" in v. 11, as the term "punishment" indicates in v. 14). This total doom is finally countered by an undeserved grace; His own people will not be exterminated! By grace Israel is saved; but the total doom and the full wrath of God are still imposed. A similar train of thought follows throughout this chapter. Verses 8-9 present a prose intrusion into the sequence of thought. They express the hope of a return from exile and a new ruler or Messianic king from the line of David to rule over God's people (compare the form of Ezek. 34:23 and Hos. 3:5). Thus total doom and total grace stand side by side here in Jeremiah. There is no bridge between them; it is not the righteous few that God saves, according to Jeremiah. Those whom God saves are the same people as those whom He has earlier damned, His helpless sinful people.

THE INCURABLE WOUND
AND THE MIRACULOUS CURE                    30:12-17

¹² "For thus says the LORD:
  Your hurt is incurable,
    and your wound is grievous.
¹³ There is none to uphold your cause,
    no medicine for your wound,
    no healing for you.
¹⁴ All your lovers have forgotten you;
    they care nothing for you;
  for I have dealt you the blow of an enemy,
    the punishment of a merciless foe,
  because your guilt is great,
    because your sins are flagrant.
¹⁵ Why do you cry out over your hurt?
  Your pain is incurable.
Because your guilt is great,
    because your sins are flagrant,
  I have done these things to you.
¹⁶ Therefore all who devour you shall be devoured,
    and all your foes, every one of them, shall go into
      captivity;
  those who despoil you shall become a spoil,
    and all who prey on you I will make a prey.
¹⁷ For I will restore health to you,
    and your wounds I will heal,
                                    says the LORD,
  because they have called you an outcast:
    'It is Zion, for whom no one cares!'

12-15 The forthright affirmation of God's relentless,
unmitigated wrath standing side by side with His totally
undeserved saving love is seen again in this oracle. Israel
is sick and her case is hopeless. None of her former

allies ("lovers") and no efforts of her own ("medicine") will be of aid. She is suffering from a wound that Yahweh Himself has inflicted; it is the deep wound of an enemy. He had punished His people to the full extent of His wrath because of their flagrant sins. There was therefore no way to escape the historical disaster that threatened their existence. Again the precise historical moment is not specified, but Judah's exile is probably meant. When God administers His judgment, He appears like a vicious cruel foe; He is no longer seen as a tender Father.

**16-17** Then follows the strange "therefore" of v. 16. How does the thought of deliverance in v. 16 follow from the message of doom in the preceding verses? Why this "therefore"? God heals His sick people not because they have now begun to improve but because He is the Physician (cf. 33:6). After His judgment His love follows. He has killed with an incurable wound, and He will bring to life with a miraculous cure. Under the wrath of God Israel was dead. By His grace she would be recreated a new people. He is her *only* enemy. All other foes He will ward off for her sake. The moment other foes begin to sneer at His people, He again becomes her jealous defender and not her enemy. Paul describes this healing of helpless ungodly men as reconciliation. Through Christ God's people are saved from the wrath of God (Rom. 5:6-11). In Christ God's plan of salvation is perfected.

## THE REVERSAL OF ISRAEL'S FORTUNES                    30:18-22

<sup>18</sup> "Thus says the LORD:
  Behold, I will restore the fortunes of the tents of
      Jacob,

and have compassion on his dwellings;
the city shall be rebuilt upon its mound,
and the palace shall stand where it used to be.
¹⁹ Out of them shall come songs of thanksgiving,
and the voices of those who make merry.
I will multiply them, and they shall not be few;
I will make them honored, and they shall not be
small.
²⁰ Their children shall be as they were of old,
and their congregation shall be established before
me;
and I will punish all who oppress them.
²¹ Their prince shall be one of themselves,
their ruler shall come forth from their midst;
I will make him draw near, and he shall approach
me,
for who would dare of himself to approach me?
says the **LORD**.
²² And you shall be my people,
and I will be your God."

This unit reflects conditions during the exile. Jerusalem seems to be in ruins. The passage promises that
the former way of life of God's people would be restored
amid great rejoicing. The "city" and "palace" would
be rebuilt, the religious "congregation" would again
assemble, and its "ruler" (for the same term see Micah
5:2) would also perform priestly functions ("approach
me," cf. Num. 16:5) as King David had once done. The
temple is conspicuous by its absence. The covenant,
however, will be restored as the "my people – your
God" formula of v. 22 implies. (See 31:1, 33)

233

## IRREVOCABLE WRATH
## AND INEXPLICABLE GRACE                    30:23 — 31:6

²³ Behold the storm of the LORD!
    Wrath has gone forth,
  a whirling tempest;
    it will burst upon the head of the wicked.
²⁴ The fierce anger of the LORD will not turn back
    until he has executed and accomplished
    the intents of his mind.
In the latter days you will understand this.

¹ "At that time, says the LORD, I will be the God of
all the families of Israel, and they shall be my people."
² Thus says the LORD:
  "The people who survived the sword
    found grace in the wilderness;
  when Israel sought for rest,
³   the LORD appeared to him *d* from afar.
  I have loved you with an everlasting love;
    therefore I have continued my faithfulness to you.
⁴ Again I will build you, and you shall be built,
  O virgin Israel!
  Again you shall adorn yourself with timbrels,
    and shall go forth in the dance of the merry-
      makers.
⁵ Again you shall plant vineyards
    upon the mountains of Samar′ia;
  the planters shall plant
    and shall enjoy the fruit.
⁶ For there shall be a day when watchmen will call
    in the hill country of E′phraim:
  'Arise, and let us go up to Zion,
    to the LORD our God.'"

    *d* Gk: Heb *me*

Once again the harsh judgment of God and the free
grace of God stand side by side. (Recall the comment on
30:4-11 and 12-17.) In this case the original historical
audience may have been the Israelites of the Northern
Kingdom. The language is somewhat similar to that
which Hosea addressed to Israel. More probably, however, the passage repeats Jeremiah's hope that the new
age would be for the exiles of the Northern Kingdom
(Israel), who had been captured a century earlier in
722 B. C., and those of the Southern Kingdom (Judah),
who were taken away in 597 and 587 B. C. He envisioned
a new and united Israel (see 31:27, 31), as did other
prophets. Both Samaria (v. 5), the capital of the North,
and Zion (v. 6), the capital of the South, are involved.
A similar orientation to the needs of the exiles of the
Northern Kingdom is reflected elsewhere in Ch. 31,
for instance, vv. 9, 15, 18, 27.

**23-24** The wrath of God is here portrayed as a
tremendous ravaging storm that will not peter out
until it has completed its destructive course. Thus God's
judgment has been fixed according to a divine plan, and
nothing can alter it now. Only when this "storm" is past
will the reason for its coming be evident to the victims.

**31:1-6** For the victims will experience a new unexpected day of salvation. History will more than repeat
itself. God will establish a new covenant (31:1) with "my
people" (cf. 31:31) as at Sinai; He will offer fresh grace
and free deliverance as in the wilderness wanderings
(v. 2); His eternal love will elect them again as His very
own (v. 3) as it had once before in Egypt; again He will
bring Israel to the promised land of Canaan and rebuild
her ruins; again He will bless her land with festive joy
(v. 4) and fertility (v. 5). On that day the watchmen of
Ephraim in the North will encourage the people to make

235

a pilgrimage to Jerusalem and there to hold a festival. For Samaria will be a place for vineyards and not for idolatry. The curses of judgment on the cities and land of Palestine are now reversed. Several terms call for special comment. "To find grace" is a frequent Old Testament expression that means receiving full acceptance by God despite one's past history of rebellion; finding grace is always an unearned discovery worked by God alone. The Hebrew terms for "love" and "faithfulness" in v. 3 (cf. 2:2) refer, respectively, to that inexplicable divine initiative which chooses an unworthy party to love and to that undaunted devotion to the chosen party despite its persistent unworthy response. This devotion to Israel was exhibited by faithfulness to the covenant bond, which Yahweh had established by His initiating love.

## The Ransom of Israel from Exile                                  31:7-14

7 For thus says the LORD:
"Sing aloud with gladness for Jacob,
  and raise shouts for the chief of the nations;
proclaim, give praise, and say,
  'The LORD has saved his people,
  the remnant of Israel.'
8 Behold, I will bring them from the north country,
    and gather them from the farthest parts of the earth,
  among them the blind and the lame,
    the woman with child and her who is in travail, together;
    a great company, they shall return here.

236

⁹ With weeping they shall come,
and with consolations ᵉ I will lead them back,
I will make them walk by brooks of water,
in a straight path in which they shall not stumble;
for I am a father to Israel,
and E′phraim is my first-born.

¹⁰ "Hear the word of the LORD, O nations,
and declare it in the coastlands afar off;
say, 'He who scattered Israel will gather him,
and will keep him as a shepherd keeps his flock.'
¹¹ For the LORD has ransomed Jacob,
and has redeemed him from hands too strong for
him.
¹² They shall come and sing aloud on the height of
Zion,
and they shall be radiant over the goodness of the
LORD,
over the grain, the wine, and the oil,
and over the young of the flock and the herd;
their life shall be like a watered garden,
and they shall languish no more.
¹³ Then shall the maidens rejoice in the dance,
and the young men and the old shall be merry.
I will turn their mourning into joy,
I will comfort them, and give them gladness for
sorrow.
¹⁴ I will feast the soul of the priests with abundance,
and my people shall be satisfied with my goodness,
says the LORD."

ᵉ Gk Compare Vg Tg: Heb *supplications*

The verses in this unit bear a marked similarity
to the latter chapters of Isaiah. Many scholars therefore

237

believe that it was written by a later prophet in the style of Isaiah 40—55 rather than by Jeremiah. The problem of authorship is not easily solved, however. Nevertheless, the ideas, if not the language, of these verses are consistent with the hope of Jeremiah elsewhere, and the concern for Ephraim fits Jeremiah's interest (cf. vv. 5 and 18), rather than those of Is. 40—55.

**7-9** The Israelite exiles, here called the "remnant" (cf. Is. 46:3), are summoned to rejoice and praise God as their Savior. Even the "chiefs of the nations" are included. This remnant is composed of the blind, the lame, pregnant mothers, and all those in need of Yahweh's help (cf. Is. 42:16). They will come from the ends of the earth (cf. Is. 43:5-6). On their return through the desert God will provide refreshing waters (cf. Is. 41:18-20). The fullness of His grace is seen when He calls the new Israel "My firstborn son," thereby electing this people as His own, as He had done once before. (See Ex. 4:22-23)

**10-14** The themes of Is. 40—55 continue in the next verses. The nations and the "coastlands" (or "isles") of the Mediterranean world are summoned to heed the message (cf. Is. 49:1). God is about to gather the exiles scattered abroad and to care for them as "a shepherd keeps his flock" (cf. Is. 40:11). As in the days of the exodus from Egypt, Yahweh will "redeem," that is, rescue His helpless people mightily and bind them to Himself. The exiles will come to Zion in radiant joy and festivity; there they will face a new world of plenty. The promised land will be like the Garden of Eden, rich, fertile, and full of happiness (cf. Is. 51:3; 58:11). Sacrifices will be so abundant that "the soul" (desire) of the priests will be more than filled. The disgrace, anguish, trials, and hardships of the exile would all be reversed by the rich mercy of God. The curses have turned to blessings. For God to restore His people without restoring the land was unthinkable.

## THE CONFESSION OF ISRAEL
## AND THE ANGUISH OF GOD                    31:15-22

15 Thus says the LORD:
"A voice is heard in Ramah,
lamentation and bitter weeping.
Rachel is weeping for her children;
she refuses to be comforted for her children,
because they are not."

16 Thus says the LORD:
"Keep your voice from weeping,
and your eyes from tears;
for your work shall be rewarded,
says the LORD,
and they shall come back from the land of the enemy.
17 There is hope for your future,
says the LORD,
and your children shall come back to their own country.
18 I have heard E'phraim bemoaning,
'Thou hast chastened me, and I was chastened,
like an untrained calf;
bring me back that I may be restored,
for thou art the LORD my God.
19 For after I had turned away I repented;
and after I was instructed, I smote upon my thigh;
I was ashamed, and I was confounded,
because I bore the disgrace of my youth.'

²⁰ Is E'phraim my dear son?
　　Is he my darling child?
　For as often as I speak against him,
　　I do remember him still.
　Therefore my heart yearns for him;
　　I will surely have mercy on him,
　　　　　　　　　　　　　　　　says the **LORD**.
²¹ "Set up waymarks for yourself,
　　make yourself guideposts;
　consider well the highway,
　　the road by which you went.
　Return, O virgin Israel,
　　return to these your cities.
²² How long will you waver,
　　O faithless daughter?
　For the **LORD** has created a new thing on the earth:
　　a woman protects a man."

This unit has a structure almost identical with
3:21 – 4:2. It is basically a confession prompted by God's
invitation to mercy. As it opens, the spirit of Rachel, the
mother of Joseph and hence a mother of the Israelite
nation, weeps bitterly at her grave in Ramah (cf. Gen.
35:16-20; 48:7; 1 Sam. 10:2) for her exiled children, the
people of Israel. (The exile of the Northern tribes in
722 B. C. may be meant here.) Yahweh answers this
lamentation with His free invitation of mercy (v. 16).
He assures Rachel that her anguish and travail for her
exiled children is not in vain. God is offering a "reward"
of free mercy. Israel still has a future; the children of
Rachel will return home from exile (v. 17). This invitation of mercy is accepted, and God hears Israel's confession (vv. 18-19). Israel acknowledges that her punishment ("Thou hast chastened me") was justified. She had

240

been like a wild calf. Next she pleads for God to help her repent ("return") so that her relationship with God will again be wholesome. She acknowledges her shame and her disgrace; she has had a change of heart ("repented"). Yahweh answers this confession in vv. 20-22, once more calling Ephraim His chosen "son" (cf. 31:9). His answer is His word of absolution. His forgiveness and mercy are not the result of Israel's confession, however, but are grounded solely in God's own love. In the midst of judgment Yahweh is constrained by His own love. The grace that comes to Israel is not earned by repentance but comes solely from this anguish and suffering love of God. "Mercy" is that inner compassion and sympathy which moves God to love amid pain. Because God has forgiven Israel, He once more addresses her as "virgin Israel" and invites her to return home from exile. As long as Israel wavers she is a "faithless" adulteress. But God's forgiveness and new plan for Israel is so radical it is a new creation; it is the unbelievable work of having a "woman returning to a man." The uncertain reading "protect" in v. 22 is rendered "return" by some, and this rendering fits the context well. The idea, then, is that the faithless woman Israel finally does return to Yahweh, her man, even though this has never happened before. (See Matt. 2:17 f.)

## A NEW LIFE IN JUDAH 31:23-26

[23] Thus says the LORD of hosts, the God of Israel: "Once more they shall use these words in the land of Judah and in its cities, when I restore their fortunes:
'The LORD bless you, O habitation of righteousness,
O holy hill!'

241

²⁴ And Judah and all its cities shall dwell there together, and the farmers and those who wander ^f^ with their flocks. ²⁵ For I will satisfy the weary soul, and every languishing soul I will replenish."

²⁶ Thereupon I woke and looked, and my sleep was pleasant to me.

^f^ Cn Compare Syr Vg Tg: Heb *and they shall wander*

While much of this chapter has been poetic oracles concerned with Israel, including especially Ephraim, the following prose narrative is concerned with the promise of restoration specifically for Judah and for the city of Jerusalem. There will be a new Zion in which the traditional exaltation of Zion as the "habitation of righteousness," that is, the abode of Yahweh the Righteous One, will again be common. Throughout the cities of Judah there will be harmony and prosperity from God. God will bring back to life those who were crushed under His judgment when Jerusalem fell. This ideal seems to clash with the perpetual demand of Jeremiah that Zion had become a barrier to the faith of God's people and must therefore be eliminated (cf. 7:14; 19:11). But by the grace of God a new age could be envisioned where a new shrine would serve its intended function.

Verse 26 is an enigma. Some view it as the casual comment of a scribe who had fallen asleep, perhaps pondering the joys of the preceding verses, and who awoke with pleasant recollections of his dream. Perhaps it is the comment of a scribe who "looked" around and saw the hard realities of his day and wished that the dreams on which he had been meditating were true in real life. Or perhaps it is a remark of Jeremiah that he received God's word through a dream even though he

242

had previously considered dreams of secondary importance. (Cf. 23:23-31)


A NEW PRINCIPLE OF LIFE          31:27-30

[27] "Behold, the days are coming, says the LORD,
when I will sow the house of Israel and the house of
Judah with the seed of man and the seed of beast.
[28] And it shall come to pass that as I have watched
over them to pluck up and break down, to overthrow,
destroy, and bring evil, so I will watch over them to
build and to plant, says the LORD. [29] In those days
they shall no longer say:
   'The fathers have eaten sour grapes,
      and the children's teeth are set on edge.'
[30] But every one shall die for his own sin; each man
who eats sour grapes, his teeth shall be set on edge.


   Verses 27-28 are dependent on the call and opening
almond rod oracle of 1:10-12. God is about to repopulate
both Judah and Israel after the ruinous captivities of
the Northern and Southern Kingdoms. In so doing He
is fulfilling His promise to be "watching" (see 1:12)
over His people to "build" and to "plant" them. (1:10)
   In the new age an old proverb will also pass away.
Ezekiel deals with the inadequacy of this proverb in
great detail (Ezek. 18:1-32). The proverb reflects the
bitterness of many of the exiles who felt that their
miserable plight was really the fault of their parents and
ancestors. They rebelled against the idea that they
seemed to be taking the rap for all the sins of their
predecessors. They, the children, are left with their
"teeth set on edge." And while there was a measure of
truth in this concept of corporate guilt (cf. Ex. 34:7),

243

Jeremiah insisted that henceforward a new principle was in effect. Each man would be held accountable for his own sins. In the future, retribution was to be primarily on an individual rather than a communal basis.

## THE NEW COVENANT                                       31:31-34

[31] "Behold, the days are coming, says the LORD, when I will make a new covenant with the house of Israel and the house of Judah, [32] not like the covenant which I made with their fathers when I took them by the hand to bring them out of the land of Egypt, my covenant which they broke, though I was their husband, says the LORD. [33] But this is the covenant which I will make with the house of Israel after those days, says the LORD: I will put my law within them, and I will write it upon their hearts; and I will be their God, and they shall be my people. [34] And no longer shall each man teach his neighbor and each his brother, saying, 'Know the LORD,' for they shall all know me, from the least of them to the greatest, says the LORD; for I will forgive their iniquity, and I will remember their sin no more."

This passage represents the climax of Jeremiah's message and theology. We shall, therefore, present a lengthier treatment of its import. This famous oracle of Jeremiah is not a flight of fancy into the distant future. It is a Word of God molded in the crucible of his own experience with a content that is immediately meaningful for his disillusioned audience. The fall of Jerusalem meant humiliation unto death. That day of judgment meant the end of an age, the end of a nation, and the removal of all the props of faith, like Zion, the ark, the

244

kingship, and the temple, which over the years had lost their true meaning for the people. Even the election had become a mechanical guarantee for security. God's people were rejected. The covenant bond of Sinai was apparently broken forever. History had come full circle. Israel no longer seemed to have the preferred status among the nations she once knew (Ex. 19:3-6). The intolerable disgrace of slavery was again imminent. There seemed to be no hope for God's people at all. But the same man who had preached unmitigated doom now proclaimed a new dawn with a new covenant between Yahweh and Israel (see above, vv. 1-6). Beyond death there was life in God's promise.

**31** This verse begins with the formula "the days are coming!" This formula points to a new era, not only a distant age. The oncoming era would be one of special divine involvement; a new beginning in history is suggested. The expression "says the Lord" is a technical formula for an oracle. This expression occurs four times in these verses and thereby underscores the authority and importance of this message. "I will make [literally, cut]" is followed by a series of verbs in the first person that emphasize God's initiative in the new covenant also. To make, or "cut," a covenant seems to stem from the practice of cutting animals in pieces to enforce the oath of the covenant (cf. Jer. 34:18-19; Gen. 15:7-10). The covenant envisioned will be made with all Israel, both the house of Judah and the house of Israel. The old rift between the Northern and Southern tribes will be forgotten (cf. 30:3; 31:27). The dream of a reunion of North (Israel) and South (Judah) persisted for generations in the minds of the Israelites, but as a political hope it died. (Hos. 1:11; Is. 11:11-13; Ezek. 37:15-24; Jer. 3:18; 50:4)

245

The idiom "a new covenant" belongs to a larger category of expressions that gained popularity because of the exile. The themes of a new exodus, a new election, a new crossing of the wilderness, and a new entry into the promised land are highlighted in Is. 40 – 55. Terms such as the "new song" (Is. 42:10) and "a new thing" (Is. 43:19) are part of this same circle of ideas. The destruction of Jerusalem meant the end of the old era. The "new," which God alone could introduce, would break sharply with the past. This "new covenant" stood in contrast to all past renewals (for example, 2 Kings 23: 1-3) of the covenant. This new covenant can hardly be defined in terms of the old.

**32** The "not like" of v. 32 makes this antithesis explicit. The "fathers" are not the patriarchs but the Israelites who had experienced the exodus from Egypt. This exodus was *the* great moment of salvation in Israel's past. This was the primary event on which the faith of the Old Testament believers was based (cf. Ex. 14:30-31; 19:3-6). The old covenant is the Sinai covenant. This Israel had flagrantly violated times without number (cf. Jer. 2:1 – 4:4; 11:1-8). "To break a covenant" means to deliberately violate a bond or trust. The bond here is described in terms of a marriage relationship between Yahweh and Israel (cf. 2:2; 3:6-14; and often in Hosea). The wording of the text presents a *double entendre* at this point. The Hebrew word *ba'al* means both "husband" and Baal! Although Yahweh was the husband of Israel, His chosen bride, she preferred to treat Him as Baal, a pagan Canaanite god instead of the true God! But Yahweh's love persisted despite Israel's unfaithfulness. (Cf. 31:20)

**33** The character of the new covenant is presented in terms of the ideal. Here we meet the superlatives of faith. The first characteristic of this new covenant is that God will put His "law within them and write it on their hearts." Several factors need to be borne in mind at this point. Throughout Jeremiah the "heart" is the religious self or center of man rather than the seat of the intellect (cf. 12:3; 11:20; 17:1; 7:24). And Israel's heart had become totally perverse. A new beginning therefore demanded a new heart, a new creation of the inner man. And this is what God was planning for His people. The second factor we need to note is that the treaty form of ancient covenants regularly incorporated laws or stipulations to give teeth to the covenant relationship. These laws were frequently inscribed on a tablet and deposited in a local shrine. The new covenant, however, will not have an external set of laws, no decalog inscribed in stone, but an innate sensitivity to the will of God. The law will be part of man's nature. Obedience will no longer be a problem. It will be instinctive. Truly a remarkable ideal! The verse closes with a traditional formula used to describe the covenant relationship, "I will be their God, and they shall be my people" (cf. Ex. 6:7). God has magnanimously chosen Israel as His people once more. The obligation to perform external rites will be gone.

**34** This verse begins by presenting the second major ideal of the new covenant. In 31:29-30 Jeremiah had pointed to the new emphasis on the personal rather than the communal aspect of man's relations with God. Now he asserts that everyone, from the smallest to the greatest, will have firsthand experience of God's reality and presence in their lives. Intimate religious experiences will not be confined to the prophet (cf. 23:18-22) or to a chosen generation such as those at Sinai, or to the assembled worshipers in the temple. But the em-

247

phasis is not primarily on this individual aspect of the new life. The new covenant is made with Israel as God's people, not just with individuals. The radical element of the second ideal is the termination of certain past traditions. The advent of the new covenant will mark the end of the old modes of education. The ancient practice of dialog and questioning in the city gate, where "each man must teach his neighbor and each his brother," will be obsolete. "Knowing" God, that is experiencing His reality, will be direct and immediate for all. It will be unnecessary to inquire about the Lord through the traditional channels of communication. Each true Israelite will have an instinctive understanding of Yahweh as his covenant Lord. Not only the Law but the Gospel will be written in men's hearts. Once again a great new hope.

The final word in this prophetic dream of hope provides the basis and ground for the entire vision. Thus it is introduced by "for," or "because." "For I will forgive their iniquity," states the Lord. In contrast to this statement stands the forthright proclamation of Jeremiah that the sins of God's people cannot be erased (17:1) and that the people are controlled by the violent forces of evil that they have set in motion. No rite could ward off this evil. Only a miracle could save Israel from final rejection under God's judgment. And that miracle is found in the free forgiveness of Yahweh. He will forgive and forget. The Hebrew term "forgive" here, like the expression "create," is used only of divine activity. Only God can forgive and remove the sin. He alone is motivated by sheer grace. "Not to remember" means to make ineffective all the force of alienation that comes into play when God marks (remembers) an offense against Himself. God is free to forgive re-

248

gardless of the circumstances. Logic is transcended, and the incredible is anticipated. Yahweh Himself will impart belief through His forgiveness. The New Testament affirms that this new covenant was made a reality in the person of Jesus Christ. He was its Mediator (Heb. 9:15) and the One through whom forgiveness was achieved. His blood ratifies the new covenant (1 Cor. 11:25; Matt. 26:28; cf. Heb. 9:15-22). His sacrifice brought forgiveness once and for all; the way of worship under the old covenant was thereby superseded (Heb. 10:8-18). Those who are in Christ are ministers of this new covenant. They are free from the law of the old covenant and are prompted by the Spirit of God from within. As such they are part of the new creation in which the promises of Jeremiah's new covenant are gradually being realized in their lives (2 Cor. 3:1-6; 5:17). Only through faith in Christ can even the hopes of Israel in the old covenant be fully grasped (2 Cor. 3:12-18). To know Christ is to know God according to the spirit of Jer. 31:31-34.

## THE NEW PROMISE OF ETERNAL BLESSING 31:35-37

<sup>35</sup> Thus says the LORD,
  who gives the sun for light by day
    and the fixed order of the moon and the stars
      for light by night,
  who stirs up the sea so that its waves roar —
    the LORD of hosts is his name:
<sup>36</sup> "If this fixed order departs
    from before me, says the LORD,
  then shall the descendants of Israel cease
    from being a nation before me for ever."

<sup>37</sup> Thus says the LORD:
"If the heavens above can be measured,
   and the foundations of the earth below can be ex-
      plored,
   then I will cast off all the descendants of Israel
   for all that they have done,
                                    says the LORD."


God had promised Abraham that his descendants
would be many and that he would become a great
nation before God (Gen. 12:1-3). Now God renews this
promise to His people with the additional clause that
this word will be as fixed as the divine order of creation.
Israel would always be God's nation. If man can ever
really fathom the mysteries of God's creation, then God
can no longer forgive Israel "for all they have done"
and erase them from the earth. In short, God's promises
of blessing for His people are as eternal as the sovereign
Lord Himself. (Cf. 33:20, 25)


## THE NEW CITY OF ZION                    31:38-40

<sup>38</sup> "Behold, the days are coming, says the LORD,
when the city shall be rebuilt for the LORD from the
tower of Han'anel to the Corner Gate. <sup>39</sup> And the
measuring line shall go out farther, straight to the
hill Gareb, and shall then turn to Go'ah. <sup>40</sup> The
whole valley of the dead bodies and the ashes, and
all the fields as far as the brook Kidron, to the corner
of the Horse Gate toward the east, shall be sacred
to the LORD. It shall not be uprooted or overthrown
any more for ever."

Compare the comment of vv. 23-25. The hope of a new Zion is again repeated. Several directions for its rebuilding and size are given (cf. Zech. 2:1-5). This time, however, it will be built "for the Lord" and not for secular reasons. It will be completely "sacred" or set apart for the Lord. But this time it would never be destroyed again! Jerusalem as we know it fell to invaders and was devastated several times after the days of Jeremiah. Could Jeremiah ever think of Jerusalem, as he knew it, as an "eternal" institution? The interpretation of passages such as this one in terms of a spiritual or heavenly Jerusalem seems to be expressed in several New Testament references. (Heb. 12:18-24; Gal. 4:26; Rev. 21)

## JEREMIAH PURCHASES THE FIELD
## OF ANATHOTH                                32:1-15

[1] The word that came to Jeremiah from the **LORD** in the tenth year of Zedeki'ah king of Judah, which was the eighteenth year of Nebuchadrez'zar. [2] At that time the army of the king of Babylon was besieging Jerusalem, and Jeremiah the prophet was shut up in the court of the guard which was in the palace of the king of Judah. [3] For Zedeki'ah king of Judah had imprisoned him, saying, "Why do you prophesy and say, 'Thus says the **LORD**: Behold, I am giving this city into the hand of the king of Babylon, and he shall take it; [4] Zedeki'ah king of Judah shall not escape out of the hand of the Chalde'ans, but shall surely be given into the hand of the king of Babylon, and shall speak with him face to face and see him eye to eye; [5] and he shall take Zedeki'ah

251

to Babylon, and there he shall remain until I visit him, says the LORD; though you fight against the Chalde'ans, you shall not succeed'?"

⁶ Jeremiah said, "The word of the LORD came to me: ⁷ Behold, Han'amel the son of Shallum your uncle will come to you and say, 'Buy my field which is at An'athoth, for the right of redemption by purchase is yours.' ⁸ Then Han'amel my cousin came to me in the court of the guard, in accordance with the word of the LORD, and said to me, 'Buy my field which is at An'athoth in the land of Benjamin, for the right of possession and redemption is yours; buy it for yourself.' Then I knew that this was the word of the LORD.

⁹ "And I bought the field at An'athoth from Han'amel my cousin, and weighed out the money to him, seventeen shekels of silver. ¹⁰ I signed the deed, sealed it, got witnesses, and weighed the money on scales. ¹¹ Then I took the sealed deed of purchase, containing the terms and conditions, and the open copy; ¹² and I gave the deed of purchase to Baruch the son of Neri'ah son of Mahsei'ah, in the presence of Han'amel my cousin, in the presence of the witnesses who signed the deed of purchase, and in the presence of all the Jews who were sitting in the court of the guard. ¹³ I charged Baruch in their presence, saying, ¹⁴ 'Thus says the LORD of hosts, the God of Israel: Take these deeds, both this sealed deed of purchase and this open deed, and put them in an earthenware vessel, that they may last for a long time. ¹⁵ For thus says the LORD of hosts, the God of Israel: Houses and fields and vineyards shall again be bought in this land.'

Jeremiah 32 is connected by the theme of hope to the two preceding chapters. It differs, however, both in date and format. The chapter relates a symbolic action of Jeremiah that took place during the final siege of Jerusalem (589–87 B. C.). The previous symbolic actions of Jeremiah were primarily to evoke messages of doom. This action speaks a dramatic message of hope.

**1-5** The opening verses are a summary of the historical situation depicted in Jer. 37 and 38. The year is 588 B. C., Jeremiah is in prison. The city is besieged by Babylon. And Jeremiah has repeated his word to King Zedekiah that the city will fall because God is fighting against it. The situation is hopeless, and total disaster is imminent. Jeremiah's prophecies of doom are about to come true. Judah is lamenting its sad plight. At that moment we might expect to hear Jeremiah crying, "I told you so!" But instead he is looking beyond doom to the dawn of God's fresh grace. Once more his words are the opposite of those the people are mouthing.

**6-8** His message of hope arose from the purchase of a piece of land. This chapter recounts the actual purchase in Jeremiah's own words (autobiographical prose) in vv. 6-15. First of all Jeremiah sensed that God was telling him that his cousin Hanamel would soon come to offer to sell him a field in his home town of Anathoth (cf. 1:1). When Hanamel came, Jeremiah recognized that what he had previously sensed was actually the word of God coming to him, and not his own personal wishes. "Then I *knew* that this was the word of the Lord," he says (v. 8). Jeremiah had a right to buy this property because of an ancient law that was designed to keep land within the family by giving the first option of purchase to the nearest of kin (see Lev. 25:25-28;

Ruth 3:6—4:12). In short, Jeremiah had the right to "redeem" this property, which in view of the Babylonian invasion would probably have been very cheap, and certainly inaccessible. To buy land under such conditions was sheer folly, it seemed. Jeremiah, moreover, had been vigorously predicting the enslavement of Judah and the destruction of the land. Why would he, of all people, buy land?

**9-15** But Jeremiah took the purchase very seriously, as the details of vv. 9-15 affirm. The exact price and procedure are given. The transaction is legal in every way. A double document was publicly prepared, whose form is known to us from archaeology. The terms of the deed were written twice on a single page with a blank space punched with small holes between the two writings. One side of the deed was signed by the purchaser (v. 10), then rolled, laced through the small holes in the center, tied, and the knots sealed. This first side became the "sealed deed" and guaranteed that the terms would not be changed. The other side containing the same information was likewise rolled but left unlaced. This was the "open copy" which the witnesses signed (v. 12). After executing the deed, Jeremiah charged Baruch to place the deed in an earthenware vessel, where it would last for a long time (v. 14). Hope there was in the face of annihilation! This deed was a public pledge that Yahweh would act in grace so that property would again belong to His people for sale and purchase. On that day life among God's people would return to normal.

## PRAYER FOR FURTHER EXPLANATION    32:16-25

[16] "After I had given the deed of purchase to Baruch the son of Neri′ah, I prayed to the LORD,

saying: [17] 'Ah Lord God! It is thou who hast made the heavens and the earth by thy great power and by thy outstretched arm! Nothing is too hard for thee, [18] who showest steadfast love to thousands, but dost requite the guilt of fathers to their children after them, O great and mighty God whose name is the LORD of hosts, [19] great in counsel and mighty in deed; whose eyes are open to all the ways of men, rewarding every man according to his ways and according to the fruit of his doings; [20] who hast shown signs and wonders in the land of Egypt, and to this day in Israel and among all mankind, and hast made thee a name, as at this day. [21] Thou didst bring thy people Israel out of the land of Egypt with signs and wonders, with a strong hand and outstretched arm, and with great terror; [22] and thou gavest them this land, which thou didst swear to their fathers to give them, a land flowing with milk and honey; [23] and they entered and took possession of it. But they did not obey thy voice or walk in thy law; they did nothing of all thou didst command them to do. Therefore thou hast made all this evil come upon them. [24] Behold, the siege mounds have come up to the city to take it, and because of sword and famine and pestilence the city is given into the hands of the Chalde'ans who are fighting against it. What thou didst speak has come to pass, and behold, thou seest it. [25] Yet thou, O Lord God, hast said to me, "Buy the field for money and get witnesses" – though the city is given into the hands of the Chalde'ans.' "

The heart of Jeremiah's prayer is in vv. 24-25. The city was in the hands of Babylon. The land purchase had "come to pass" as Yahweh had said. Yet Jeremiah cries for further explanations. The preliminary expressions of faith in vv. 17-23 of the prayer are general in nature and do not seem to touch Jeremiah's problem directly. Many therefore consider them a later addition. In any case, these verses praise Yahweh in traditional fashion for His creative power, His mercy, and His justice. He is the God of the exodus from Egypt and the conquest of Canaan. It was His word that Israel disobeyed. How different is this prayer from the bold and vehement cries of Jeremiah elsewhere. (11:20; 12:1-3; 15:15-18)

## JEREMIAH RECEIVES
## AN EXPLANATION                                  32:26-44

<sup>26</sup> The word of the LORD came to Jeremiah: <sup>27</sup> "Behold, I am the LORD, the God of all flesh; is anything too hard for me? <sup>28</sup> Therefore, thus says the LORD: Behold, I am giving this city into the hands of the Chalde'ans and into the hand of Nebuchadrez'zar king of Babylon, and he shall take it. <sup>29</sup> The Chalde'ans who are fighting against this city shall come and set this city on fire, and burn it, with the houses on whose roofs incense has been offered to Ba'al and drink offerings have been poured out to other gods, to provoke me to anger. <sup>30</sup> For the sons of Israel and the sons of Judah have done nothing but evil in my sight from their youth; the sons of Israel have done nothing but provoke me to anger by the work of their hands, says the LORD. <sup>31</sup> This city has aroused my anger and wrath, from the day it was built to this day, so that I will remove it from my sight <sup>32</sup> because of all the evil of the sons of Israel and the sons of Judah which they did to provoke me to anger—their kings and their princes, their priests

and their prophets, the men of Judah and the inhabitants of Jerusalem. [33] They have turned to me their back and not their face; and though I have taught them persistently they have not listened to receive instruction. [34] They set up their abominations in the house which is called by my name, to defile it. [35] They built the high places of Ba'al in the valley of the son of Hinnom, to offer up their sons and daughters to Molech, though I did not command them, nor did it enter into my mind, that they should do this abomination, to cause Judah to sin.

[36] "Now therefore thus says the LORD, the God of Israel, concerning this city of which you say, 'It is given into the hand of the king of Babylon by sword, by famine, and by pestilence': [37] Behold, I will gather them from all the countries to which I drove them in my anger and my wrath and in great indignation; I will bring them back to this place, and I will make them dwell in safety. [38] And they shall be my people, and I will be their God. [39] I will give them one heart and one way, that they may fear me for ever, for their own good and the good of their children after them. [40] I will make with them an everlasting covenant, that I will not turn away from doing good to them; and I will put the fear of me in their hearts, that they may not turn from me. [41] I will rejoice in doing them good, and I will plant them in this land in faithfulness, with all my heart and all my soul.

[42] "For thus says the LORD: Just as I have brought all this great evil upon this people, so I will bring upon them all the good that I promise them. [43] Fields shall be bought in this land of which you are saying, It is a desolation, without man or beast; it is given into the hands of the Chalde'ans. [44] Fields

shall be bought for money, and deeds shall be signed and sealed and witnessed, in the land of Benjamin, in the places about Jerusalem, and in the cities of Judah, in the cities of the hill country, in the cities of the Shephe'lah, and in the cities of the Negeb; for I will restore their fortunes, says the LORD."

**26, 42-44** The answer to Jeremiah's question in vv. 24-25 is found here. Yahweh is the sovereign Lord; He can do anything He wishes. Just as He brought the total doom He had threatened, so He can bring the undeserved goodness He now promises (v. 42). Jeremiah's symbolic action of purchasing his cousin's field gave public assurance that what once was completely desolate would again become desirable land for God's people to buy and sell as before. Various regions of Judah and Benjamin are promised this blessing.

**28-35** Prior to the direct answer of vv. 42-44, the text offers two lengthy digressions. The first of these (vv. 28-35) designates the Chaldeans (Babylonians) as the destroyers of Jerusalem and consequently of all the corrupt religious practices it harbored. All the city would perish by fire. Baal worship and the practice of burning children in the fires of the god Molech are mentioned as typical of Israel's perversity (cf. 19:5). "From their youth" the Israelites rebelled; their leaders likewise turned their backs on God. None of them would heed Yahweh and take instruction. Therefore God was about to vent His anger through the agency of Babylon.

**36-41** The second digression (vv. 36-41) repeats the promise of gathering the Babylonian exiles from distant lands and bringing them back to "this place," Jerusalem (cf. 31:8, 10). This passage also reaffirms the message of a covenant between "their God" and "my people" (cf. 31:1, 33). The promise of an "everlasting covenant" according to which God gives His people "one heart" that would automatically fear God forever is treated above in connection with 31:31-34. This new "way" of life under the new covenant is portrayed as completely ideal. God's people will never slip back into sin, God will give them a heart of perfect obedience, and they will live in a land that is overflowing with Yahweh's rich mercies. And this state of affairs will go on indefinitely. (For the New Testament associations with the new covenant, see pages 248 – 249.)

## NEW HOPE FOR COMPLETE
## RESTORATION                                    33:1-9

**¹ The word of the LORD came to Jeremiah a second time, while he was still shut up in the court of the guard: ² "Thus says the LORD who made the earth,*ᵍ* the LORD who formed it to establish it – the LORD is his name: ³ Call to me and I will answer you, and will tell you great and hidden things which you have not known. ⁴ For thus says the LORD, the God of Israel, concerning the houses of this city and the houses of the kings of Judah which were torn down to make a defense against the siege mounds and before the sword:*ʰ* ⁵ The Chalde'ans are coming in to fight*ⁱ* and to fill them with the dead bodies of men whom I shall smite in my anger and my wrath, for I have hidden my face from this city because of all their wickedness. ⁶ Behold, I will bring to it health and healing, and I will heal them and reveal to them abundance*ʲ* of prosperity and security. ⁷ I will restore**

*ᵍ* Gk: Heb it   *ʰ* Heb obscure
*ⁱ* Cn: Heb *They are coming in to fight against the Chaldeans*
*ʲ* Heb uncertain

259

the fortunes of Judah and the fortunes of Israel, and rebuild them as they were at first. ⁸ I will cleanse them from all the guilt of their sin against me, and I will forgive all the guilt of their sin and rebellion against me. ⁹ And this city ᵏ shall be to me a name of joy, a praise and a glory before all the nations of the earth who shall hear of all the good that I do for them; they shall fear and tremble because of all the good and all the prosperity I provide for it.

1-4 Jeremiah 33 embraces a collection of prose oracles of hope. The first of these presents words of doom and words of hope in juxtaposition. Verses 1-4 offer an unusual preface. Verse 1 links this oracle with the preceding chapter. Jeremiah is still confined to the court of the guard (cf. 32:2). The oracle the prophet is about to receive will reveal "hidden things" (cf. Is. 48:6), which presumably deal with the rebuilding of Judah and Israel. This message of unknown mysteries was given when the city of Zion was about to be ravished and destroyed. For even in that moment the God whose name was Yahweh, that is, the God who revealed His name to Israel, was still in control despite appearances to the contrary.

5-9 The message itself consists of two parts: the preliminary doom (v. 5) and the ultimate hope (vv. 6-9). The doom oracle repeats the frequent cry of Jeremiah that Babylon was about to kill the people in Jerusalem because of their great wickedness. This judgment has not been eliminated. But after judgment there will be hope. The word of hope is very comprehensive. Yahweh will heal the mortal wounds inflicted by His judgment (see 30:17) and make His people well once more. Judah

ᵏ Heb *and it*

and Israel will be reestablished and prosperous (cf. 30:3). Their ruins will be rebuilt. All of this will be indicative of Yahweh's forgiving love; their guilt will be erased by the free grace of Yahweh (see 31:34). Jerusalem will again be renowned, but this time because of the rich mercy of God to His people. Then all nations will express their fearful belief in Yahweh as the true God.

## THE REMOVAL OF THE OLD CURSE    33:10-13

[10] "Thus says the LORD: In this place of which you say, 'It is a waste without man or beast,' in the cities of Judah and the streets of Jerusalem that are desolate, without man or inhabitant or beast, there shall be heard again [11] the voice of mirth and the voice of gladness, the voice of the bridegroom and the voice of the bride, the voices of those who sing, as they bring thank offerings to the house of the LORD:
'Give thanks to the LORD of hosts,
    for the LORD is good,
    for his steadfast love endures for ever!'
For I will restore the fortunes of the land as at first, says the LORD.
[12] "Thus says the LORD of hosts: In this place which is waste, without man or beast, and in all of its cities, there shall again be habitations of shepherds resting their flocks. [13] In the cities of the hill country, in the cities of the Shephe'lah, and in the cities of the Negeb, in the land of Benjamin, the places about Jerusalem, and in the cities of Judah, flocks shall again pass under the hands of the one who counts them, says the LORD.

261

Ancient covenants and treaties had curses attached to the end of them. Any who broke the covenant stood under those curses. God's people, too, stood under the divine curse for breaking its covenant with Yahweh (cf. 11:3). These curses had certain traditional wordings in the ancient world. One of these was the curse that threatened to remove all mirth, gladness, and the voices of the bride and bridegroom from society. This curse had been pronounced on Judah (16:9; 25:10). But now it was about to terminate; joy and jubilant voices would soon be heard again. The song of God's people would be one of thanks for the undeserved "steadfast (covenant) love" of God (see the comment on "faithfulness" in 31:3). The accursed waste regions of Palestine that once stood under God's wrath would again be inhabited by people and peaceful flocks. For vv. 12-13 see 32:43-44. The tense and sense of v. 10 suggest that Jerusalem had fallen.

## THE RIGHTEOUS BRANCH
## AND THE LEVITICAL PRIESTS                33:14-26

**¹⁴ "Behold, the days are coming, says the LORD, when I will fulfil the promise I made to the house of Israel and the house of Judah. ¹⁵ In those days and at that time I will cause a righteous Branch to spring forth for David; and he shall execute justice and righteousness in the land. ¹⁶ In those days Judah will be saved and Jerusalem will dwell securely. And this is the name by which it will be called: 'The LORD is our righteousness.'**

**¹⁷ "For thus says the LORD: David shall never lack a man to sit on the throne of the house of Israel,**

<sup>18</sup> and the Levitical priests shall never lack a man in my presence to offer burnt offerings, to burn cereal offerings, and to make sacrifices for ever."

<sup>19</sup> The word of the LORD came to Jeremiah: <sup>20</sup> "Thus says the LORD: If you can break my covenant with the day and my covenant with the night, so that day and night will not come at their appointed time, <sup>21</sup> then also my covenant with David my servant may be broken, so that he shall not have a son to reign on his throne, and my covenant with the Levitical priests my ministers. <sup>22</sup> As the host of heaven cannot be numbered and the sands of the sea cannot be measured, so I will multiply the descendants of David my servant, and the Levitical priests who minister to me."

<sup>23</sup> The word of the LORD came to Jeremiah: <sup>24</sup> "Have you not observed what these people are saying, 'The LORD has rejected the two families which he chose'? Thus they have despised my people so that they are no longer a nation in their sight. <sup>25</sup> Thus says the LORD: If I have not established my covenant with day and night and the ordinances of heaven and earth, <sup>26</sup> then I will reject the descendants of Jacob and David my servant and will not choose one of his descendants to rule over the seed of Abraham, Isaac, and Jacob. For I will restore their fortunes, and will have mercy upon them."


14-17 These verses are absent from the Greek (Septuagint) version of the Old Testament, which may reflect an earlier stage of this chapter. The oracles of vv. 14-26 were apparently written during the exile, although they cannot be dated exactly. Verses 14-16

263

represent a minor variation of the same promise in 23:5-6 (see the comment there). The major change in the present form of the oracle is that Jerusalem, not the Messianic king, is to bear the title, "The Lord is our Righteousness." Thus the community rather than an individual is seen as the fulfillment of this oracle. The additional explanation of v. 17 seems to indicate that God is also promising an unbroken line of Messianic rulers on the throne of David.

**18-22** The promise of an unbroken Davidic dynasty is supplemented by the promise of an unbroken line of legitimate priests in Israel. These priests will perpetually perform the necessary rituals of the temple service (v. 18). This promise is as unbreakable as Yahweh's agreement to sustain the order of creation (Gen. 8:22). Recalling the promises of numerous progeny for Abraham (Gen. 22:17), God promises the same for David's household and that of the Levitical (legitimate) priests of Jerusalem. One wonders how the promise of a priesthood to minister to Yahweh eternally complements 31:31-34, which envisioned a new covenant in which all men would instinctively know Yahweh and require none of the former traditional modes of mediation between man and God.

**23-26** With the fall of Jerusalem, the throne of David became vacant and Judah was thrown into exile. God had apparently terminated His covenant with David (2 Sam. 7:12-14) and with His people Israel (Jacob). The dejected cries of the people were not to be taken seriously, however. For in reality Yahweh no more would reject the descendants of Jacob or of David eternally than reverse the order of day and night. His undying mercy was about to demonstrate this fact by restoring the fortunes of His people again. The New

Testament proclaims that these promises (33:14-26) of God's operation through the community of Jerusalem, priests, kings and the seed of Jacob, are fulfilled in the church, the new Israel. (1 Peter 2:4-10; Rom. 4:16-17)

# Experiences of Jeremiah
# Under Jehoiakim and Zedekiah

## Jeremiah 34—38

Chapters 34—38 are composed of prose narratives, primarily biographical in nature. Most of the incidents recorded, whether by Baruch or someone else, took place during the years immediately before the fall of Jerusalem in 587 B. C. Chapter 36, however, is strangely out of place and is dated in the 4th year of Jehoiakim after the ominous Battle of Carchemish (see the comment). All of these chapters demonstrate how Jeremiah's message made its impact, in one way or another, on the kings and political leaders of the city. Whether they heeded Jeremiah or not, they were forced to take measures to counteract his preaching. The word of Jeremiah finally had some real effect, despite his claim that before 605 B. C. no one had listened to him (25:3). Now Jehoiakim was exposed for what he really was, a godless tyrant (Ch. 36); the conscience of Zedekiah was pricked even though he was too weak to follow what he knew was right (Ch. 37); faithful followers began to show their hand (38:7-13), and some people actually followed Jeremiah's advice and defected to Babylon in order to survive in exile as God's people (38:19). And miraculously, through all the anarchy of those final years, that prophet who had been accused of treason survived to see his message of judgment come true.

## JEREMIAH REBUKES ZEDEKIAH
## FOR HIS TREATMENT OF SLAVES            34:1-22

¹ The word which came to Jeremiah from the LORD, when Nebuchadrez'zar king of Babylon and all his army and all the kingdoms of the earth under his dominion and all the people were fighting against Jerusalem and all of its cities: ² "Thus says the LORD, the God of Israel: Go and speak to Zedeki'ah king of Judah and say to him, 'Thus says the LORD: Behold, I am giving this city into the hand of the king of Babylon, and he shall burn it with fire. ³ You shall not escape from his hand, but shall surely be captured and delivered into his hand; you shall see the king of Babylon eye to eye and speak with him face to face; and you shall go to Babylon.' ⁴ Yet hear the word of the LORD, O Zedeki'ah king of Judah! Thus says the LORD concerning you: 'You shall not die by the sword. ⁵ You shall die in peace. And as spices were burned for your fathers, the former kings who were before you, so men shall burn spices for you and lament for you, saying, "Alas, lord!"' For I have spoken the word, says the LORD."

⁶ Then Jeremiah the prophet spoke all these words to Zedeki'ah king of Judah, in Jerusalem, ⁷ when the army of the king of Babylon was fighting against Jerusalem and against all the cities of Judah that were left, Lachish and Aze'kah; for these were the only fortified cities of Judah that remained.

⁸ The word which came to Jeremiah from the LORD, after King Zedeki′ah had made a covenant with all the people in Jerusalem to make a proclamation of liberty to them, ⁹ that every one should set free his Hebrew slaves, male and female, so that no one should enslave a Jew, his brother. ¹⁰ And they obeyed, all the princes and all the people who had entered into the covenant that every one would set free his slave, male or female, so that they would not be enslaved again; they obeyed and set them free. ¹¹ But afterward they turned around and took back the male and female slaves they had set free, and brought them into subjection as slaves. ¹² The word of the LORD came to Jeremiah from the LORD: ¹³ "Thus says the LORD, the God of Israel: I made a covenant with your fathers when I brought them out of the land of Egypt, out of the house of bondage, saying, ¹⁴ 'At the end of six *ˡ* years each of you must set free the fellow Hebrew who has been sold to you and has served you six years; you must set him free from your service.' But your fathers did not listen to me or incline their ears to me. ¹⁵ You recently repented and did what was right in my eyes by proclaiming liberty, each to his neighbor, and you made a covenant before me in the house which is called by my name; ¹⁶ but then you turned around and profaned my name when each of you took back his male and female slaves, whom you had set free according to their desire, and you brought them into subjection to be your slaves. ¹⁷ Therefore, thus says the LORD: You have not obeyed me by proclaiming liberty, every one to his brother and to his neighbor; behold, I proclaim to you liberty to the sword, to pestilence, and to famine,

*ˡ* Gk: Heb *seven*

says the LORD. I will make you a horror to all the kingdoms of the earth. <sup>18</sup> And the men who transgressed my covenant and did not keep the terms of the covenant which they made before me, I will make like <sup>m</sup> the calf which they cut in two and passed between its parts — <sup>19</sup> the princes of Judah, the princes of Jerusalem, the eunuchs, the priests, and all the people of the land who passed between the parts of the calf; <sup>20</sup> and I will give them into the hand of their enemies and into the hand of those who seek their lives. Their dead bodies shall be food for the birds of the air and the beasts of the earth. <sup>21</sup> And Zedeki'ah king of Judah, and his princes I will give into the hand of their enemies and into the hand of those who seek their lives, into the hand of the army of the king of Babylon which has withdrawn from you. <sup>22</sup> Behold, I will command, says the LORD, and will bring them back to this city; and they will fight against it, and take it, and burn it with fire. I will make the cities of Judah a desolation without inhabitant."

<sup>m</sup> Cn: Heb lacks *like*

1-7   The action of this chapter takes place during the siege of Jerusalem (in 588–87 B. C.). Nebuchadnezzar had surrounded the city with the "kingdoms of the earth" as Jeremiah had predicted (1:15; 25:9); Nebuchadnezzar's vassals had come from many countries for the fray. This was no normal conquest. And Jeremiah made this plain to King Zedekiah (cf. 21:1-10). God Himself was "giving the city into the hand of" the enemy, just as He had given cities "into the hand of" Israel during the conquest of Canaan (cf. Joshua 6:2; 8:1; 10:30, 32). The Israelites who had burned cities with fire as part of the divine curse on the conquered land

269

would now see their own holy city burned to the ground. The process of that glorious conquest of Canaan was being reversed. The only comfort Zedekiah could find was in the prediction that he would not be killed in the battle. For his lot was exile in Babylon. There he would receive the appropriate rites of burial when he finally passed away "in peace." Yet even that promise was conditional upon the king's surrender. When this message was delivered, the situation was already critical. Beside Jerusalem only Lachish and Azekah (20—23 miles southwest of Jerusalem) remained in the hands of Judah. Letters written on potsherds that describe the turmoil of this period have been found in the ruins of Lachish. But despite Jeremiah's oracle, Zedekiah refused to surrender his city as God demanded.

**8-11** Early in the siege of Jerusalem King Zedekiah issued an edict for the liberation of all Hebrew slaves (apparently in accordance with the law of Deut. 15:1, 12-18). For most of them this release was long overdue (cf. v. 14). Slaves were a liability when food became scarce. Moreover, as free men they would be more willing to join in the defense of the city. All the leaders of Jerusalem affirmed their approval of liberation by a covenant. Later, however, the Egyptian army invaded from the south. Nebuchadnezzar was then forced to lift the siege of Jerusalem for a short time (see 37:1-10). During this lull in the campaign the Israelite masters broke their covenant promise and subjugated their slaves again. Slave labor was needed again to refortify the city.

**12-22** This despicable action evoked another strong attack by Jeremiah. He reminded his people of the law of slavery (Deut. 15:1, 12-18) to which they were committed. The people, however, had not released their

slaves as the law demanded. The liberation of slaves
under Zedekiah's edict was a step in the right direction.
Judah seemed penitent; she had made a covenant about
the matter in the temple. Then she deliberately and
sacrilegiously broke her word. Nevertheless, Yahweh
Himself would enforce the intent of the covenant any-
how; He would effect a liberty for all, but a liberty that
none expected. He would free His people from their ties
to Himself so that they would be at the mercy of the
sword, pestilence, and famine. Judah now stood under
the curse of the covenant. The covenant ceremony
apparently involved dividing a calf (or some such animal)
into parts. The parties of the covenant walked between
these animal pieces (cf. Gen. 15:7-17). Yahweh was
about to enforce the oath of that ceremony and make the
parties who had broken this covenant sacred victims
like the divided calf. For many that meant death without
burial; for others it meant disgrace in exile. For all it
meant that Nebuchadnezzar would soon be back to
finish the job of razing Jerusalem.

JEREMIAH TEACHES A LESSON FROM
THE EXAMPLE OF THE RECHABITES          35:1-19

¹ The word which came to Jeremiah from the
LORD in the days of Jehoi'akim the son of Josi'-
ah, king of Judah: ² "Go to the house of the Re'-
chabites, and speak with them, and bring them to
the house of the LORD, into one of the chambers;
then offer them wine to drink." ³ So I took Ja-azani'ah
the son of Jeremiah, son of Habazzini'ah, and his
brothers, and all his sons, and the whole house of
the Re'chabites. ⁴ I brought them to the house of the

271

LORD into the chamber of the sons of Hanan the son Igdali'ah, the man of God, which was near the chamber of the princes, above the chamber of Ma-asei'ah the son of Shallum, keeper of the threshold. 5 Then I set before the Re'chabites pitchers full of wine, and cups; and I said to them, "Drink wine." 6 But they answered, "We will drink no wine, for Jon'adab the son of Rechab, our father, commanded us, 'You shall not drink wine, neither you nor your sons for ever; 7 you shall not build a house; you shall not sow seed; you shall not plant or have a vineyard; but you shall live in tents all your days, that you may live many days in the land where you sojourn.' 8 We have obeyed the voice of Jon'adab the son of Rechab, our father, in all that he commanded us, to drink no wine all our days, ourselves, our wives, our sons, or our daughters, 9 and not to build houses to dwell in. We have no vineyard or field or seed; 10 but we have lived in tents, and have obeyed and done all that Jon'adab our father commamded us. 11 But when Nebuchadrez'zar king of Babylon came up against the land, we said, 'Come, and let us go to Jerusalem for fear of the army of the Chalde'ans and the army of the Syrians.' So we are living in Jerusalem."

12 Then the word of the LORD came to Jeremiah: 13 "Thus says the LORD of hosts, the God of Israel: Go and say to the men of Judah and the inhabitants of Jerusalem, Will you not receive instruction and listen to my words? says the LORD. 14 The command which Jon'adab the son of Rechab gave to his sons, to drink no wine, has been kept; and they drink none to this day, for they have obeyed their father's command. I have spoken to you persistently, but you have not listened to me. 15 I have sent to you all my

servants the prophets, sending them persistently, saying, 'Turn now every one of you from his evil way, and amend your doings, and do not go after other gods to serve them, and then you shall dwell in the land which I gave to you and your fathers.' But you did not incline your ear or listen to me. ¹⁶ The sons of Jon'adab the son of Rechab have kept the command which their father gave them, but this people has not obeyed me. ¹⁷ Therefore, thus says the LORD, the God of hosts, the God of Israel: Behold, I am bringing on Judah and all the inhabitants of Jerusalem all the evil that I have pronounced against them; because I have spoken to them and they have not listened, I have called to them and they have not answered."

¹⁸ But to the house of the Re'chabites Jeremiah said, "Thus says the LORD of hosts, the God of Israel: Because you have obeyed the command of Jon'adab your father, and kept all his precepts, and done all that he commanded you, ¹⁹ therefore thus says the LORD of hosts, the God of Israel: Jon'adab the son of Rechab shall never lack a man to stand before me."

1-11 The lesson of this chapter was taught by Jeremiah a short time before the first campaign of Nebuchadnezzar against Judah in 598 B.C. The king of Babylon had urged neighboring hordes to harass Judah until such time as he could send his specialized army (cf. 2 Kings 24:2). This situation is indicated by the reference to Syrian hordes in 35:11. The Rechabites were religious fanatics. They were a major force behind the bloodbath under Jehu (2 Kings 10:15-28). They avoided many aspects of settled life in Canaan, such as vineyards, wine, solid houses, and the like. The ancient desert way of life was still their ideal of pure devotion to

Yahweh. They apparently took a vow (similar to that of the Nazirites in Num. 6:1-8) to remain faithful to their ideals. Jeremiah's task was to challenge their faithfulness. He was to summon them to a public chamber in the temple grounds where wine was available. The chamber in question apparently belonged to a friend of Jeremiah who is designated a "man of God." This title usually designates a prophet and in this case probably a professional prophet. Wine was sometimes used by these prophets to induce an ecstatic or delirious state conducive to prophesying. Jeremiah here offers the wine to the Rechabites. The Rechabites, in turn, reaffirm the demands of their founder ("father") Jonadab, son of Rechab, not to drink but to sojourn in the land as a stranger and not as a native. The Rechabites are proud of how well they have kept their vow of allegiance. It was only the hordes sent by Nebuchadnezzar that forced them to find refuge in a city with permanent houses. But although these circumstances had caused them temporarily to modify one part of their oath and to live in a city, they would not break the other part by drinking wine.

**12-17** The Rechabites were staunchly obedient to their deceased human ancestor. That was praiseworthy in itself. Such an example afforded an excellent opportunity to prick the conscience of Judah. God's people had received directions from their covenant Overlord. They had made their vow of allegiance in the covenant to a much greater living master. But they refused to obey His demands. They were just the opposite of the Rechabites despite the repeated efforts of God to reform them by the message of the prophets. The previously announced day of doom for God's household was therefore inevitable. God had planned a catas-

274

trophe ("evil"), and His word could not be broken. A similar lesson of complete surrender and obedience is emphasized by the symbolic actions of Jer. 27 – 28.

**18-19** The story has an unexpected ending. The devotion of the Rechabites in God's telling illustration is not secondary. For the Rechabites also receive the promise of an unbroken succession of servants to perform appropriate cultic rites, that is, they "shall never lack a man to stand before me."

## JEREMIAH DICTATES A SCROLL, AND JEHOIAKIM BURNS IT     36:1-26

¹ In the fourth year of Jehoi'akim the son of Josi'ah, king of Judah, this word came to Jeremiah from the LORD: ² "Take a scroll and write on it all the words that I have spoken to you against Israel and Judah and all the nations, from the day I spoke to you, from the days of Josi'ah until today. ³ It may be that the house of Judah will hear all the evil which I intend to do to them, so that every one may turn from his evil way, and that I may forgive their iniquity and their sin."

⁴ Then Jeremiah called Baruch the son of Neri'ah, and Baruch wrote upon a scroll at the dictation of Jeremiah all the words of the LORD which he had spoken to him. ⁵ And Jeremiah ordered Baruch, saying, "I am debarred from going to the house of the LORD; ⁶ so you are to go, and on a fast day in the hearing of all the people in the LORD'S house you shall read the words of the LORD from the scroll which you have written at my dictation. You shall read them also in the hearing of all the men of Judah who come out of their cities. ⁷ It may be that their

275

supplication will come before the LORD, and that every one will turn from his evil way, for great is the anger and wrath that the LORD has pronounced against this people." ⁸ And Baruch the son of Neri'ah did all that Jeremiah the prophet ordered him about reading from the scroll the words of the LORD in the LORD'S house.

⁹ In the fifth year of Jehoi'akim the son of Josi'ah, king of Judah, in the ninth month, all the people in Jerusalem and all the people who came from the cities of Judah to Jerusalem proclaimed a fast before the LORD. ¹⁰ Then, in the hearing of all the people, Baruch read the words of Jeremiah from the scroll, in the house of the LORD, in the chamber of Gemari'ah the son of Shaphan the secretary, which was in the upper court, at the entry of the New Gate of the LORD'S house.

¹¹ When Micai'ah the son of Gemari'ah, son of Shaphan, heard all the words of the LORD from the scroll, ¹² he went down to the king's house, into the secretary's chamber; and all the princes were sitting there: Eli'shama the secretary, Delai'ah the son of Shemai'ah, Elna'than the son of Achbor, Gemari'ah the son of Shaphan, Zedeki'ah the son of Hanani'ah, and all the princes. ¹³ And Micai'ah told them all the words that he had heard, when Baruch read the scroll in the hearing of the people. ¹⁴ Then all the princes sent Jehu'di the son of Nethani'ah, son of Shelemi'ah, son of Cushi, to say to Baruch, "Take in your hand the scroll that you read in the hearing of the people, and come." So Baruch the son of Neri'ah took the scroll in his hand and came to them. ¹⁵ And they said to him, "Sit down and read it." So Baruch read it to them. ¹⁶ When they heard all

the words, they turned one to another in fear; and they said to Baruch, "We must report all these words to the king." ¹⁷ Then they asked Baruch, "Tell us, how did you write all these words? Was it at his dictation?" ¹⁸ Baruch answered them, "He dictated all these words to me, while I wrote them with ink on the scroll." ¹⁹ Then the princes said to Baruch, "Go and hide, you and Jeremiah, and let no one know where you are."

²⁰ So they went into the court to the king, having put the scroll in the chamber of Eli'shama the secretary; and they reported all the words to the king. ²¹ Then the king sent Jehu'di to get the scroll, and he took it from the chamber of Eli'shama the secretary; and Jehu'di read it to the king and all the princes who stood beside the king. ²² It was the ninth month, and the king was sitting in the winter house and there was a fire burning in the brazier before him. ²³ As Jehu'di read three or four columns, the king would cut them off with a penknife and throw them into the fire in the brazier, until the entire scroll was consumed in the fire that was in the brazier. ²⁴ Yet neither the king, nor any of his servants who heard all these words, was afraid, nor did they rend their garments. ²⁵ Even when Elna'than and Delai'ah and Gemari'ah urged the king not to burn the scroll, he would not listen to them. ²⁶ And the king commanded Jerah'meel the king's son and Serai'ah the son of Az'ri-el and Shelemi'ah the son of Abdeel to seize Baruch the secretary and Jeremiah the prophet, but the LORD hid them.

1-8 Writing a book or a scroll was a significant undertaking in the days of Jeremiah, when sayings, sermons, and traditions were usually preserved by word of mouth. To fix an oracle in writing meant intensifying its force. At Jeremiah's dictation all the curses and words of doom pronounced against Israel, Judah, and the foreign nations were therefore fixed in writing. The year was 605 B. C., perhaps the most crucial date in all of Jeremiah's preaching. Babylon had just won world supremacy (see the comment on 46:1-12). Jeremiah's proclamation of doom for Judah seemed about to be vindicated. The course of disaster seemed inescapable. Fulfillment had apparently begun. The public had to know; God's people had to be warned again. The situation was critical. There was always a chance, a possibility that the total impact of these forthright oracles of doom would move the heart of God's people to repentance. "It may be!" And God can always reverse His decision and forgive. Alas, the possibility is remote, and the weight of God's wrath upon Judah is great indeed (cf. Amos 5:15). God's written Word would be powerful, however, even if Baruch, Jeremiah's personal scribe, read the text. Jeremiah, it seems, had been forbidden to return to the temple environment. His messages, as often, were apparently considered disruptive, false, and blasphemous.

9-19 Some time elapsed between the writing of the scroll and the proclamation of a fast day, when large crowds would assemble in Jerusalem. Whether the fast was announced because of drought (cf. Joel 1:14) or impending invasion, or whether it was an annual fast, is not certain. However, at about this time the Babylonian army was already plundering the Philistine coastal plain. Baruch, who stemmed from a relatively important family (51:59), suddenly stepped into the limelight (see the comment on Ch. 45). The scroll was read

278

in the chamber of Gemariah, who was apparently among Jeremiah's small circle of supporters (cf. v. 25). Ahikam, Gemariah's brother, had previously saved Jeremiah's life (26:24). The chamber in question probably opened into a courtyard before the New Gate of the temple, where the crowd which Baruch addressed was assembled (cf. 26:10-11). The fact that the ninth month (v. 9) is in the wintertime (v. 22) indicates that Judah was then following the Babylonian calendar, which begins in April, rather than her former calendar, which commenced in October. (Ex. 34:22)

Gemariah's son reported the incident to the princes, the leading political and administrative leaders (cf. 26:16). Jehudi was sent as a messenger to summon Baruch, who was obliged to read the document to the princes as well. The consternation of the princes, especially in the light of Babylon's sudden rise to power, was understandable. The situation was urgent, and the king would have to be informed, but in the meantime it was advisable to guarantee the safety of Jeremiah and his scribe. The intolerant character of King Jehoiakim was known to them all (26:20-23). Once more Jeremiah's life is in danger.

**20-26** Jehudi had the unpleasant task of reading this scroll before the king, who was calmly enjoying the comfort of his winter quarters. As Jehudi read, the king nonchalantly and sacrilegiously cut pieces off Jeremiah's scroll and disdainfully threw them into the flames of his brazier. But the words which had terrified the princes had no effect on the confident king and his household. Jehoiakim, who had previously been in league with Egypt, would simply transfer allegiance to Babylon and welcome the marching army of Nebuchadnezzar. The protests of the princes were pointless. His plan to imprison Jeremiah, however, was thwarted.

## JEREMIAH DICTATES ANOTHER
## SCROLL                                    36:27-32

²⁷ Now, after the king had burned the scroll with the words which Baruch wrote at Jeremiah's dictation, the word of the LORD came to Jeremiah: ²⁸ "Take another scroll and write on it all the former words that were in the first scroll, which Jehoi′akim the king of Judah has burned. ²⁹ And concerning Jehoi′akim king of Judah you shall say, 'Thus says the LORD, You have burned this scroll, saying, "Why have you written in it that the king of Babylon will certainly come and destroy this land, and will cut off from it man and beast?" ³⁰ Therefore thus says the LORD concerning Jehoi′akim king of Judah, He shall have none to sit upon the throne of David, and his dead body shall be cast out to the heat by day and the frost by night. ³¹ And I will punish him and his offspring and his servants for their iniquity; I will bring upon them, and upon the inhabitants of Jerusalem, and upon the men of Judah, all the evil that I have pronounced against them, but they would not hear.'"

³² Then Jeremiah took another scroll and gave it to Baruch the scribe, the son of Neri′ah, who wrote on it at the dictation of Jeremiah all the words of the scroll which Jehoi′akim king of Judah had burned in the fire; and many similar words were added to them.

Jeremiah's reaction to the blatant rejection of God's will by Jehoiakim was twofold. The prophet pronounced a curse on the king and had the scroll rewritten. The curse is comprised of two stereotype pronouncements: the disgrace of death without burial (cf. 22:18-19) and the ignominy of seeing his sons lose their right to the throne (cf. 22:30). The second edition of Jeremiah's scroll was expanded. Its precise contents are not known. However, Jer. 25:13 refers to a book that seems to be concluded at that point. Both Jer. 25 and the scroll of Jer. 36 are dated in the same year. The subject of the scroll of Jer. 36 is apparently primarily doom and judgment, and the topic concluded in Jer. 25 is similar. It seems quite plausible, therefore, that much of Jer. 1:4 – 25:13 was included in the scroll of Jer. 36. That Jer. 25:13 is the end of a collection or book is confirmed by the fact that the Greek version of Jeremiah (the Septuagint) includes a collection of oracles against the foreign nations (Jer. 46 – 51) at this point. By rewriting the scroll Jeremiah reasserts his authority to speak God's will despite the authority and challenge of the king (v. 29). This chapter also gives us a deep insight into the way in which the living word of Yahweh was preserved for us despite hazards and often because of them.

## JEREMIAH ACCUSED OF TREASON 37:1-15

¹ Zedeki'ah the son of Josi'ah, whom Nebuchad-rez'zar king of Babylon made king in the land of Judah, reigned instead of Coni'ah the son of Jehoi'akim. ² But neither he nor his servants nor the people of the land listened to the words of the LORD which he spoke through Jeremiah the prophet.

³ King Zedeki'ah sent Jehu'cal the son of Shel-emi'ah, and Zephani'ah the priest, the son of Ma-asei'ah, to Jeremiah the prophet, saying, "Pray for

us to the LORD our God." ⁴ Now Jeremiah was still
going in and out among the people, for he had not
yet been put in prison. ⁵ The army of Pharaoh had
come out of Egypt; and when the Chalde'ans who
were besieging Jerusalem heard news of them, they
withdrew from Jerusalem.

⁶ Then the word of the LORD came to Jeremiah
the prophet: ⁷ "Thus says the LORD, God of Israel:
Thus shall you say to the king of Judah who sent you
to me to inquire of me, 'Behold, Pharaoh's army which
came to help you is about to return to Egypt, to its
own land. ⁸ And the Chalde'ans shall come back and
fight against this city; they shall take it and burn it
with fire. ⁹ Thus says the LORD, Do not deceive yourselves, saying, "The Chalde'ans will surely stay away
from us," for they will not stay away. ¹⁰ For even if
you should defeat the whole army of Chalde'ans who
are fighting against you, and there remained of them
only wounded men, every man in his tent, they would
rise up and burn this city with fire.' "

¹¹ Now when the Chalde'an army had withdrawn
from Jerusalem at the approach of Pharaoh's army,
¹² Jeremiah set out from Jerusalem to go to the land
of Benjamin to receive his portion ⁿ there among the
people. ¹³ When he was at the Benjamin Gate, a sentry
there named Iri'jah the son of Shelemi'ah, son of
Hanani'ah, seized Jeremiah the prophet, saying,
"You are deserting to the Chalde'ans." ¹⁴ And Jeremiah said, "It is false; I am not deserting to the Chalde'ans." But Iri'jah would not listen to him, and
seized Jeremiah and brought him to the princes.
¹⁵ And the princes were enraged at Jeremiah, and

ⁿ Heb obscure

they beat him and imprisoned him in the house of
Jonathan the secretary, for it had been made a prison.

Chapter 37 has much in common with 34. They both
belong to the same period. The Egyptian army had invaded from the south and forced Nebuchadnezzar to
break his siege of Jerusalem at least temporarily (588
B. C.). Zedekiah had periodically turned to Jeremiah
for advice and intercession on behalf of his people. But
he was too weak an individual ever to follow Jeremiah's
demands. On this occasion Jeremiah's answer remained
consistent. The appearance of the Egyptian forces on
the scene naturally suggested the downfall of Nebuchadnezzar in the mind of some. But Jeremiah insists that
the Egyptians will soon flee and that Nebuchadnezzar
will soon return to execute the Lord's judgment on Jerusalem. That judgment was final and fixed. Hence even
if Nebuchadnezzar did lose to Egypt, God would bring
his wounded men back to destroy the holy city. There
was no escape.

Jeremiah's preaching probably sounded like treason to many. One of Jeremiah's actions was also interpreted as treacherous. During that break in the siege
mentioned above, Jeremiah took the opportunity to go
to his hometown of Anathoth "in the land of Benjamin"
to attend to a business transaction in connection with
his inherited property. Whether this deal was connected
with the purchase of property mentioned in Jer. 32 is
not indicated. Some connection is likely, however. As
Jeremiah left the city, he was arrested by the sentry at
the northern city gate and charged with deserting to
the Babylonian enemy. The princes who controlled the
city (and the weak Zedekiah) at that time beat Jeremiah
and threw him into an emergency prison to stop his

283

politically dangerous activities. This incident gave the leaders a "legal" excuse to get rid of a prophet whose preaching had weakened the defense of the city. (Cf. 38:4)

## JEREMIAH REBUKES ZEDEKIAH
## SHARPLY                                    37:16-21

16 When Jeremiah had come to the dungeon cells, and remained there many days, 17 King Zedeki'ah sent for him, and received him. The king questioned him secretly in his house, and said, "Is there any word from the LORD?" Jeremiah said, "There is." Then he said, "You shall be delivered into the hand of the king of Babylon." 18 Jeremiah also said to King Zedeki'ah, "What wrong have I done to you or your servants or this people, that you have put me in prison? 19 Where are your prophets who prophesied to you, saying, 'The king of Babylon will not come against you and against this land'? 20 Now hear, I pray you, O my lord the king: let my humble plea come before you, and do not send me back to the house of Jonathan the secretary, lest I die there." 21 So King Zedeki'ah gave orders, and they committed Jeremiah to the court of the guard; and a loaf of bread was given him daily from the bakers' street, until all the bread of the city was gone. So Jeremiah remained in the court of the guard.

Jeremiah was moved from his temporary prison to the dungeon cells. The situation in Jerusalem became progressively worse. The siege of the city by Nebuchadnezzar was renewed. Jeremiah had repeatedly told King Zedekiah and the rest of the city that God's word was final. The city would fall! But the pathetic and scared Zedekiah kept running back to Jeremiah, hoping for a new "word" (that is, message) from God. But the answer was always the same! On the occasion mentioned here Jeremiah took the opportunity to rebuke Zedekiah for his unfair treatment of the prophet. The other prophets had predicted falsely; Jeremiah's prophecy about the invasion of Babylon had come true. Ironically, it is Jeremiah who is in prison! Jeremiah uses this hold he has over the king to good advantage and requests a new location, where he will be safer. The king grants his request and places him in the "court of the guard," an enclosure adjacent to the palace itself. There Jeremiah would receive the ration of other prisoners while there was still food in the city. But siege usually led to famine, and for Jerusalem that day was not far off.

JEREMIAH IS RESCUED
FROM A CISTERN                                    38:1-13

¹ Now Shephati'ah the son of Mattan, Gedali'ah the son of Pashhur, Jucal the son of Shelemi'ah, and Pashhur the son of Malchi'ah heard the words that Jeremiah was saying to all the people, ² "Thus says the LORD, He who stays in this city shall die by the sword, by famine, and by pestilence; but he who goes out to the Chalde'ans shall live; he shall have his life as a prize of war, and live. ³ Thus says the LORD, This city shall surely be given into the hand of the army of the king of Babylon and be taken." ⁴ Then the princes said to the king, "Let this man be put

to death, for he is weakening the hands of the soldiers who are left in this city, and the hands of all the people, by speaking such words to them. For this man is not seeking the welfare of this people, but their harm." 5 King Zedeki′ah said, "Behold, he is in your hands; for the king can do nothing against you." 6 So they took Jeremiah and cast him into the cistern of Mal-chi′ah, the king's son, which was in the court of the guard, letting Jeremiah down by ropes. And there was no water in the cistern, but only mire, and Jeremiah sank in the mire.

7 When E′bed-mel′ech the Ethiopian, a eunuch, who was in the king's house, heard that they had put Jeremiah into the cistern—the king was sitting in the Benjamin Gate—8 E′bed-mel′ech went from the king's house and said to the king, 9 "My lord the king, these men have done evil in all that they did to Jeremiah the prophet by casting him into the cistern, and he will die there of hunger, for there is no bread left in the city." 10 Then the king commanded E′bed-mel′ech, the Ethiopian, "Take three men with you from here, and lift Jeremiah the prophet out of the cistern before he dies." 11 So E′bed-mel′ech took the men with him and went to the house of the king, to a wardrobe of*o* the storehouse, and took from there old rags and worn-out clothes, which he let down to Jeremiah in the cistern by ropes. 12 Then E′bed-mel′ech the Ethiopian said to Jeremiah, "Put the rags and clothes between your armpits and the ropes." Jeremiah did so. 13 Then they drew Jeremiah up with ropes and lifted him out of the cistern. And Jeremiah remained in the court of the guard.

*o* Cn: Heb *to under*

**1-6** While Jeremiah was in the court of the guard, he was apparently permitted contact with the public. His messages still circulated through the city. As the trials of the siege increased, Jeremiah's words became more meaningful. The fall of Jerusalem was God's will. If anyone wanted to save his neck, he had better defect to the Babylonians. This kind of talk sounded like treason in the ears of the political leaders. Accordingly these leaders summoned Jeremiah to appear before them. Jeremiah was condemned for undermining the spirit of the people. Despite his personal feelings King Zedekiah admitted he could not do anything to counter the decision of the princes handling the case. Jeremiah was thereupon thrown into the cistern of Malchiah, which had a layer of mud but no water at the bottom. If Jeremiah had died there, it would have been legal murder, and the city would have removed an obnoxious left-wing agitator. In any case the prophet was left to rot!

**7-13** Ebedmelech is the "good Samaritan" of the Old Testament. He was an Ethiopian servant of the king. He may actually have been a eunuch, or a high official, as the term sometimes implies. When he heard of Jeremiah's plight, he went directly to the king. The king was in the Benjamin gate at the time, presumably handling law cases according to the Israelite custom. At great risk to his own life Ebedmelech informed the king of Jeremiah's imminent death. There was no more food for the prisoners. The description of the rescue operation which follows is vivid and realistic. The weak old prophet is tenderly pulled out of the mud by long ropes. Old rags are placed under his armpits to prevent injury. Jeremiah is then returned to the "court of the guard" (cf. 37:21), where the king's household could care for him. Once again the prophet's life had been saved!

287

## JEREMIAH HEARS ZEDEKIAH'S
## FINAL PLEA                                    38:14-28

[14] King Zedeki'ah sent for Jeremiah the prophet and received him at the third entrance of the temple of the LORD. The king said to Jeremiah, "I will ask you a question; hide nothing from me." [15] Jeremiah said to Zedeki'ah, "If I tell you, will you not be sure to put me to death? And if I give you counsel, you will not listen to me." [16] Then King Zedeki'ah swore secretly to Jeremiah, "As the LORD lives, who made our souls, I will not put you to death or deliver you into the hand of these men who seek your life."

[17] Then Jeremiah said to Zedeki'ah, "Thus says the LORD, the God of hosts, the God of Israel, If you will surrender to the princes of the king of Babylon, then your life shall be spared, and this city shall not be burned with fire, and you and your house shall live. [18] But if you do not surrender to the princes of the king of Babylon, then this city shall be given into the hand of the Chalde'ans, and they shall burn it with fire, and you shall not escape from their hand." [19] King Zedeki'ah said to Jeremiah, "I am afraid of the Jews who have deserted to the Chalde'ans, lest I be handed over to them and they abuse me." [20] Jeremiah said, "You shall not be given to them. Obey now the voice of the LORD in what I say to you, and it shall be well with you, and your life shall be spared. [21] But if you refuse to surrender, this is the vision which the LORD has shown to me: [22] Behold, all the women left in the house of the king of Judah were being led out to the princes of the king of Babylon and were saying,

'Your trusted friends have deceived you

and prevailed against you;
now that your feet are sunk in the mire,
they turn away from you.'
²³ All your wives and your sons shall be led out to the
Chalde'ans, and you yourself shall not escape from
their hand, but shall be seized by the king of Babylon;
and this city shall be burned with fire."

²⁴ Then Zedeki'ah said to Jeremiah, "Let no one
know of these words and you shall not die. ²⁵ If the
princes hear that I have spoken with you and come to
you and say to you, 'Tell us what you said to the king
and what the king said to you; hide nothing from us
and we will not put you to death,' ²⁶ then you shall
say to them, 'I made a humble plea to the king that
he would not send me back to the house of Jonathan
to die there.'" ²⁷ Then all the princes came to Jeremiah and asked him, and he answered them as the
king had instructed him. So they left off speaking
with him, for the conversation had not been over-
heard. ²⁸ And Jeremiah remained in the court of the
guard until the day that Jerusalem was taken.

14-23 And once again Zedekiah comes to Jeremiah
for an oracle from God. The king is at his wit's end. But
he does not have the strength of character to take a stand.
He hopes for a miraculous solution from God. Jeremiah,
who had previously been deserted by Zedekiah (38:5),
now demands an oath from this spineless king that if
he was told the truth, Jeremiah would not be put to
death as a result. Zedekiah swears by the God who
"made our souls," or more accurately "who made us
living beings," that Jeremiah would not die. Jeremiah's
oracle from God does not change, however. "Surrender"
to Babylon is the only way to save both king and city.

289

Zedekiah, although he knew the wisdom of Jeremiah's advice, was afraid to follow it. He feared those Jews who had defected earlier (perhaps following Jeremiah's counsel). They were likely to abuse the king for his hypocrisy. Jeremiah's answer was biting and pointed. Zedekiah would not suffer mistreatment at the hands of those who defected but would be ridiculed by the women who remained in Jerusalem. Their dirge would expose the sad story of a king who had followed the advice of the wrong friends. They had taken advantage of him and in the end had left him floundering in the mire, as it were. Perhaps Jeremiah still had the mud from the filthy pit covering him (v. 13) and used his own condition to describe the king's fate. Zedekiah would not be rescued from the mire as Jeremiah had been. The king and his family were destined for exile, come what may!

24-28 Zedekiah was now more fearful than ever. How would the princes, who had convicted Jeremiah and thrown him in the cistern, react to Zedekiah's asking such a man for advice? The king therefore extracted a promise from Jeremiah that if the princes questioned him, he would not disclose the topic of their conversation but tell them that he had pleaded not to be sent back to his former cell in the house of Jonathan. (See 37:15)

# Oracles and Incidents
# of Jerusalem During and After the Fall

## Jeremiah 39—44

Little comment is called for in the following chapters. The text consists of simple biographical accounts and prose discourses. Unlike most sections of the book, they follow a strict chronological sequence. Many portions are simple records of the events that took place during and after the fall of Jerusalem in 587 B. C. The final discourse of Jeremiah in Ch. 44 was obviously delivered some time before the death of Pharaoh Hophra in 569 B. C. We do not know how these materials were returned to Palestine from Egypt. It is quite probable, however, that Baruch was also the editor who compiled these chapters.

### THE SIEGE AND FALL
### OF JERUSALEM                                        39:1-10

¹ In the ninth year of Zedeki'ah king of Judah, in the tenth month, Nebuchadrez'zar king of Babylon and all his army came against Jerusalem and besieged it; ² in the eleventh year of Zedeki'ah, in the

fourth month, on the ninth day of the month, a breach was made in the city. ³ When Jerusalem was taken,ᵖ all the princes of the king of Babylon came and sat in the middle gate: Ner'gal-share'zer, Sam'gar-ne'bo, Sar'sechim the Rab'saris, Ner'gal-share'zer the Rab-mag, with all the rest of the officers of the king of Babylon. ⁴ When Zedeki'ah king of Judah and all the soldiers saw them, they fled, going out of the city at night by way of the king's garden through the gate between the two walls; and they went toward the Arabah. ⁵ But the army of the Chalde'ans pursued them, and overtook Zedeki'ah in the plains of Jericho; and when they had taken him, they brought him up to Nebuchadrez'zar king of Babylon, at Riblah, in the land of Hamath; and he passed sentence upon him. ⁶ The king of Babylon slew the sons of Zedeki'ah at Riblah before his eyes; and the king of Babylon slew all the nobles of Judah. ⁷ He put out the eyes of Zedeki'ah, and bound him in fetters to take him to Babylon. ⁸ The Chalde'ans burned the king's house and the house of the people, and broke down the walls of Jerusalem. ⁹ Then Nebu'-zarad'an, the captain of the guard, carried into exile to Babylon the rest of the people who were left in the city, those who had deserted to him, and the people who remained. ¹⁰ Nebu'zarad'an, the captain of the guard, left in the land of Judah some of the poor people who owned nothing, and gave them vineyards and fields at the same time.

ᵖ This clause has been transposed from the end of Chapter 38

The same narrative appears with minor variations in Jer. 52:4-16 (2 Kings 25:1-12). The fall of Jerusalem was the dramatic verification of Jeremiah's harsh words of judgment. The day of the Lord had come for Judah. A simple unbiased report of that event is therefore appropriate. The siege began in the 9th year of Zedekiah (December 589 B. C.) and ended in his 11th year (June 587 B. C.). The Babylonian army of Nebuchadnezzar had done its job, and the leaders of the Babylonian forces entered the city to divide the spoil. Some of these leaders are given technical Babylonian titles. The location of the "middle gate" where they set up their quarters is uncertain. Zedekiah and his army fled through another gate between two of the city walls. The Arabah region, to which they fled, is the Jordan valley, which abounds in caves. Zedekiah, the king who deserted his people, suffers a tragic fate. He is captured, taken to the campaign headquarters of Nebuchadnezzar at Riblah on the river Orontes in Syria, forced to witness the massacre of his sons, have his own eyes blinded, and be taken in chains to Babylon. His end is the epitome of disgrace, as Jeremiah had foreseen (34:3; 38:22). Nebuzaradan, the captain of Nebuchadnezzar's personal army, supervised the final operations. The royal palace was burnt, along with other public buildings, city walls were knocked down, and additional captives were taken. According to Jer. 52:29, the number of captives was 832. Those left behind in Judah were farmers rather than political or religious leaders who might urge further revolt.

## JEREMIAH IS RELEASED 39:11-14

[11] Nebuchadrez'zar king of Babylon gave command concerning Jeremiah through Nebu'zarad'an, the captain of the guard, saying, [12] "Take him, look after him well and do him no harm, but deal with

293

him as he tells you." ¹³ So Nebu'zarad'an the captain of the guard, Nebushaz'ban the Rab'saris, Ner'gal-share'zer the Rabmag, and all the chief officers of the king of Babylon ¹⁴ sent and took Jeremiah from the court of the guard. They entrusted him to Geda-li'ah the son of Ahi'kam, son of Shaphan, that he should take him home. So he dwelt among the people.

Verses 13-14 present an account of Jeremiah's release. According to this account, the Babylonian officials meet after the fall of the city, remove Jeremiah from prison, summon him before their council, and leave him in the hands of Gedaliah, who was appointed governor over Judah (40:5). The final comment of v. 14 is significant. Jeremiah "dwelt among the people" who needed him the most, those people whom God had once called the "bad figs," the condemned hypocrites of Judah (24:1-7). Jeremiah did not go to Babylon with those people for whom God had planned "a future and a hope" (29:11). Verses 11-12 indicate that Nebuchadnezzar was well aware of Jeremiah's efforts to save the city and its people by surrendering to Babylon. Such an unexpected ally deserved special consideration. Hence his wishes were to be honored. Nebuchadnezzar put Nebuzaradan in charge of this special case. The story of Nebuzaradan's discussion with Jeremiah in 40:1-6 seems to follow logically after 39:11-12.

## AN ORACLE FOR EBEDMELECH          39:15-18

¹⁵ The word of the LORD came to Jeremiah while he was shut up in the court of the guard: ¹⁶ "Go, and say to E'bed-mel'ech the Ethiopian, 'Thus says the LORD of hosts, the God of Israel: Behold, I will

294

fulfil my words against this city for evil and not for good, and they shall be accomplished before you on that day. [17] But I will deliver you on that day, says the LORD, and you shall not be given into the hand of the men of whom you are afraid. [18] For I will surely save you, and you shall not fall by the sword; but you shall have your life as a prize of war, because you have put your trust in me, says the LORD.'"

Verses 15-18 are a brief appendix concerning the fate of Ebedmelech who had been instrumental in saving Jeremiah's life (in 38:7-13). As a reward for that unselfish act he was promised that his life would be spared when the city was finally taken. The recording of this oracle at this point suggests that Ebedmelech did survive the ordeal. His personal "trust," or faith, had saved him. How different are the figures of Ebedmelech, the unselfish slave, and King Zedekiah, his pitiful master, who fled to save his skin.

## JEREMIAH CHOOSES TO REMAIN IN PALESTINE                    40:1-6

[1] The word that came to Jeremiah from the LORD after Nebu'zarad'an the captain of the guard had let him go from Ramah, when he took him bound in chains along with all the captives of Jerusalem and Judah who were being exiled to Babylon. [2] The captain of the guard took Jeremiah and said to him, "The LORD your God pronounced this evil against this place; [3] the LORD has brought it about, and has done as he said. Because you sinned against the LORD, and did not obey his voice, this thing has come upon you. [4] Now, behold, I release you today

295

**from the chains on your hands. If it seems good to you to come with me to Babylon, come, and I will look after you well; but if it seems wrong to you to come with me to Babylon, do not come. See, the whole land is before you; go wherever you think it good and right to go. 5 If you remain,[q] then return to Gedali'ah the son of Ahi'kam, son of Shaphan, whom the king of Babylon appointed governor of the cities of Judah, and dwell with him among the people; or go wherever you think it right to go." So the captain of the guard gave him an allowance of food and a present, and let him go. 6 Then Jeremiah went to Gedali'ah the son of Ahi'kam, at Mizpah, and dwelt with him among the people who were left in the land.**

[q] Syr: Heb obscure

Nebuzaradan, the captain of Nebuchadnezzar's army, had been given orders to honor Jeremiah's wishes (39:11-12). Jeremiah had apparently been confined for a time in the temporary prison camps at Ramah, about five miles north of Jerusalem. Whether this confinement occurred after Jeremiah had been taken from the court of the guard and committed into the care of Gedaliah (according to 39:14) is not clear. Perhaps Jeremiah was picked up later by soldiers who had not known of the prophet's release by Nebuzaradan. Nebuzaradan's opening remarks to Jeremiah at Ramah are couched in the language of Jeremiah's preaching and reflect Nebuzaradan's offer (v. 3). Jeremiah is given a free choice because of his privileged position (see the comment on 39:11-14). He can leave for Babylon with the other leaders or remain in the devastated land of Judah. In exile the prophet would have been esteemed highly; in Judah life would be one of great hardship.

But the old prophet chose the latter, took his rations, went to Gedaliah, and lived with the poor survivors. Gedaliah, moreover, belonged to a leading family that had befriended Jeremiah. Gedaliah's father Ahikam had once saved the prophet's life (26:24). Nebuchadnezzar had appointed Gedaliah governor of the province of Judah. After the fall of Jerusalem the government under Gedaliah was located in Mizpah, which is probably a site about eight miles north of Jerusalem.

## GEDALIAH RULES FROM MIZPAH          40:7-16

**7** When all the captains of the forces in the open country and their men heard that the king of Babylon had appointed Gedali'ah the son of Ahi'kam governor in the land, and had committed to him men, women, and children, those of the poorest of the land who had not been taken into exile to Babylon, **8** they went to Gedali'ah at Mizpah – Ish'mael the son of Nethani'ah, Joha'nan the son of Kare'ah, Serai'ah the son of Tanhu'meth, the sons of Ephai the Netoph'athite, Jezani'ah the son of the Maac'athite, they and their men. **9** Gedali'ah the son of Ahi'kam, son of Shaphan, swore to them and their men, saying, "Do not be afraid to serve the Chalde'ans. Dwell in the land, and serve the king of Babylon, and it shall be well with you. **10** As for me, I will dwell at Mizpah, to stand for you before the Chalde'ans who will come to us; but as for you, gather wine and summer fruits and oil, and store them in your vessels, and dwell in your cities that you have taken." **11** Likewise, when all the Jews who were in Moab and among the Ammonites and in Edom and in other lands heard that the king of Babylon had left a remnant in Judah and had appointed Gedali'ah the son of Ahi'kam, son of Shaphan, as governor over them, [12] then all the Jews returned from all the places to which they had been driven and came to the land of Judah, to Gedali'ah at Mizpah; and they gathered wine and summer fruits in great abundance.

[13] Now Joha'nan the son of Kare'ah and all the leaders of the forces in the open country came to Gedali'ah at Mizpah [14] and said to him, "Do you know that Ba'alis the king of the Ammonites has sent Ish'mael the son of Nethani'ah to take your life?" But Gedali'ah the son of Ahi'kam would not believe them. [15] Then Joha'nan the son of Kare'ah spoke secretly to Gedali'ah at Mizpah, "Let me go and slay Ish'mael the son of Nethani'ah, and no one will know it. Why should he take your life, so that all the Jews who are gathered about you would be scattered, and the remnant of Judah would perish?" [16] But Gedali'ah the son of Ahi'kam said to Joha'nan the son of Kare'ah, "You shall not do this thing, for you are speaking falsely of Ish'mael."

7-12 Once Gedaliah had established himself as governor in Mizpah over the survivors of Judah, various refugee forces that had escaped the army of Nebuchadnezzar began to congregate at Mizpah. The leaders of these groups are mentioned by name. Other Israelite refugees from the nearby countries of Moab, Ammon, and Edom also returned to Judah and helped with the harvest. Gedaliah, in turn, swore to uphold the rights of the people before their Babylonian masters and promised a fair deal from their hands. Further, he urged them to take advantage of the ripe crops and to settle in the abandoned cities. Apparently Nebuchadnezzar had not ravaged the countryside, as many of his Assyrian predecessors had done on their campaigns.

**13-16** Under Gedaliah peace and prosperity seemed assured. Other smaller nations, however, were ready to take advantage of Judah's weak condition. Baalis, king of the Ammonites to the east of the Jordan, was one such opportunist. His precise motives were not given. He dispatched a certain Ishmael, a member of the royal family of Judah (41:1), as his henchman to slay the unsuspecting Gedaliah. Even when Gedaliah was informed of the plot by Johanan, one of the leaders of the surviving forces (v. 8), the governor refused to heed the warning. After the horrible debacle at the hands of Babylon Gedaliah apparently could not conceive of any ruler incurring further reprisals from Nebuchadnezzar by murdering his governor. He therefore crushed Johanan's plan to intercept Ishmael and kill him first. That action was Gedaliah's undoing.

## ISHMAEL SLAYS GEDALIAH AND OTHERS  41:1-10

¹ In the seventh month, Ish'mael the son of Nethani'ah, son of Eli'shama, of the royal family, one of the chief officers of the king, came with ten men to Gedali'ah the son of Ahi'kam, at Mizpah. As they ate bread together there at Mizpah, ² Ish'mael the son of Nethani'ah and the ten men with him rose up and struck down Gedali'ah the son of Ahi'kam, son of Shaphan, with the sword, and killed him, whom the king of Babylon had appointed governor in the land. ³ Ish'mael also slew all the Jews who were with Gedali'ah at Mizpah, and the Chalde'an soldiers who happened to be there.

⁴ On the day after the murder of Gedali'ah, be-

299

fore any one knew of it, ⁵ eighty men arrived from Shechem and Shiloh and Samar'ia, with their beards shaved and their clothes torn, and their bodies gashed, bringing cereal offerings and incense to present at the temple of the LORD. ⁶ And Ish'mael the son of Nethani'ah came out from Mizpah to meet them, weeping as he came. As he met them, he said to them, "Come in to Gedali'ah the son of Ahi'kam." ⁷ When they came into the city, Ish'mael the son of Nethani'ah and the men with him slew them and cast them into a cistern. ⁸ But there were ten men among them who said to Ish'mael, "Do not kill us, for we have stores of wheat, barley, oil, and honey hidden in the fields." So he refrained and did not kill them with their companions.

⁹ Now the cistern into which Ish'mael cast all the bodies of the men whom he had slain was the large cistern ʳ which King Asa had made for defense against Ba'asha king of Israel; Ish'mael the son of Nethani'ah filled it with the slain. ¹⁰ Then Ish'mael took captive all the rest of the people who were in Mizpah, the king's daughters and all the people who were left at Mizpah, whom Nebu'zarad'an, the captain of the guard, had committed to Gedali'ah the son of Ahi'kam. Ish'mael the son of Nethani'ah took them captive and set out to cross over to the Ammonites.

ʳ Gk: Heb *he had slain by the hand of Gedaliah*

1-3 The murder of Gedaliah was a vicious atrocity. Ishmael and 10 of his followers were dining with Gedaliah when the killing was accomplished. The meal, which was a symbol of fellowship, was desecrated by these bloodthirsty men who slaughtered all the personnel living with Gedaliah at the time. Even the Babylonian soldiers were killed and the rule of Nebuchadnezzar further flouted. Reprisals for such action would be inevitable. The dastardly crime took place in the seventh month. Whether this was the same year as the fall of Jerusalem, or a year or two later, is not clear. The month, however, was long remembered with a fast as one of the blackest hours of Judah's disgrace. (Cf. Zech. 7:5; 8:19)

4-8 Another tragedy follows on the next day. Eighty pilgrims from Northern cities came to the temple in Jerusalem. Their appearance reflected their attitude of penitence and mourning over the fall of Jerusalem. Although the temple was in ruins, it was still a sacred shrine even for Northern Israelites. They were probably bringing sacrifices for the Feast of Booths, which was the cultic New Year (comparable to the beginning of the modern church year) for Israel. Ishmael added deception to his crimes by pretending to be sympathetic to the cause of the pilgrims. He invited them to pay their respects to Gedaliah, the governor. The reason for murdering these pilgrims is not given; Ishmael's action only incensed the inhabitants of Judah further and led to his own undoing. Ten men saved their lives bribing Ishmael with hidden treasure and goods. The murder of the other 70 seems senseless and sadistic.

The murdered bodies were thrown in a well-known cistern built by King Asa some 300 years earlier as part of the city's defenses (cf. 1 Kings 15:32). The members of the royal household and the other people of Mizpah were taken captive. Jeremiah seems to have been among them (cf. 42:2). Ishmael intended to deliver these captives to King Baalis of Ammon, who had hired Ishmael to perform the initial killing of Gedaliah. (40:14)

## JOHANAN SEEKS TO AVENGE
## GEDALIAH'S DEATH                     41:11-18

¹¹ But when Joha'nan the son of Kare'ah and all the leaders of the forces with him heard of all the evil which Ish'mael the son of Nethani'ah had done, ¹² they took all their men and went to fight against Ish'mael the son of Nethani'ah. They came upon him at the great pool which is in Gib'eon. ¹³ And when all the people who were with Ish'mael saw Joha'nan the son of Kare'ah and all the leaders of the forces with him, they rejoiced. ¹⁴ So all the people whom Ish'mael had carried away captive from Mizpah turned about and came back, and went to Joha'nan the son of Kare'ah. ¹⁵ But Ish'mael the son of Nethani'ah escaped from Joha'nan with eight men, and went to the Ammonites. ¹⁶ Then Joha'nan the son of Kare'ah and all the leaders of the forces with him took all the rest of the people whom Ish'-mael the son of Nethani'ah had carried away captive ˢ from Mizpah after he had slain Gedali'ah the son of Ahi'kam — soldiers, women, children, and eunuchs, whom Joha'nan brought back from Gib'eon. ¹⁷ And they went and stayed at Geruth Chimham near Bethlehem, intending to go to Egypt ¹⁸ because of the Chalde'ans; for they were afraid of them, because Ish'mael the son of Nethani'ah had slain Gedali'ah the son of Ahi'kam, whom the king of Babylon had made governor over the land.

ˢ Cn: Heb *whom he recovered from Ishmael*

Johanan became the leader of the remaining forces. He and his men overtook Ishmael and his captives at Gibeon, about six miles northwest of Jerusalem. The

302

captives immediately revolted and joined forces with
Johanan. In the confusion Ishmael and eight of his men
escaped to Baalis of Ammon, where they could expect
protection. The released captives and the followers
of Johanan then camped at a small place near Bethlehem. Their plan was to leave Judah and go to Egypt.
Their own safety was more important than pursuing
Ishmael any further. They naturally feared that the
murder of Gedaliah and the apparent revolt under
Ishmael would evoke harsh retaliation on the part of
the Babylonian overlords. The campaign of Nebuzaradan, the captain of Nebuchadnezzar's guard forces, in
582 B. C. may well have been a reprisal for this un-
warranted uprising. (See 52:30)

## THE REMNANT ASKS JEREMIAH'S
## ADVICE                                        42:1-22

¹ Then all the commanders of the forces, and
Joha'nan the son of Kare'ah and Azari'ah ' the son
of Hoshai'ah, and all the people from the least to
the greatest, came near ² and said to Jeremiah the
prophet, "Let our supplication come before you,
and pray to the LORD your God for us, for all this
remnant (for we are left but a few of many, as your
eyes see us), ³ that the LORD your God may show
us the way we should go, and the thing that we should
do." ⁴ Jeremiah the prophet said to them, "I have
heard you; behold, I will pray to the LORD your
God according to your request, and whatever the
LORD answers you I will tell you; I will keep nothing
back from you." ⁵ Then they said to Jeremiah, "May
the LORD be a true and faithful witness against us

' Gk: Heb *Jezaniah*

if we do not act according to all the word with which the LORD your God sends you to us. ⁶ Whether it is good or evil, we will obey the voice of the LORD our God to whom we are sending you, that it may be well with us when we obey the voice of the LORD our God."

⁷ At the end of ten days the word of the LORD came to Jeremiah. ⁸ Then he summoned Joha′nan the son of Kare′ah and all the commanders of the forces who were with him, and all the people from the least to the greatest, ⁹ and said to them, "Thus says the LORD, the God of Israel, to whom you sent me to present your supplication before him: ¹⁰ If you will remain in this land, then I will build you up and not pull you down; I will plant you, and not pluck you up; for I repent of the evil which I did to you. ¹¹ Do not fear the king of Babylon, of whom you are afraid; do not fear him, says the LORD, for I am with you, to save you and to deliver you from his hand. ¹² I will grant you mercy, that he may have mercy on you and let you remain in your own land. ¹³ But if you say, 'We will not remain in this land,' disobeying the voice of the LORD your God ¹⁴ and saying, 'No, we will go to the land of Egypt, where we shall not see war, or hear the sound of the trumpet, or be hungry for bread, and we will dwell there,' ¹⁵ then hear the word of the LORD, O remnant of Judah. Thus says the LORD of hosts, the God of Israel: If you set your faces to enter Egypt and go to live there, ¹⁶ then the sword which you fear shall overtake you there in the land of Egypt; and the famine of which you are afraid shall follow hard after you to Egypt; and there you shall die. ¹⁷ All the men who set their faces to go to Egypt to live there shall

die by the sword, by famine, and by pestilence; they shall have no remnant or survivor from the evil which I will bring upon them.

18 "For thus says the LORD of hosts, the God of Israel: As my anger and my wrath were poured out on the inhabitants of Jerusalem, so my wrath will be poured out on you when you go to Egypt. You shall become an execration, a horror, a curse, and a taunt. You shall see this place no more. 19 The LORD has said to you, O remnant of Judah, 'Do not go to Egypt.' Know for a certainty that I have warned you this day 20 that you have gone astray at the cost of your lives. For you sent me to the LORD your God, saying, 'Pray for us to the LORD our God, and whatever the LORD our God says declare to us and we will do it.' 21 And I have this day declared it to you, but you have not obeyed the voice of the LORD your God in anything that he sent me to tell you. 22 Now therefore know for a certainty that you shall die by the sword, by famine, and by pestilence in the place where you desire to go to live."

1-6 The remnant, that is, those survivors who remained in Judah after the campaigns of Nebuchadnezzar, had all but decided to desert their homeland. They feared another campaign by the Babylonian army in retaliation for the murder of Gedaliah (see 41:18). Before departing, these survivors hoped to get an oracle from God to justify their plans. Jeremiah is approached on the matter. He promises to give God's answer without reservations. The people, in turn, promise to follow God's decision, regardless of the consequences.

**7-17** Verse 7 is very significant. It states that the word of the Lord came to Jeremiah "at the end of ten days." A prophet like Jeremiah did not apparently know precisely how God felt on a subject immediately. Only after the prophet has mulled over the problem for several days is he given to know God's verdict. (Compare a similar situation in 28:5-12.) Jeremiah is more than just a mechanical spokesman for a heavenly voice. He must wrestle with God in prayer for his answers (compare his confessions in 11:18 – 12:6). Jeremiah delivers the answer of God to all the people. The answer is given in the form of an option. If the remnant will stay in Judah instead of fleeing, God will establish them as a people again. He will "build" and "plant" them instead of "plucking" them up (cf. 1:10). God will not bring further destruction ("evil") upon them (as He had threatened in 24:8). They need not fear Babylon any more because Yahweh would live up to His name as the great "I AM WITH YOU" to rescue them. Jeremiah knew what that promise meant from his own call (1:8), as Moses had long before (Ex. 3:12, 14). But if the people refused to stay in Judah, then the curse of destruction they deserved would overtake them in Egypt. They had the alternative of a new covenant: obedience and the way of life or rebellion and the way of death. Compare the covenant alternative of Deut. 30:15-20.

**18-22** The seriousness of the decision is reinforced by reminding the people of their long history of rebelliousness and the horrible curses that would ensue if they persisted in this course of action. God was giving them an undeserved final choice, another last chance. And Jeremiah's words had come true so dramatically when Jerusalem fell. They had never heeded him before. Surely they would now.

## THE REMNANT TAKES JEREMIAH
## TO EGYPT
43:1-7

¹ When Jeremiah finished speaking to all the people all these words of the LORD their God, with which the LORD their God had sent him to them, ² Azari'ah the son of Hoshai'ah and Joha'nan the son of Kare'ah and all the insolent men said to Jeremiah, "You are telling a lie. The LORD our God did not send you to say, 'Do not go to Egypt to live there'; ³ but Baruch the son of Neri'ah has set you against us, to deliver us into the hand of the Chalde'ans, that they may kill us or take us into exile in Babylon." ⁴ So Joha'nan the son of Kare'ah and all the commanders of the forces and all the people did not obey the voice of the LORD, to remain in the land of Judah. ⁵ But Joha'nan the son of Kare'ah and all the commanders of the forces took all the remnant of Judah who had returned to live in the land of Judah from all the nations to which they had been driven — ⁶ the men, the women, the children, the princesses, and every person whom Nebu'zarad'an the captain of the guard had left with Gedali'ah the son of Ahi'kam, son of Shaphan; also Jeremiah the prophet and Baruch the son of Neri'ah. ⁷ And they came into the land of Egypt, for they did not obey the voice of the LORD. And they arrived at Tah'panhes.

When Jeremiah delivered God's demand to remain in Judah, two of the leaders and the unruly element in the crowd accused Jeremiah of "telling a lie." They employ the same term that Jeremiah had often used in describing Judah's hypocrisy before the fall of Jerusalem. They also try to involve Baruch, Jeremiah's faithful scribe, in the scheme. Apparently Baruch was a man of some influence among the remnant and preferred to cooperate with Babylon. The upshot of the argument was that God's Word was again rejected and the men of Judah set out for Egypt taking Jeremiah and Baruch with them. They settled at Tahpanhes, a fortress on the eastern branch of the Nile. With both Jeremiah and Baruch in Egypt, we wonder how the book of Jeremiah was preserved by the people of Judah. Did Baruch return to Judah later?

## THE PARABLE OF THE LARGE
## STONES IN THE PAVEMENT                          43:8-13

**8 Then the word of the LORD came to Jeremiah in Tah'panhes: 9 "Take in your hands large stones, and hide them in the mortar in the pavement which is at the entrance to Pharaoh's palace in Tah'panhes, in the sight of the men of Judah, 10 and say to them, 'Thus says the LORD of hosts, the God of Israel: Behold, I will send and take Nebuchadrez'zar the king of Babylon, my servant, and he " will set his throne above these stones which I have hid, and he will spread his royal canopy over them. 11 He shall come and smite the land of Egypt, giving to the pestilence those who are doomed to the pestilence, to captivity those who are doomed to captivity, and to the sword those who are doomed to the sword. 12 He ʳ shall kindle a fire in the temples of the gods of Egypt; and he shall burn them and carry them away captive; and he shall clean the land of Egypt, as a shepherd cleans his cloak of vermin; and he shall go away from there in peace. 13 He shall break**

" Gk Syr: Heb *I*   ʳ Gk Syr Vg: Heb *I*

the obelisks of Heliop'olis which is in the land of
Egypt; and the temples of the gods of Egypt he shall
burn with fire.'"

The final symbolic action performed by Jeremiah
is perhaps the most bizarre of all. This action rein-
forces his earlier assertion that doom would overtake
God's people if they went to Egypt. The new Pharaoh
(Hophra) of Egypt would not save them. The prophet
is told to bury large stones somewhere in front of the
royal house in Tahpanhes. The precise meaning of the
Hebrew words translated "the mortar in the pavement"
is uncertain. The royal house is not the palace of Pharaoh, in this case, but some kind of official building
used by the king when he visited this frontier city. The
burying was to be witnessed by the people of Judah
who would be involved in the message. Nebuchadnezzar would one day come, predicted Jeremiah, and
pitch his canopy (or battle tents) over the very stones
Jeremiah had buried. These would be like foundation
stones for his throne. And the people who were marked
by God for judgment would receive their appropriate
dues. Egypt, moreover, would be ravaged, its temples
burned to the ground, and the famous tall stone pillars
("Obelisks") for the sun god at Heliopolis would fall.
The number of captives taken would be so great that
the country would appear to be picked clean in the way
that a shepherd picks his cloak clean of vermin. When
Nebuchadnezzar did invade Egypt in 568 B.C., he
forced Egypt's submission but did not completely devastate the land or deport all the people. The extent to
which his campaign affected the Israelites we do not
know.

## JEREMIAH PREDICTS THE END
## OF THE REMNANT IN EGYPT                    44:1-30

¹ The word that came to Jeremiah concerning all the Jews that dwelt in the land of Egypt, at Migdol, at Tah'panhes, at Memphis, and in the land of Pathros, ² "Thus says the LORD of hosts, the God of Israel: You have seen all the evil that I brought upon Jerusalem and upon all the cities of Judah. Behold, this day they are a desolation, and no one dwells in them, ³ because of the wickedness which they committed, provoking me to anger, in that they went to burn incense and serve other gods that they knew not, neither they, nor you, nor your fathers. ⁴ Yet I persistently sent to you all my servants the prophets, saying, 'Oh, do not do this abominable thing that I hate!' ⁵ But they did not listen or incline their ear, to turn from their wickedness and burn no incense to other gods. ⁶ Therefore my wrath and my anger were poured forth and kindled in the cities of Judah and in the streets of Jerusalem; and they became a waste and a desolation, as at this day. ⁷ And now thus says the LORD God of hosts, the God of Israel: Why do you commit this great evil against yourselves, to cut off from you man and woman, infant and child, from the midst of Judah, leaving you no remnant? ⁸ Why do you provoke me to anger with the works of your hands, burning incense to other gods in the land of Egypt where you have come to live, that you may be cut off and become a curse and a taunt among all the nations of the earth? ⁹ Have you forgotten the wickedness of your fathers, the wickedness of the kings of Judah, the wickedness of their ʷ wives, your

ʷ Heb *his*

310

own wickedness, and the wickedness of your wives, which they committed in the land of Judah and in the streets of Jerusalem? [10] They have not humbled themselves even to this day, nor have they feared, nor walked in my law and my statutes which I set before you and before your fathers.

[11] "Therefore thus says the LORD of hosts, the God of Israel: Behold, I will set my face against you for evil, to cut off all Judah. [12] I will take the remnant of Judah who have set their faces to come to the land of Egypt to live, and they shall all be consumed; in the land of Egypt they shall fall; by the sword and by famine they shall be consumed; from the least to the greatest, they shall die by the sword and by famine; and they shall become an execration, a horror, a curse, and a taunt. [13] I will punish those who dwell in the land of Egypt, as I have punished Jerusalem, with the sword, with famine, and with pestilence, [14] so that none of the remnant of Judah who have come to live in the land of Egypt shall escape or survive or return to the land of Judah, to which they desire to return to dwell there; for they shall not return, except some fugitives."

[15] Then all the men who knew that their wives had offered incense to other gods, and all the women who stood by, a great assembly, all the people who dwelt in Pathros in the land of Egypt, answered Jeremiah: [16] "As for the word which you have spoken to us in the name of the LORD, we will not listen to you. [17] But we will do everything that we have vowed, burn incense to the queen of heaven and pour out libations to her, as we did, both we and our fathers, our kings and our princes, in the cities of Judah and in the streets of Jerusalem; for then we had plenty

311

of food, and prospered, and saw no evil. [18] But since we left off burning incense to the queen of heaven and pouring out libations to her, we have lacked everything and have been consumed by the sword and by famine." [19] And the women said,[x] "When we burned incense to the queen of heaven and poured out libations to her, was it without our husbands' approval that we made cakes for her bearing her image and poured out libations to her?"

[20] Then Jeremiah said to all the people, men and women, all the people who had given him this answer: [21] "As for the incense that you burned in the cities of Judah and in the streets of Jerusalem, you and your fathers, your kings and your princes, and the people of the land, did not the LORD remember it? [y] Did it not come into his mind? [22] The LORD could no longer bear your evil doings and the abominations which you committed; therefore your land has become a desolation and a waste and a curse, without inhabitant, as it is this day. [23] It is because you burned incense, and because you sinned against the LORD and did not obey the voice of the LORD or walk in his law and in his statutes and in his testimonies, that this evil has befallen you, as at this day."

[24] Jeremiah said to all the people and all the women, "Hear the word of the LORD, all you of Judah who are in the land of Egypt, [25] Thus says the LORD of hosts, the God of Israel: You and your wives have declared with your mouths, and have fulfilled it with your hands, saying, 'We will surely perform our vows that we have made, to burn incense to the queen of heaven and to pour out libations to her.' Then con-

---

[x] Compare Syr: Heb lacks *And the women said*
[y] Syr: Heb *them*

firm your vows and perform your vows! <sup>26</sup> Therefore hear the word of the LORD, all you of Judah who dwell in the land of Egypt: Behold, I have sworn by my great name, says the LORD, that my name shall no more be invoked by the mouth of any man of Judah in all the land of Egypt, saying, 'As the LORD God lives.' <sup>27</sup> Behold, I am watching over them for evil and not for good; all the men of Judah who are in the land of Egypt shall be consumed by the sword and by famine, until there is an end of them. <sup>28</sup> And those who escape the sword shall return from the land of Egypt to the land of Judah, few in number; and all the remnant of Judah, who came to the land of Egypt to live, shall know whose word will stand, mine or theirs. <sup>29</sup> This shall be the sign to you, says the LORD, that I will punish you in this place, in order that you may know that my words will surely stand against you for evil: <sup>30</sup> Thus says the LORD, Behold, I will give Pharaoh Hophra king of Egypt into the hand of his enemies and into the hand of those who seek his life, as I gave Zedeki'ah king of Judah into the hand of Nebuchadrez'zar king of Babylon, who was his enemy and sought his life."

1-14 By the time this final oracle of Jeremiah was delivered, there were at least four different colonies of Jews in Egypt. Migdol was probably near Tahpanhes in northeast Egypt, Memphis was the capital city, and Pathros was in upper Egypt. Jeremiah's message is in the form of a long prose discourse. He begins by reminding the people of why and how God brought His judgment down on the cities of Judah and Jerusalem. This precedent ought to have taught them a lesson (vv. 2-7). Alas, the end of the remnant is also impending.

313

The people are still worshiping false gods, placating them with incense. These people have never repented of their past wickedness; they are as stubborn as ever. God's law meant nothing to them (vv. 8-10). God's cruel judgment would therefore fall on the remnant in Egypt. It would suffer all the curses of warfare, famine, pestilence, and the like. None would escape and return to the homeland in Judah. "Except some fugitives," adds the writer. The sense is that they are so few they are hardly worth mentioning. The doom of the remnant in Egypt would be horrible and final.

**15-19** The men and women devotees of the queen of heaven (see 7:18) publicly scorned Jeremiah. They asserted that when their forefathers had been worshiping this fertility goddess, the people had prospered but after the fall of Jerusalem the worship of Yahweh had brought them nothing but anguish. They therefore intended to resume the worship of the queen of heaven with all her distinctive rites. One of these was the practice of offering cakes that bore a replica of her image. The women apparently had an unusually active part in this idolatrous religion. From one perspective the people seemed correct. There were periods of peace and material prosperity under both Manasseh and Jehoiakim when idolatry was practiced.

**20-30** Jeremiah showed that the evidence could be interpreted differently. The fall of Jerusalem and the devastation of Judah was the result of worshiping these false gods. The troubles they experienced were to be recognized as God's punishment for their disobedience, not the proof of how Yahweh would bless them materially (vv. 20-23). Jeremiah therefore employs the last tactic he has at his disposal. He uses a sarcastic exhortation. He encourages the people to make good their vows

314

to the queen of heaven and see what will happen. At the same time he gives God's final oath of doom. God has made a vow to bring the evil of His judgment upon the remnant in Egypt. And those who survive and return to Judah to publicly testify to what happened will be just a handful. Was Baruch one of them? Unfortunately the people had to learn the hard way that in the end God's Word proves itself authentic and true. God even goes further than usual to impress His message here. He provides an additional sign to substantiate His threat against his people. Hophra, the mighty Pharaoh of Egypt, would be taken by his enemies just as Zedekiah had been taken captive by Nebuchadnezzar. History records the murder of Hophra by his rivals in 570 B. C. Jeremiah stayed with his people to the end. He warned them to the end. But even after all his vindicated prophecies and glorious words of hope, he was rejected and alone among the refugees. Truly he was a man of sorrows and acquainted with grief!

# A Brief Personal Note to Baruch

## Jeremiah 45:1-5

[1] The word that Jeremiah the prophet spoke to Baruch the son of Neri'ah, when he wrote these words in a book at the dictation of Jeremiah, in the fourth year of Jehoi'akim the son of Josi'ah, king of Judah: [2] "Thus says the LORD, the God of Israel, to you, O Baruch: [3] You said, 'Woe is me! for the LORD has added sorrow to my pain; I am weary with my groaning, and I find no rest.' [4] Thus shall you say to him, Thus says the LORD: Behold, what I have built I am breaking down, and what I have planted I am plucking up – that is, the whole land. [5] And do you seek great things for yourself? Seek them not; for, behold, I am bringing evil upon all flesh, says the LORD; but I will give you your life as a prize of war in all places to which you may go."

Chapter 45 is addressed by Jeremiah to the scribe Baruch, who no doubt recorded much of the biographical material from Ch. 34 to Ch. 44. At the end of this collection he places, as it were, his signature in this note. In short, it says that by the grace of God I, too, survived the judgment on Jerusalem and Judah. The situation that gave rise to the message of this post-script is to be found in the critical fourth year of Jehoiakim, when Jeremiah dictated a scroll to be read to the crowd at a festival (see Ch. 36). Because of the circumstances, Baruch was chosen to read the scroll in public. That was his big day. He was no longer just a scribe for Jeremiah. But for some unstated reason Baruch met with nothing but trouble, and he felt sorry for himself. Jeremiah, who had been through similar trials, brought the Word of God home to him. Why should you feel anguish? Think of the suffering of God over the destructive punishment He is bringing upon His people. In a crisis like that, Baruch's personal ambitions had to be suppressed. Further, he ought to be thankful that despite the terrible vengeance about to be imposed on God's people, his life would be spared. His life would be a "prize of war" (cf. 21:9), like part of the booty that was rescued from the ruins. He survived by the grace of God. And this personal note of thanks he adds at the end of his work.

317

# The Oracles Concerning the Nations

Jeremiah 46–51

## CONCERNING EGYPT AT CARCHEMISH    46:1-12

¹ The word of the LORD which came to Jeremiah the prophet concerning the nations.

² About Egypt. Concerning the army of Pharaoh Neco, king of Egypt, which was by the river Eu-phra'tes at Car'chemish and which Nebuchadrez'zar king of Babylon defeated in the fourth year of Jehoi'akim the son of Josi'ah, king of Judah:

³ "Prepare buckler and shield,
   and advance for battle!
⁴ Harness the horses;
   mount, O horsemen!
 Take your stations with your helmets,
   polish your spears,
   put on your coats of mail!
⁵ Why have I seen it?
 They are dismayed
   and have turned backward.
 Their warriors are beaten down,
   and have fled in haste;

they look not back—
  terror on every side!

says the LORD.

⁶ The swift cannot flee away,
  nor the warrior escape;
in the north by the river Eu-phra'tes
  they have stumbled and fallen.

⁷ "Who is this, rising like the Nile,
  like rivers whose waters surge?
⁸ Egypt rises like the Nile,
  like rivers whose waters surge.
He said, I will rise, I will cover the earth,
  I will destroy cities and their inhabitants.
⁹ Advance, O horses,
  and rage, O chariots!
Let the warriors go forth:
  men of Ethiopia and Put who handle the shield,
  men of Lud, skilled in handling the bow.
¹⁰ That day is the day of the Lord GOD of hosts,
  a day of vengeance,
  to avenge himself on his foes.
The sword shall devour and be sated,
  and drink its fill of their blood.
For the Lord GOD of hosts holds a sacrifice
  in the north country by the river Eu-phra'tes.
¹¹ Go up to Gilead, and take balm,
  O virgin daughter of Egypt!
In vain you have used many medicines;
  there is no healing for you.
¹² The nations have heard of your shame,
  and the earth is full of your cry;
for warrior has stumbled against warrior;
  they have both fallen together."

319

In 605 B. C. Pharaoh Neco of Egypt was decisively beaten by King Nebuchadnezzar of Babylon at Carchemish on the River Euphrates. The greatest threat to the encroaching Babylonian Empire was thereby removed. For Judah this event had a twofold significance. It represented Yahweh's personal vindication upon Egypt and pointed ahead to Yahweh's retribution upon Judah itself at the hands of Babylon, the enemy from the north. The oracles of 46:3-12 are concerned primarily with the former aspect. In 609 B. C. Neco planned an earlier onslaught on the forces of Babylon. En route he was confronted by the army of Josiah, a hero king of Judah (cf. 2 Kings 23:25), who was killed in the course of the battle. For this act and all preceding acts of violence against the people of God, the defeat of Egypt was interpreted as a day of the Lord, a day of vengeance. It was a day for the sacrifice of Judah's foes that God Himself had planned and celebrated. (Cf. Zeph. 1:7)

The oracles begin with a vivid description of the battle. The infantry and cavalry are summoned to prepare for attack (vv. 3-4). In the next instant the army is stricken with panic. There is "terror on every side," and the army cannot escape from the ominous north (vv. 5-6; cf. 6:22-25). To heighten the ignominy of Egypt's collapse, the poet next revives the presumptuous boasts of the mighty Pharaoh whose army had once surged forward like the Nile in flood. "I will cover the earth," he cries, echoing the attitude of his predecessor who had once tried to cross the Red Sea in pursuit of Israel (vv. 7-9; cf. Ex. 15:9-10). In the last analysis the reason for Egypt's defeat was the plan and intervention of Yahweh, the God of Israel. He had picked a day for Egypt's downfall. And this was that day (v. 10). The poem closes with a victory satire against the fallen foe. There was no cure for Egypt's wounds, and all the world knew it. Even medicinal balsam from Gilead would prove futile. (Vv. 11-12; cf. 8:22)

## CONCERNING EGYPT'S HUMILIATION
## BEFORE NEBUCHADNEZZAR                    46:13-28

¹³ The word which the LORD spoke to Jeremiah the prophet about the coming of Nebuchadrez'zar king of Babylon to smite the land of Egypt:
¹⁴ "Declare in Egypt, and proclaim in Migdol;
    proclaim in Memphis and Tah'panhes;
Say, 'Stand ready and be prepared,
    for the sword shall devour round about you.'
¹⁵ Why has Apis fled? ᶻ
    Why did not your bull stand?
    Because the LORD thrust him down.
¹⁶ Your multitude stumbled ᵃ and fell,
    and they said one to another,
'Arise, and let us go back to our own people
    and to the land of our birth,
    because of the sword of the oppressor.'
¹⁷ Call the name of Pharaoh, king of Egypt,
    'Noisy one who lets the hour go by.'

¹⁸ "As I live, says the King,
    whose name is the LORD of hosts,
like Tabor among the mountains,
    and like Carmel by the sea, shall one come.
¹⁹ Prepare yourselves baggage for exile,
    O inhabitants of Egypt!

---

ᶻ Gk: Heb *Why was it swept away*
ᵃ Gk: Heb *He made many stumble*

For Memphis shall become a waste,
a ruin, without inhabitant.
20 "A beautiful heifer is Egypt,
but a gadfly from the north has come upon her.
21 Even her hired soldiers in her midst
are like fatted calves;
yea, they have turned and fled together,
they did not stand;
for the day of their calamity has come upon them,
the time of their punishment.

22 "She makes a sound like a serpent gliding away;
for her enemies march in force,
and come against her with axes,
like those who fell trees.
23 They shall cut down her forest,

says the LORD,

though it is impenetrable,
because they are more numerous than locusts;
they are without number.
24 The daughter of Egypt shall be put to shame,
she shall be delivered into the hand of a people
from the north."

25 The LORD of hosts, the God of Israel, said:
"Behold, I am bringing punishment upon Amon of
Thebes, and Pharaoh, and Egypt and her gods and
her kings, upon Pharaoh and those who trust in him.
26 I will deliver them into the hand of those who seek
their life, into the hand of Nebuchadrez'zar king of
Babylon and his officers. Afterward Egypt shall be
inhabited as in the days of old, says the LORD.

27 "But fear not, O Jacob my servant,
nor be dismayed, O Israel;

for lo, I will save you from afar,
and your offspring from the land of their captivity.
Jacob shall return and have quiet and ease,
and none shall make him afraid.
²⁸ Fear not, O Jacob my servant,
says the LORD,
for I am with you.
I will make a full end of all the nations
to which I have driven you,
but of you I will not make a full end.
I will chasten you in just measure,
and I will by no means leave you unpunished."

Egypt, the traditional foe of God's people, is the unifying theme of the various oracles in Ch. 46. The defeat of Egypt at Carchemish in 605 B. C made Nebuchadnezzar supreme in the Near East (46:2). His ultimate invasion of Egypt in 568 B. C. was delayed but not unexpected. The oracles of Jer. 46:13-24 and 25-26 are apparently related to this invasion. The details of Jeremiah's extradition to Egypt and his activities there are recorded in Chs. 42 – 44.

13-24 The satire against Egypt in 46:13-24 is composed of a series of mocking summons to prepare for destruction (v. 14) or exile (v. 19) and of vivid portraits depicting Egypt's disgrace. The northern cities of Egypt are warned to prepare for their fate. This warning is colored by the taunting questions which follow. "Why has Apis fled?" "Why did your bull not stand?" Apis, the mighty bull-god of Egypt, had been rendered ineffective by Yahweh at Carchemish. Now Egypt's downfall could not be averted. Pharaoh had missed his opportunity and deserved the ignominious title, "The loud-

323

mouth who let his chances slip" (v. 17.). Because Egypt's fate was sealed, the great and glorious land of Egypt, like a beautiful heifer, would be humiliated by Nebuchadnezzar, even though he was nothing but a little gadfly in the hands of Yahweh. Yahweh had set the day of doom for Egypt. Her degradation was but a matter of time. On that day her professional soldiers would panic like domestic animals, and she would act like an accursed snake fleeing before an army of irate woodcutters. Egypt's fate would be truly an object of international scorn. The enemy from the north would claim another victim. (Vv. 20-24)

25-28 Appended to this colorful taunt is a brief prose announcement of the same event. Nebuchadnezzar is the agent of Yahweh's punitive action against Egypt and all her gods (cf. 43:8-13). At the same time Yahweh is Lord over Egypt's destiny and promises a new age of prosperity and hope even for this idolatrous nation (vv. 25-26). The people of God who suffered punishment and exile at the hand of Nebuchadnezzar in Egypt as well as in Babylon could take courage from the oracle of 30:10-11, which is repeated in this new context (vv. 27-28). Israel had to be punished, but as God's chosen servant (cf. Is. 44:21-22) it could be assured now of an ultimate return to the comfort of Canaan, irrespective of where its people had been exiled.

## CONCERNING THE PHILISTINES 47:1-7

¹ The word of the LORD that came to Jeremiah the prophet concerning the Philistines, before Pharaoh smote Gaza.
² "Thus says the LORD:
Behold, waters are rising out of the north,

and shall become an overflowing torrent;
   they shall overflow the land and all that fills it,
     the city and those who dwell in it.
Men shall cry out,
   and every inhabitant of the land shall wail.
3 At the noise of the stamping of the hoofs of his
     stallions,
   at the rushing of his chariots, at the rumbling of
     their wheels,
the fathers look not back to their children,
   so feeble are their hands,
4 because of the day that is coming to destroy
   all the Philistines,
to cut off from Tyre and Sidon
   every helper that remains.
For the LORD is destroying the Philistines,
   the remnant of the coastland of Caphtor.
5 Baldness has come upon Gaza,
   Ash'kelon has perished.
O remnant of the Anakim,[b]
   how long will you gash yourselves?
6 Ah, sword of the LORD!
   How long till you are quiet?
Put yourself into your scabbard,
   rest and be still!
7 How can it [c] be quiet,
   when the LORD has given it a charge?
Against Ash'kelon and against the seashore
   he has appointed it."

   [b] Gk: Heb *their valley*   [c] Gk Vg: Heb *you*

Jeremiah's message of judgment against the Philistines is as colorful and uncompromising as those of his predecessors (Amos 1:6-8; Is. 14:28-31; Zeph. 2:4-7).

325

This perennial foe of Israel is described as originating from Caphtor (Amos 9:7), which is probably Crete. The superscription (v. 1) relates the downfall of Gaza, one of the major Philistine cities, to the attack of an Egyptian Pharaoh. Such an attack may have occurred when Pharaoh Neco returned from the battle of Megiddo in 609 B. C. or the battle of Carchemish in 605 B. C. In either case his normal return route to Egypt would have been along the coastal plain of Palestine where the Philistine cities were located. Other scholars argue that the invasions of Nebuchadnezzar are being described inasmuch as Babylon is usually the enemy from the north (v. 2) and the agent of Yahweh's judgment (v. 4) in Jeremiah.

The onslaught of the enemy is depicted as an overpowering flood that inundates the entire land and leaves the inhabitants helpless. The very sound of the onrushing chariotry demoralizes the people to such an extent that they cannot even muster enough courage to help their own abandoned children. Why this abnormal terror? Because this was Yahweh's day of retribution upon the entire seacoast. Tyre and Sidon to the north would experience a similar agony (vv. 1-4). The rites of mourning performed by the Philistine cities would prove futile. Their cries of anguish addressed to Yahweh's sword of judgment are answered with an unrelenting message of hopelessness. Their fate is sealed by order of Yahweh. (Vv. 5-7)

CONCERNING MOAB                                    48:1-47

<sup>1</sup> Concerning Moab.
Thus says the **LORD** of hosts, the God of Israel:
"Woe to Nebo, for it is laid waste!

Kiriatha'im is put to shame, it is taken;
the fortress is put to shame and broken down;
2     the renown of Moab is no more.
In Heshbon they planned evil against her:
'Come, let us cut her off from being a nation!'
You also, O Madmen, shall be brought to silence;
the sword shall pursue you.

3 Hark! a cry from Horona'im,
'Desolation and great destruction!'
4 Moab is destroyed;
a cry is heard as far as Zo'ar.$^d$
5 For at the ascent of Luhith
they go up weeping; $^e$
for at the descent of Horona'im
they have heard the cry $^f$ of destruction.
6 Flee! Save yourselves!
Be like a wild ass $^g$ in the desert!
7 For, because you trusted in your strongholds $^h$ and
your treasures,
you also shall be taken;
and Chemosh shall go forth into exile,
with his priests and his princes.
8 The destroyer shall come upon every city,
and no city shall escape;
the valley shall perish,
and the plain shall be destroyed,
as the LORD has spoken.

9 "Give wings to Moab,
for she would fly away;

$^d$ Gk: Heb *her little ones*
$^e$ Cn: Heb *weeping goes up with weeping*
$^f$ Gk Compare Is 15. 5: Heb *the distress of the cry*
$^g$ Gk Aquila: Heb *like Aroer*   $^h$ Gk: Heb *works*

327

her cities shall become a desolation,
    with no inhabitant in them.

[10] "Cursed is he who does the work of the LORD with slackness; and cursed is he who keeps back his sword from bloodshed.

[11] "Moab has been at ease from his youth
    and has settled on his lees;
he has not been emptied from vessel to vessel,
    nor has he gone into exile;
so his taste remains in him,
    and his scent is not changed.

[12] "Therefore, behold, the days are coming, says the LORD, when I shall send to him tilters who will tilt him, and empty his vessels, and break his [i] jars in pieces. [13] Then Moab shall be ashamed of Chemosh, as the house of Israel was ashamed of Bethel, their confidence.

[14] "How do you say, 'We are heroes
    and mighty men of war'?
[15] The destroyer of Moab and his cities has come up,
    and the choicest of his young men have gone down
        to slaughter,
    says the King, whose name is the LORD of hosts.
[16] The calamity of Moab is near at hand
    and his affliction hastens apace.
[17] Bemoan him, all you who are round about him,
    and all who know his name;
say, 'How the mighty scepter is broken,
    the glorious staff.'

[18] "Come down from your glory,
    and sit on the parched ground,

    [i] Gk Aquila: Heb *their*

O inhabitant of Dibon!
For the destroyer of Moab has come up against you;
  he has destroyed your strongholds.
¹⁹ Stand by the way and watch,
  O inhabitant of Aro'er!
Ask him who flees and her who escapes;
  say, 'What has happened?'
²⁰ Moab is put to shame, for it is broken;
  wail and cry!
Tell it by the Arnon,
  that Moab is laid waste.

²¹ "Judgment has come upon the tableland, upon Holon, and Jahzah, and Meph'a-ath, ²² and Dibon, and Nebo, and Beth-diblatha'im, ²³ and Kiriatha'im, and Beth-ga'mul, and Beth-me'on, ²⁴ and Ker'i-oth, and Bozrah, and all the cities of the land of Moab, far and near. ²⁵ The horn of Moab is cut off, and his arm is broken, says the LORD.

²⁶ "Make him drunk, because he magnified himself against the LORD; so that Moab shall wallow in his vomit, and he too shall be held in derision. ²⁷ Was not Israel a derision to you? Was he found among thieves, that whenever you spoke of him you wagged your head?

²⁸ "Leave the cities, and dwell in the rock,
  O inhabitants of Moab!
Be like the dove that nests
  in the sides of the mouth of a gorge.
²⁹ We have heard of the pride of Moab—
  he is very proud—
of his loftiness, his pride, and his arrogance,
  and the haughtiness of his heart.
³⁰ I know his insolence, says the LORD;

  his boasts are false,
  his deeds are false.
³¹ Therefore I wail for Moab;
  I cry out for all Moab;
  for the men of Kir-he'res I mourn.
³² More than for Jazer I weep for you,
  O vine of Sibmah!
 Your branches passed over the sea,
  reached as far as Jazer;ʲ
 upon your summer fruits and your vintage
  the destroyer has fallen.
³³ Gladness and joy have been taken away
  from the fruitful land of Moab;
 I have made the wine cease from the wine presses;
  no one treads them with shouts of joy;
  the shouting is not the shout of joy.

³⁴ "Heshbon and Ele-a'leh cry out;ᵏ as far as Jahaz they utter their voice, from Zo'ar to Horona'im and Eg'lath-shelish'iyah. For the waters of Nimrim also have become desolate. ³⁵ And I will bring to an end in Moab, says the LORD, him who offers sacrifice in the high place and burns incense to his god. ³⁶ Therefore my heart moans for Moab like a flute, and my heart moans like a flute for the men of Kir-he'res; therefore the riches they gained have perished.

³⁷ "For every head is shaved and every beard cut off; upon all the hands are gashes, and on the loins is sackcloth. ³⁸ On all the housetops of Moab and in the squares there is nothing but lamentation; for I have broken Moab like a vessel for which no one cares, says the LORD. ³⁹ How it is broken! How they

ʲ Cn: Heb *the sea of Jazer*
ᵏ Cn: Heb *From the cry of Heshbon to Elealeh*

wail! How Moab has turned his back in shame! So
Moab has become a derision and a horror to all that
are round about him."

40 For thus says the LORD:
  "Behold, one shall fly swiftly like an eagle,
    and spread his wings against Moab;
41 the cities shall be taken
    and the strongholds seized.
  The heart of the warriors of Moab shall be in that
      day
    like the heart of a woman in her pangs;
42 Moab shall be destroyed and be no longer a people,
    because he magnified himself against the LORD.
43 Terror, pit, and snare
    are before you, O inhabitant of Moab!
                                        says the LORD.

44 He who flees from the terror
    shall fall into the pit,
  and he who climbs out of the pit
    shall be caught in the snare.
  For I will bring these things ' upon Moab
    in the year of their punishment,
                                        says the LORD.


45 "In the shadow of Heshbon
    fugitives stop without strength;
  for a fire has gone forth from Heshbon,
    a flame from the house of Sihon;
  it has destroyed the forehead of Moab,
    the crown of the sons of tumult.
46 Woe to you, O Moab!
    The people of Chemosh is undone;

  ' Gk Syr: Heb to her

331

for your sons have been taken captive,
and your daughters into captivity.
⁴⁷ Yet I will restore the fortunes of Moab
in the latter days, says the LORD."
Thus far is the judgment on Moab.

Moab was another of Israel's traditional adversaries.
The history of the conflict between Israel and Moab
precedes the conquests of Joshua. Allusions to Moab
are scattered throughout the Old Testament (see, for
example, Amos 2:1-3; Ezek. 25:8-11). Jeremiah 48, however, has the most extensive collection of oracles and
messages relating to Moab. The origin and date of these
messages are quite diverse. Some sections, it would
seem, are dependent on or taken from other Biblical
works (compare v. 5 with Is. 15:5, vv. 43-44 with Is. 24:
17-18, vv. 45-46 with Num. 21:28-29, and vv. 29-39 with
sections of Is. 15 – 16). During the lifetime of Jeremiah
the Moabites had joined forces with the marauding
hordes sent by Nebuchadnezzar to subdue Jehoiakim
in 602 B. C. (2 Kings 24:2; compare the note on 12:7-13).
On another occasion Moabite emissaries had visited
Jerusalem to discuss plans of revolt against Babylon
(Jer. 27:1-11) relatively early in the reign of Zedekiah.

1-10 The opening oracle is a description of an anonymous "destroyer" invading one Moabite city after
another. With monotonous regularity cries of hopeless
despair rise from each of these cities, until the Moabite
god Chemosh has been taken into exile along with the
Moabite leaders. Moab's trust had been completely
misplaced. If Moab could fly, she might escape! But a
curse lay heavily upon the destroyer to complete his
task of devastating Moab so that the punitive work of
Yahweh could be satisfactorily concluded.

**11-13** Moab's wine was rich and her lot a fortunate one. Like quality wine which is left to settle undisturbed on its "lees" (sediment), Moab had retained its flavor and aroma. Moab's life was still rich and full. But Yahweh would soon change all that and send His workmen to upset Moab. She would be emptied and broken like a wine flagon. Her misplaced confidence in Chemosh, her god (cf. 1 Kings 11:7, 33), would be as evident as Israel's distorted attitude toward worship in the shattered shrine at Bethel, where the calf of Jeroboam once stood (1 Kings 12:28-29; Amos 5:5; 7:10-17). Moab would soon be demolished.

**14-28** Moab cannot rest on her laurels as a mighty nation of warriors. Yahweh, the King of a greater host, is about to send a mightier force to effect Moab's downfall (vv. 14-16). It is fitting, therefore, that Moab's neighbors mourn the passing of this great kingdom (v. 17) and that the inhabitants of Moab in the cities of Dibon and Aroer and along the Arnon river humble themselves and promote a nationwide lament when Yahweh sends His "destroyer" (vv. 18-20). For all the cities of Moab are involved in Yahweh's plan to break the "horn," that is, the might of Moab (vv. 21-25). Moab will become drunk, not with her own rich wines, but with the cup of Yahweh's wrath (cf. 25:27-29), which leads to vomiting and a disgusting state of shame. By proudly exalting herself against Yahweh and by sneering at Israel, His people, when they were disgraced, Moab deserves the fate that awaits her. The survivors of Moab have only one option left: to flee to some desolate mountain cave. (Vv. 26-28)

**29-33** Pride is frequently condemned by the prophets as an intolerable attitude before God (cf. Is. 2:12-19). National pride or arrogance seems to be related to treacherous political conduct and inhumane actions. The author of this passage employs the message and wording of Is. 16:6-10 to characterize Moab's haughtiness and subsequent downfall. The fall is so great that even Yahweh is described as joining the chorus of wailing. Moab's destruction means the end of her vineyards and her wine, the very thing that symbolized and fostered her vitality and joy (see the comment on vv. 11-13 above). The agent of Moab's doom is once again "the destroyer" of vv. 8, 15, and 18 above. By introducing this figure, the author interprets the oracle of Is. 16:6-10 to meet a new situation.

**34-39** In the following prose oracle v. 34 stems from Is. 15:4-6; v. 36 from Is. 16:11; and vv. 37-38 from Is. 15:2-3. These verses depict the cries of anguish rising from desolated places in Moab known to the listeners. The Moabites employ every rite of repentance they know to evoke the response of their god. Yahweh's own heart is touched by the pathetic scene (v. 36), even though He was the one who shattered Moab as a man would smash an undesirable pot (v. 38). The revolting shame of Moab can hardly be imagined by her friends (v. 39). In addition to these secondary materials, the prophet adds one pungent remark in v. 35. Yahweh's intervention will also mean the removal of all the objectionable sacrifices to Chemosh, the pagan deity of Moab. When Yahweh punishes, He purges as well!

**40-44** In summarizing the character of the "destroyer" and the futility of flight from his onslaughts, the prophet again utilizes materials from several sources. Verses 40 and 41b are almost the same as Jer. 49:22, vv. 43-44 are taken from Is. 24:17-18, and vv. 45-46 from Num. 21:28-29; 24:17. The enemy is portrayed as an eagle that swoops down and carries off the cities of Moab as prey. The warriors of Moab are petrified with pain, like a woman in childbirth (cf. 4:31). The cause of Moab's downfall is again characterized as pride (see vv. 26, 29). The fugitives are trapped wherever they flee. For Moab's calamitous end is a planned day of the Lord, her "year of retribution" (cf. 46:10). Such a disaster is a warning to every nation to beware of inordinate pride.

**45-47** Heshbon was the capital of King Sihon, who was defeated by the Israelites under Moses. The destruction of Heshbon was so renowned that the ancient ballad singers had recalled it in song (Num. 21:21-30). Now history was repeating itself. A similar humiliation had already been determined by Yahweh. It was therefore useless for Moabites to flee north to Heshbon. Captivity (in Babylon?) awaited all the worshipers of Chemosh, the god of Moab. Yahweh had spoken His irreversible "woe" upon Moab. Yet despite this message of total judgment, a new era of prosperity would one day be granted by Yahweh Himself. Such is the inexplicable generosity of the grace of God.

## CONCERNING AMMON                    49:1-6

¹ Concerning the Ammonites. Thus says the
LORD:
  "Has Israel no sons?
   Has he no heir?
  Why then has Milcom dispossessed Gad,
    and his people settled in its cities?
² Therefore, behold, the days are coming,
    says the LORD,
  when I will cause the battle cry to be heard
    against Rabbah of the Ammonites;
  it shall become a desolate mound,
    and its villages shall be burned with fire;

335

then Israel shall dispossess those who dispossessed
   him,
says the **LORD**.

3 "Wail, O Heshbon, for Ai is laid waste!
   Cry, O daughters of Rabbah!
Gird yourselves with sackcloth,
   lament, and run to and fro among the hedges!
For Milcom shall go into exile,
   with his priests and his princes.
4 Why do you boast of your valleys,[m]
   O faithless daughter,
who trusted in her treasures, saying,
   'Who will come against me?'
5 Behold, I will bring terror upon you,
   says the Lord God of hosts,
   from all who are round about you,
and you shall be driven out, every man straight before him,
   with none to gather the fugitives.
6 But afterward I will restore the fortunes of the
Ammonites, says the **LORD**."

[m] Heb *valleys, your valley flows*

The transgression of Ammon is defined as "unlaw-
ful" occupation of Israelite territory. Border disputes
between Israel and Ammon had a long history (cf. Judg.
11:24-27; Amos 1:13-15; and elsewhere). The checkered
course of Israel-Ammon relations was not aided by
Israel's kinship with Ammon (Gen. 19:30-38). During the
campaigns of Tiglath-pileser III, 734–732 B. C., Gilead
(Gad) was conquered and its people deported. Ammon
seized the opportunity to take possession of this area
in the name of her national god Milcom (who is else-

where known as Molech; cf. Lev. 18:21). This reprehensible action is given as the major reason for Ammon's later misfortunes (v. 1). Yahweh therefore announces a day when Ammon would be punished and God's people would repossess their rightful land. In the process Rabbah, the modern city of Amman and the ancient capital of Ammon, will become a "desolate mound" or tell. Both Rabbah and Heshbon, which was apparently captured from the Moabites for a period (cf. 48:45), are urged to render a fitting lament. For Ammon's exile means the exile of the cherished idol of Milcom. Her fertile valleys offer no guarantee of protection against the terror ordained by Yahweh. There will be no escape. Even this announcement, however, does not preclude the possibility of a later restoration of Ammon. The agent of Yahweh's punishment is presumably Babylon. But whether the destructive action of Babylon preceded or followed the treacherous move of the Ammonites in Jer. 40:14 is not clear.

## CONCERNING EDOM                    49:7-22

⁷ Concerning Edom.
  Thus says the LORD of hosts:
  "Is wisdom no more in Teman?
    Has counsel perished from the prudent?
    Has their wisdom vanished?
⁸ Flee, turn back, dwell in the depths,
    O inhabitants of Dedan!
  For I will bring the calamity of Esau upon him,
    the time when I punish him.
⁹ If grape-gatherers came to you,
    would they not leave gleanings?
  If thieves came by night,

would they not destroy only enough for themselves?
<sup>10</sup> But I have stripped Esau bare,
I have uncovered his hiding places,
and he is not able to conceal himself.
His children are destroyed, and his brothers,
and his neighbors; and he is no more.
<sup>11</sup> Leave your fatherless children, I will keep them
alive;
and let your widows trust in me."

<sup>12</sup> For thus says the LORD: "If those who did
not deserve to drink the cup must drink it, will you
go unpunished? You shall not go unpunished, but
you must drink. <sup>13</sup> For I have sworn by myself, says
the LORD, that Bozrah shall become a horror, a taunt,
a waste, and a curse; and all her cities shall be perpetual wastes."
<sup>14</sup> I have heard tidings from the LORD,
and a messenger has been sent among the nations:
"Gather yourselves together and come against her,
and rise up for battle!
<sup>15</sup> For behold, I will make you small among the na-
tions,
despised among men.
<sup>16</sup> The horror you inspire has deceived you,
and the pride of your heart,
you who live in the clefts of the rock,<sup>n</sup>
who hold the height of the hill.
Though you make your nest as high as the eagle's,
I will bring you down from there,
says the LORD.
<sup>17</sup> "Edom shall become a horror; every one who
passes by it will be horrified and will hiss because of

<sup>n</sup> Or *Sela*

all its disasters. ¹⁸ As when Sodom and Gomor'rah and their neighbor cities were overthrown, says the LORD, no man shall dwell there, no man shall sojourn in her. ¹⁹ Behold, like a lion coming up from the jungle of the Jordan against a strong sheepfold, I will suddenly make them ᵒ run away from her; and I will appoint over her whomever I choose. For who is like me? Who will summon me? What shepherd can stand before me? ²⁰ Therefore hear the plan which the LORD has made against Edom and the purposes which he has formed against the inhabitants of Teman: Even the little ones of the flock shall be dragged away; surely their fold shall be appalled at their fate. ²¹ At the sound of their fall the earth shall tremble; the sound of their cry shall be heard at the Red Sea. ²² Behold, one shall mount up and fly swiftly like an eagle, and spread his wings against Bozrah, and the heart of the warriors of Edom shall be in that day like the heart of a woman in her pangs."

ᵒ Gk Syr: Heb *him*

The Israelites traced the ancestry of the Edomites to Esau, the twin brother of Jacob (Gen. 25:25-26). The animosity of Jacob and Esau persisted for centuries between the Israelites and Edomites (see Num. 20:14-21; 2 Kings 8:20-22; and often). One of the most despicable acts of the Edomites was their seizure of Israelite territory after the fall of Jerusalem in 587 B. C. (see Obad. 11-14; Ezek. 35:1-15). Edom was a perennial foe of Israel, and numerous oracles are directed against her (even as late as Mal. 1:2-4). The precise occasion for the oracles of this chapter, however, is not made explicit. The Edomites were not ravaged by the Babylonian army, despite their probable part in the coalition of 2

Kings 24:2 against Babylon. The territory of Edom was finally overrun by the Nabatean Arabs late in the 5th century (cf. Mal.1:2-4). There are strong linguistic similarities between vv. 9-10 of this chapter and Obad. 5-6, as well as between vv. 14-16 and Obad. 1-4. The degree of literary dependency, however, is uncertain.

**7-13** Wise men were an important segment of most ancient Near Eastern societies. Jeremiah is amazed that the wise men in Teman, a city of Edom, cannot foresee the impending catastrophe by which Yahweh will strip Edom of all its inhabitants. It is normal for grape gatherers to leave a few grapes. Yahweh's action will be quite abnormal; even the children will not escape (cf. 6:9). Any helpless survivors are completely at His mercy as the people try to flee. Like Moab (48:26) and the other nations (25:17-26), Edom must drink the cup of wrath prepared by Yahweh. Yahweh's personal oath makes this cruel punishment unavoidable. Bozrah, the capital of Edom, will experience this divine fury in full measure.

**14-22** Despite Edom's terrifying pride and her relatively inaccessible cities and fortresses, Yahweh will tear her down from her high nest. He has even summoned warriors from many nations to execute His plan of belittling and humiliating Edom (vv. 14-16). Her disgrace will equal that of Sodom and Gomorrah (cf. 19:8; 50:40). Yahweh the Judge is depicted both as a lion (cf. 4:7) destroying the sheepfold of Edom and as the master who chooses shepherds over the sheep of Edom (cf. Zech. 11). For Yahweh controls the history of Edom also, and His plans call for breaking up the fold of Edom and dragging off the lambs as prey. On that day the earth will tremble in sympathy, and people afar off will be amazed. And one nation, like a carrion eagle (cf. 48:40), will circle above the broken sheepfold of Edom to seek the terrified and homeless survivors until all are destroyed. (Vv. 17-22)

## CONCERNING DAMASCUS         49:23-27

**23 Concerning Damascus.**
   **"Hamath and Arpad are confounded,**
      **for they have heard evil tidings;**
   **they melt in fear, they are troubled like the sea** [p]
      **which cannot be quiet.**
**24 Damascus has become feeble, she turned to flee,**
      **and panic seized her;**
   **anguish and sorrows have taken hold of her,**
      **as of a woman in travail.**
**25 How the famous city is forsaken,** [q] **the joyful city!** [r]
**26 Therefore her young men shall fall in her squares,**
      **and all her soldiers shall be destroyed in that day,**
                    **says the LORD of hosts.**
**27 And I will kindle a fire in the wall of Damascus,**
      **and it shall devour the stronghold of Ben-ha'-dad."**

[p] Cn: Heb *there is trouble in the sea*    [q] Vg: Heb *not forsaken*
[r] Syr Vg Tg: Heb *city of my joy*

After the subjugation of Damascus, the capital of Syria, by the Assyrians in the 8th century, that "famous city" played little part in the course of Israel's history. She is not condemned to drink of the cup of wrath in 25:17-26 but seems to be added here for the sake of completion in pronouncing judgment on all of Judah's traditional foes. The ideas of the text are quite general. The Syrian cities of Hamath and Arpad will be overwhelmed with fear, the warriors of Damascus will fall,

341

and its fortifications will be demolished. Benhadad is a throne name used by several kings of Damascus (1 Kings 15:18; 2 Kings 13:24). The wording of v. 26 is taken from 50:30, and that of v. 27 from Amos 1:4.

## CONCERNING KEDAR AND HAZOR    49:28-33

<sup>28</sup> Concerning Kedar and the kingdoms of Hazor which Nebuchadrez'zar king of Babylon smote.
  Thus says the LORD:
  "Rise up, advance against Kedar!
  Destroy the people of the east!
<sup>29</sup> Their tents and their flocks shall be taken,
    their curtains and all their goods;
  their camels shall be borne away from them,
    and men shall cry to them: 'Terror on every side!'
<sup>30</sup> Flee, wander far away, dwell in the depths,
    O inhabitants of Hazor!
                                        says the LORD.
  For Nebuchadrez'zar king of Babylon
    has made a plan against you,
    and formed a purpose against you.

<sup>31</sup> "Rise up, advance against a nation at ease,
    that dwells securely,
                                        says the LORD,
  that has no gates or bars,
    that dwells alone.
<sup>32</sup> Their camels shall become booty,
    their herds of cattle a spoil.
  I will scatter to every wind
    those who cut the corners of their hair,
  and I will bring their calamity
    from every side of them,
                                        says the LORD.

342

³³ Hazor shall become a haunt of jackals,
and everlasting waste;
no man shall dwell there,
no man shall sojourn in her."

Kedar (cf. Gen. 25:13) and Hazor are designations
for a seminomadic people of the Arabian desert and their
territory respectively. They are called "people of the
East" who dwell in tents (v. 29) and possess camels
(v. 32). Hazor is not to be identified with the Palestinian
city of Joshua 11. Nebuchadnezzar, the special agent
of God's purposes, is summoned to campaign against
this tribe and give one of Jeremiah's favorite cries:
"Terror on every side!" (cf. 6:25; 20:3, 10; 46:5). The
people of Hazor, in turn, are urged to flee for safety.
The reason for the punishment of this people is somewhat hazy. Perhaps the words "at ease" and "securely"
in v. 31 are intended to suggest a false confidence in the
freedom of the open desert as their home. Nebuchadnezzar's invasion, however, will mean ample booty
for his army, dispersion of these seminomads, and the
desolation of their homeland (cf. 9:11). Precisely when
Nebuchadnezzar invaded the Arabian desert is not
known. The practice of clipping the hair on the corners
of the forehead was characteristic of certain tribes
(cf. 9:25-26) and considered an objectionable pagan custom by the Israelites. (Lev. 19:27)

CONCERNING ELAM                          49:34-39

³⁴ The word of the LORD that came to Jeremiah
the prophet concerning Elam, in the beginning of the
reign of Zedeki'ah king of Judah.
³⁵ Thus says the LORD of hosts: "Behold, I will

343

break the bow of Elam, the mainstay of their might; [36] and I will bring upon Elam the four winds from the four quarters of heaven; and I will scatter them to all those winds, and there shall be no nation to which those driven out of Elam shall not come. [37] I will terrify Elam before their enemies, and before those who seek their life; I will bring evil upon them, my fierce anger, says the LORD. I will send the sword after them, until I have consumed them; [38] and I will set my throne in Elam, and destroy their king and princes, says the LORD.

[39] "But in the latter days I will restore the fortunes of Elam, says the LORD."

This is the only oracle against the foreign nations that is explicitly dated in the reign of Zedekiah. It was especially during his regime that the people of Judah who had been exiled in 598 B. C. (2 Kings 24:10-14) expected a reversal of Babylon's fortunes and the opportunity to return to Jerusalem (cf. 29:21). Elam was a probable agent of Babylon's downfall in the mind of these men of Judah. Elam's relations with God's people hark back to the expedition of Gen. 14:1. The Elamites seem to have been famous for their archery (Is. 22:6). For Yahweh to "break the bow" of Elam, therefore, means to render her helpless. Like the people of Kedar (v. 32), the Elamites will be scattered in every direction. The catastrophe ("evil") of Elam's military downfall will be obvious evidence of Yahweh's intense wrath against them. Just as Yahweh had once summoned all the nations to set up thrones in Jerusalem to judge God's people (Jer. 1:15-16), in like manner Yahweh Himself will judge Elam and execute the sentence of death. This oracle of Jeremiah was no doubt intended

344

to reinforce the advice given in the letter of Jeremiah (Ch. 29) to settle down for a long stay in captivity. For the Elamites, however, there would be another day of prosperity (compare the additions in 48:47 and 49:6). The devastation of Elam is also reported by Ezekiel. (32:24)

## CONCERNING BABYLON
## AND THE FATE OF GOD'S PEOPLE             50:1-46

[1] The word which the LORD spoke concerning Babylon, concerning the land of the Chalde'ans, by Jeremiah the prophet:

[2] "Declare among the nations and proclaim,
      set up a banner and proclaim,
      conceal it not, and say:
   'Babylon is taken,
      Bel is put to shame,
      Mer'odach is dismayed.
   Her images are put to shame,
      her idols are dismayed.'

[3] "For out of the north a nation has come up against her, which shall make her land a desolation, and none shall dwell in it; both man and beast shall flee away.

[4] "In those days and in that time, says the LORD, the people of Israel and the people of Judah shall come together, weeping as they come; and they shall seek the LORD their God. [5] They shall ask the way to Zion, with faces turned toward it, saying, 'Come, let us join ourselves to the LORD in an everlasting covenant which will never be forgotten.'

[6] "My people have been lost sheep; their shepherds have led them astray, turning them away on

345

the mountains; from mountain to hill they have gone, they have forgotten their fold. ⁷ All who found them have devoured them, and their enemies have said, 'We are not guilty, for they have sinned against the LORD, their true habitation, the LORD, the hope of their fathers.'

⁸ "Flee from the midst of Babylon, and go out of the land of the Chalde′ans, and be as he-goats before the flock. ⁹ For behold, I am stirring up and bringing against Babylon a company of great nations, from the north country; and they shall array themselves against her; from there she shall be taken. Their arrows are like a skilled warrior who does not return empty-handed. ¹⁰ Chalde′a shall be plundered; all who plunder her shall be sated, says the LORD.

¹¹ "Though you rejoice, though you exult,
　　O plunderers of my heritage,
　though you are wanton as a heifer at grass,
　　and neigh like stallions,
¹² your mother shall be utterly shamed,
　　and she who bore you shall be disgraced.
　Lo, she shall be the last of the nations,
　　a wilderness dry and desert.
¹³ Because of the wrath of the LORD she shall not
　　　be inhabited,
　　but shall be an utter desolation;
　every one who passes by Babylon shall be appalled,
　　and hiss because of all her wounds.
¹⁴ Set yourselves in array against Babylon round
　　　about,
　　all you that bend the bow;
　shoot at her, spare no arrows,
　　for she has sinned against the LORD.

346

<sup>15</sup> Raise a shout against her round about,
  she has surrendered;
 her bulwarks have fallen,
  her walls are thrown down.
 For this is the vengeance of the LORD:
  take vengeance on her,
  do to her as she has done.
<sup>16</sup> Cut off from Babylon the sower,
  and the one who handles the sickle in time of
   harvest;
 because of the sword of the oppressor,
  every one shall turn to his own people,
  and every one shall flee to his own land.

<sup>17</sup> "Israel is a hunted sheep driven away by lions. First the king of Assyria devoured him, and now at last Nebuchadrez'zar king of Babylon has gnawed his bones. <sup>18</sup> Therefore, thus says the LORD of hosts, the God of Israel: Behold, I am bringing punishment on the king of Babylon and his land, as I punished the king of Assyria. <sup>19</sup> I will restore Israel to his pasture, and he shall feed on Carmel and in Bashan, and his desire shall be satisfied on the hills of E'phraim and in Gilead. <sup>20</sup> In those days and in that time, says the LORD, iniquity shall be sought in Israel, and there shall be none; and sin in Judah, and none shall be found; for I will pardon those whom I leave as a remnant.

<sup>21</sup> "Go up against the land of Meratha'im, <sup>s</sup>
  and against the inhabitants of Pekod. <sup>t</sup>
 Slay, and utterly destroy after them,
                  says the LORD,
  and do all that I have commanded you.

<sup>s</sup> Or *Double Rebellion*    <sup>t</sup> Or *Punishment*

347

²² The noise of battle is in the land,
  and great destruction!
²³ How the hammer of the whole earth
  is cut down and broken!
  How Babylon has become
  a horror among the nations!
²⁴ I set a snare for you and you were taken, O Babylon,
  and you did not know it;
  you were found and caught,
  because you strove against the LORD.
²⁵ The LORD has opened his armory,
  and brought out the weapons of his wrath,
  for the Lord GOD of hosts has a work to do
  in the land of the Chalde'ans.
²⁶ Come against her from every quarter;
  open her granaries;
  pile her up like heaps of grain, and destroy her
    utterly;
  let nothing be left of her.
²⁷ Slay all her bulls,
  let them go down to the slaughter.
  Woe to them, for their day has come,
  the time of their punishment.


²⁸ "Hark! they flee and escape from the land of Babylon, to declare in Zion the vengeance of the LORD our God, vengeance for his temple.

²⁹ "Summon archers against Babylon, all those who bend the bow. Encamp round about her; let no one escape. Requite her according to her deeds, do to her according to all that she has done; for she has proudly defied the LORD, the Holy One of Israel. ³⁰ Therefore her young men shall fall in her squares,

and all her soldiers shall be destroyed on that day,
says the LORD.

<sup>31</sup> "Behold, I am against you, O proud one,
  says the Lord GOD of hosts;
 for your day has come,
   the time when I will punish you.
<sup>32</sup> The proud one shall stumble and fall,
   with none to raise him up,
 and I will kindle a fire in his cities,
   and it will devour all that is round about him.

<sup>33</sup> "Thus says the LORD of hosts: The people of
Israel are oppressed, and the people of Judah with
them; all who took them captive have held them fast,
they refuse to let them go. <sup>34</sup> Their Redeemer is
strong; the LORD of hosts is his name. He will surely
plead their cause, that he may give rest to the earth,
but unrest to the inhabitants of Babylon.
<sup>35</sup> "A sword upon the Chalde'ans, says the LORD,
   and upon the inhabitants of Babylon,
   and upon her princes and her wise men!
<sup>36</sup> A sword upon the diviners,
   that they may become fools!
 A sword upon her warriors,
   that they may be destroyed!
<sup>37</sup> A sword upon her horses and upon her chariots,
   and upon all the foreign troops in her midst,
   that they may become women!
 A sword upon all her treasures,
   that they may be plundered!
<sup>38</sup> A drought upon her waters,
   that they may be dried up!
 For it is a land of images,
   and they are mad over idols.

39 "Therefore wild beasts shall dwell with hyenas in Babylon, and ostriches shall dwell in her; she shall be peopled no more for ever, nor inhabited for all generations. 40 As when God overthrew Sodom and Gomor'rah and their neighbor cities, says the LORD, so no man shall dwell there, and no son of man shall sojourn in her.

41 "Behold, a people comes from the north;
    a mighty nation and many kings
    are stirring from the farthest parts of the earth.
42 They lay hold of bow and spear;
    they are cruel, and have no mercy.
The sound of them is like the roaring of the sea;
    they ride upon horses,
arrayed as a man for battle
    against you, O daughter of Babylon!

43 "The king of Babylon heard the report of them,
    and his hands fell helpless;
anguish seized him,
    pain as of a woman in travail.

44 "Behold, like a lion coming up from the jungle of the Jordan against a strong sheepfold, I will suddenly make them run away from her; and I will appoint over her whomever I choose. For who is like me? Who will summon me? What shepherd can stand before me? 45 Therefore hear the plan which the LORD has made against Babylon, and the purposes which he has formed against the land of the Chalde'ans: Surely the little ones of their flock shall be dragged away; surely their fold shall be appalled at their fate. 46 At the sound of the capture of Babylon the earth shall tremble, and her cry shall be heard among the nations."

Throughout Jeremiah Babylon is the great world power, the instrument of Yahweh's international plans, the agent of personal retribution upon Israel, and the hero of Yahweh's immediate purposes. A brief portent of Babylon's ultimate judgment is given in 25:26. It is significant that such a large collection of pronouncements against or concerning this great "destroyer," the enemy from the north, should be included in Jeremiah's book. The nation that inflicted Judah's greatest injury would naturally become the object of prolific prophetic condemnation. Some scholars raise the question as to how many of these oracles can be attributed to the pen of Jeremiah. Most of them stem from the exilic period, but some of them seem to be the work of another prophetic hand according to these scholars. The Medes are seen as a formidable threat on the world scene (51:11). The actual fall of Babylon came at the hands of Cyrus, king of Persia in 538, after he had absorbed the Medes into his empire. The materials in general are marked by a strong vindictive spirit and a vehement urgency to return from exile. The defeat of Babylon seems to be imminent rather than in the distant future, as Jeremiah had once said (29:10). These facts suggest to many that one of Jeremiah's disciples may have been responsible for many of the oracles of these chapters. The present sequence of messages is marked by certain repetitions and a lack of topical arrangement. It is perhaps noteworthy that the Septuagint does not attribute these two chapters to Jeremiah as does the Hebrew text but has the general title "The Word of the Lord which He spoke against Babylon."

2-7 The downfall of Babylon is good reason for an international news release. The humiliation of Marduk (sometime addressed as Bel), the chief god of the Baby-

351

lonian empire, is cause for great glee. And the irony of it all is that Babylon, the illustrious "enemy from the north" (4:6; 6:22), will also be deposed by a nation from the north (50:2-3). At the same time the penitent people of both Israel and Judah will return to Yahweh and seek salvation through an eternal covenant with Yahweh in Zion (cf. 31:31-34). The former broken covenant can then be forgotten (50:4-5). In the meantime God's people suffer in exile. Their leaders had followed their own interests and led them astray to become an easy prey for their gloating enemies (cf. 23:1-4), who pointed the finger of guilt directly at God's people (50:6-7). Alas, they had failed to realize that neither the temple of Zion nor Jerusalem nor Canaan offered eternally secure homes; Yahweh alone was Israel's enduring habitation.

**8-10** Instead of being urged to dwell contentedly in exile as previously (29:4-7), the people of God are now bidden to depart aggressively like he-goats taking the lead in a flock. For the Babylonians or Chaldeans will soon be confronted by a mass of mighty nations with skilled marksmen poised for the kill. (Cf. 1:15)

**11-16** Israel, the people of God, was the "heritage" or chosen and precious possession of Yahweh, and any who dared to harm it incurred the "wrath of Yahweh" (see the note on 10:16). In short, Israel was still "holy to the Lord" (2:3). And the Babylonians had not only plundered Israel but had enjoyed doing so. "Their mother," the land of Babylonia itself, would be ashamed of her own. She would soon experience "the vengeance of the Lord" in full measure. Shame, desolation, siege, demolition of property, and abandonment, the very things that "she had done," would be her just deserts. In the last analysis, Babylon, like Israel, "had sinned against the Lord."

352

17-20 Resuming the metaphor of v. 6, the prophet sees a day of retribution upon the king of Babylon for having devoured Israel, the hunted sheep of Yahweh. The punishment of the king of Assyria (by Babylon in 612 B. C.) offers a pertinent precedent for this prediction. The unmotivated grace of Yahweh will thereafter be revealed. Yahweh will dispense free forgiveness and abundant life to the remnant, the chosen survivors of His flock. On that day Israel's restoration will be so complete, so ideal, that no sign of her past guilt and disgrace will be evident.

21-28 Yahweh's new agent of destruction, presumably the nation from the north (vv. 3 and 9), is now commissioned to advance upon Merathaim and Pekod. These names mean "double rebellion" and "punishment," or "visitation," and are apparently veiled allusions to regions of Babylon with similar names. Babylon, which had once been Yahweh's mighty weapon, "the hammer" of the whole earth (cf. 51:20-23), must now be smashed by the new weapons of Yahweh's wrath. Babylon had begun to "strive" against God instead of for Him. Unawares, it had fallen into the trap Yahweh had set. Now, for the inhabitants of "Pekod" there was a "time of punishment," desolation and woe (50:21-27). When that happens, many of the Israelites will view this as just retribution upon Babylon for destroying Zion and the temple of Jerusalem rather than the necessary "work" (v. 25) of Yahweh to execute His plan of reviving Israel. With glee they will shout (v. 28), "vengeance for his temple." In Jer. 7:1-15 and elsewhere the prophet's attitude was somewhat different: "the temple must go," he cried. Verse 28 is missing in the Greek (Septuagint) translation and may be the note of a later scribe.

**29-46** The remaining units of Jer. 50 repeat the same refrain of Babylon's doom. Her oncoming foe stems from the north in battle array (vv. 41-42; cf. vv. 3, 9), to besiege her with archers (v. 29; cf. vv. 9, 14) and destroy all her inhabitants with the sword (vv. 30, 35-37; cf. v. 21). This enemy is the jungle lion destined to execute Yahweh's plan (vv. 44-46; see the comment on 49: 19-22). The king of Babylon will collapse with fear (v. 43), the curse of drought will ensue (v. 38), and the land will become the desolate haunt of wild animals (vv. 39-40). This is a just reward (v. 29; cf. v. 15) for Babylon's proud defiance of Yahweh, the God of Israel (vv. 29, 31-32). For Yahweh is the "Holy One," the strong "Redeemer" who will not tolerate relentless oppression even of those He Himself has delivered into captivity (vv. 29, 33-34). As the Redeemer, Yahweh is the kinsman of Israel, who is concerned with buying back His property, that is, the people of Israel. As the "Holy One" He cannot be treated like any other deity (cf. Is. 5:16; 43:14-15), nor can He be expected to act as man might expect (Hos. 11:8-9). To be the Holy One means to be the Unique One, who reveals Himself as the one living God.

## CONCERNING BABYLON
## AND THE ADVENT OF THE MEDES          51:1-58

[1] Thus says the LORD:
"Behold, I will stir up the spirit of a destroyer
    against Babylon,
    against the inhabitants of Chalde′a; [u]
[2] and I will send to Babylon winnowers,
    and they shall winnow her,
    and they shall empty her land,

[u] Heb Leb-qamai. a cipher for Chaldea

354

when they come against her from every side
  on the day of trouble.
³ Let not the archer bend his bow,
  and let him not stand up in his coat of mail.
Spare not her young men;
  utterly destroy all her host.
⁴ They shall fall down slain in the land of the Chal-
    de'ans,
  and wounded in her streets.
⁵ For Israel and Judah have not been forsaken
  by their God, the LORD of hosts;
but the land of the Chalde'ans ʳ is full of guilt
  against the Holy One of Israel.

⁶ "Flee from the midst of Babylon,
  let every man save his life!
Be not cut off in her punishment,
  for this is the time of the LORD'S vengeance,
  the requital he is rendering her.
⁷ Babylon was a golden cup in the LORD'S hand,
  making all the earth drunken;
the nations drank of her wine,
  therefore the nations went mad.
⁸ Suddenly Babylon has fallen and been broken;
  wail for her!
Take balm for her pain;
  perhaps she may be healed.
⁹ We would have healed Babylon,
  but she was not healed.
Forsake her, and let us go
  each to his own country;
for her judgment has reached up to heaven
  and has been lifted up even to the skies.

ʳ Heb *their land*

355

<sup>10</sup> The LORD has brought forth our vindication;
  come, let us declare in Zion
  the work of the LORD our God.


<sup>11</sup> "Sharpen the arrows!
  Take up the shields!
The LORD has stirred up the spirit of the kings of the Medes, because his purpose concerning Babylon is to destroy it, for that is the vengeance of the LORD, the vengeance for his temple.
<sup>12</sup> Set up a standard against the walls of Babylon;
  make the watch strong;
 set up watchmen;
  prepare the ambushes;
 for the LORD has both planned and done
  what he spoke concerning the inhabitants of
  Babylon.
<sup>13</sup> O you who dwell by many waters,
  rich in treasures,
 your end has come,
  the thread of your life is cut.
<sup>14</sup> The LORD of hosts has sworn by himself:
 Surely I will fill you with men, as many as locusts,
  and they shall raise the shout of victory over you.


<sup>15</sup> "It is he who made the earth by his power,
  who established the world by his wisdom,
 and by his understanding stretched out the heavens.
<sup>16</sup> When he utters his voice there is a tumult of waters
   in the heavens,
  and he makes the mist rise from the ends of the
  earth.
 He makes lightnings for the rain,
  and he brings forth the wind from his storehouses.

17 Every man is stupid and without knowledge;
 every goldsmith is put to shame by his idols;
for his images are false,
 and there is no breath in them.
18 They are worthless, a work of delusion;
 at the time of their punishment they shall perish.
19 Not like these is he who is the portion of Jacob,
 for he is the one who formed all things,
and Israel is the tribe of his inheritance;
 the LORD of hosts is his name.

20 "You are my hammer and weapon of war:
 with you I break nations in pieces;
 with you I destroy kingdoms;
21 with you I break in pieces the horse and his rider;
 with you I break in pieces the chariot and the
  charioteer;
22 with you I break in pieces man and woman;
 with you I break in pieces the old man and the
  youth;
 with you I break in pieces the young man and the
  maiden;
23  with you I break in pieces the shepherd and his
  flock;
 with you I break in pieces the farmer and his team;
 with you I break in pieces governors and commanders.

24 "I will requite Babylon and all the inhabitants
of Chalde'a before your very eyes for all the evil that
they have done in Zion, says the LORD.

25 "Behold, I am against you, O destroying mountain,
           says the LORD,
 which destroys the whole earth;

357

I will stretch out my hand against you,
  and roll you down from the crags,
  and make you a burnt mountain.
<sup>26</sup> No stone shall be taken from you for a corner
  and no stone for a foundation,
but you shall be a perpetual waste,
  says the LORD.


<sup>27</sup> "Set up a standard on the earth,
  blow the trumpet among the nations;
prepare the nations for war against her,
  summon against her the kingdoms,
  Ar'arat, Minni, and Ash'kenaz;
appoint a marshal against her,
  bring up horses like bristling locusts.
<sup>28</sup> Prepare the nations for war against her,
  the kings of the Medes, with their governors and
    deputies,
  and every land under their dominion.
<sup>29</sup> The land trembles and writhes in pain,
  for the LORD'S purposes against Babylon stand,
to make the land of Babylon a desolation,
  without inhabitant.
<sup>30</sup> The warriors of Babylon have ceased fighting,
  they remain in their strongholds;
their strength has failed,
  they have become women;
her dwellings are on fire,
  her bars are broken.
<sup>31</sup> One runner runs to meet another,
  and one messenger to meet another,
to tell the king of Babylon
  that his city is taken on every side;
<sup>32</sup> the fords have been seized,

the bulwarks are burned with fire,
and the soldiers are in panic.
33 For thus says the LORD of hosts, the God of Israel:
The daughter of Babylon is like a threshing floor
at the time when it is trodden;
yet a little while
and the time of her harvest will come."

34 "Nebuchadrez'zar the king of Babylon has devoured
me,
he has crushed me;
he has made me an empty vessel,
he has swallowed me like a monster;
he has filled his belly with my delicacies,
he has rinsed me out.
35 The violence done to me and to my kinsmen be
upon Babylon,"
let the inhabitant of Zion say.
"My blood be upon the inhabitants of Chalde'a,"
let Jerusalem say.
36 Therefore thus says the LORD:
"Behold, I will plead your cause
and take vengeance for you.
I will dry up her sea
and make her fountain dry;
37 and Babylon shall become a heap of ruins,
the haunt of jackals,
a horror and a hissing,
without inhabitant.

38 "They shall roar together like lions;
they shall growl like lions' whelps.
39 While they are inflamed I will prepare them a feast
and make them drunk, till they swoon away [w]

[w] Gk Vg: Heb *rejoice*

359

and sleep a perpetual sleep
and not wake, says the LORD.
⁴⁰ I will bring them down like lambs to the slaughter,
like rams and he-goats.

⁴¹ "How Babylon ˣ is taken,
the praise of the whole earth seized!
How Babylon has become
a horror among the nations!
⁴² The sea has come up on Babylon;
she is covered with its tumultuous waves.
⁴³ Her cities have become a horror,
a land of drought and a desert,
a land in which no one dwells,
and through which no son of man passes.
⁴⁴ And I will punish Bel in Babylon,
and take out of his mouth what he has swallowed.
The nations shall no longer flow to him;
the wall of Babylon has fallen.
⁴⁵ "Go out of the midst of her, my people!
Let every man save his life
from the fierce anger of the LORD!
⁴⁶ Let not your heart faint, and be not fearful
at the report heard in the land,
when a report comes in one year
and afterward a report in another year,
and violence is in the land,
and ruler is against ruler.

⁴⁷ "Therefore, behold, the days are coming
when I will punish the images of Babylon;
her whole land shall be put to shame,
and all her slain shall fall in the midst of her.
⁴⁸ Then the heavens and the earth,

ˣ Heb *Sheshach,* a cipher for Babylon

and all that is in them,
shall sing for joy over Babylon;
for the destroyers shall come against them out
of the north,
says the LORD.
⁴⁹ Babylon must fall for the slain of Israel,
as for Babylon have fallen the slain of all the
earth.

⁵⁰ "You that have escaped from the sword,
go, stand not still!
Remember the LORD from afar,
and let Jerusalem come into your mind:
⁵¹ 'We are put to shame, for we have heard reproach;
dishonor has covered our face,
for aliens have come
into the holy places of the LORD'S house.'

⁵² "Therefore, behold, the days are coming, says the
LORD,
when I will execute judgment upon her images,
and through all her land
the wounded shall groan.
⁵³ Though Babylon should mount up to heaven,
and though she should fortify her strong height,
yet destroyers would come from me upon her,
says the LORD.

⁵⁴ "Hark! a cry from Babylon!
The noise of great destruction from the land of
the Chalde'ans!
⁵⁵ For the LORD is laying Babylon waste,
and stilling her mighty voice.
Their waves roar like many waters,
the noise of their voice is raised;

361

⁵⁶ for a destroyer has come upon her,
     upon Babylon;
   her warriors are taken,
     their bows are broken in pieces;
   for the LORD is a God of recompense,
     he will surely requite.
⁵⁷ I will make drunk her princes and her wise men,
     her governors, her commanders, and her warriors;
   they shall sleep a perpetual sleep and not wake,
     says the King, whose name is the LORD of hosts.

⁵⁸ "Thus says the LORD of hosts:
   The broad wall of Babylon
     shall be leveled to the ground
   and her high gates
     shall be burned with fire.
   The peoples labor for nought,
     and the nations weary themselves only for fire."

The themes of Jer. 50 persist in Jer. 51:1-58 (see the comments on these verses). Verses 15-19 appeared in 10:12-16 and were discussed at that point. They are employed here to underscore the might and majesty of Yahweh, who can demolish the terrible mountain of Babylon with ease (vv. 25-26). For Babylon, who had once been "the destroyer" (v. 25) and the "hammer" in Yahweh's hand (50:23) must now face her own deafening "destroyer" (vv. 1, 54-57) and be completely shattered by a new "hammer" at Yahweh's disposal (vv. 20-23). She who had once been the "golden cup" of splendor and wrath in Yahweh's hand (v. 7; cf. 25:15-26) will herself feast at Yahweh's expense, become drunk and sleep forever (vv. 38-40, 57). Her downfall will result from a full-scale military campaign (vv. 12-14, 27-33). Her adversaries are now identified as the kings of the

362

Medes (vv. 11, 28) and the adjacent kingdoms of Ararat and Minni in Armenia and of Ashkenaz (v. 27). The actual fall of Babylon came in 539 B. C. at the hands of Cyrus, king of Persia (cf. Is. 45:1), who ruled these territories. The annihilation of Babylon will be like a winnowing of all chaff from the threshing floor (v. 2, cf. v. 33). In this historical event God's people can see the fulfillment of God's plans (v. 12), the vindication of His chosen ones (vv. 8-10, 34-49), a fitting punishment for the "guilt" and "evil" of Babylon (vv. 5, 24), a bloody vengeance for the desecration of Zion (vv. 11, 34-37), and a demonstration of Yahweh's superiority over the idols and gods of Babylon (vv. 44, 47-48, 52-53). When that day comes, the Israelite exiles are to flee home, despite their misgivings (vv. 6, 45-46, 50-51). The whole world will "sing for joy" over Babylon's disgrace (v. 48); her condition could not be healed. (V. 9)

## CONCERNING BABYLON
## AND ZEDEKIAH'S VISIT                    51:59-64

59 The word which Jeremiah the prophet commanded Serai'ah the son of Neri'ah, son of Mahsei'ah, when he went with Zedeki'ah king of Judah to Babylon, in the fourth year of his reign. Serai'ah was the quartermaster. 60 Jeremiah wrote in a book all the evil that should come upon Babylon, all these words that are written concerning Babylon. 61 And Jeremiah said to Serai'ah: "When you come to Babylon, see that you read all these words, 62 and say, 'O LORD, thou hast said concerning this place that thou wilt cut it off, so that nothing shall dwell in it, neither man nor beast, and it shall be desolate for ever.' 63 When you finish reading this book, bind a stone to

363

it, and cast it into the midst of the Eu-phra′tes, [64] and say, 'Thus shall Babylon sink, to rise no more, because of the evil that I am bringing upon her.'" [y]
Thus far are the words of Jeremiah.

[y] Gk: Heb *upon her. And they shall weary themselves*

During the fourth year of his reign Zedekiah is summoned to Babylon, presumably to reassert his personal loyalty after the formation of the rebellious coalition of 27:1-11. Jeremiah takes advantage of this royal mission to solicit the services of Seraiah, a brother of his scribe Baruch, to take a written prophecy with him and cast it into the Euphrates River in Babylon. Although Jeremiah's public message to the people of Judah during the reign of Zedekiah was primarily one of surrender to Babylon as Yahweh's servant (27:6; cf. 38:1-4), he took measures to affirm Yahweh's involvement in the later phases of the divine plan. By the symbolic act of throwing the oracles against Babylon into the Euphrates, Jeremiah asserted Yahweh's ultimate control of Babylon's fate. A few years later, during the last stages of the siege of Jerusalem, he purchased property as a forceful prediction that Yahweh would one day restore activities to normal in Jerusalem (Ch. 32). Symbolic actions of this nature are typical of Jeremiah's message (13:1-11; 19:1-15; 27:2; 28:10, 13). The message of conquest and desolation upon Babylon is elaborated in the later oracles of 50:1 – 51:58. This common theme explains the presence of this incident here in the book as a fitting finale to the prophecies of Jeremiah. The final statement that the words of Jeremiah end at this point can be understood to mean either that an earlier collection of Jeremiah's oracles concluded at this juncture or that the following chapter is to be considered the work of a prophetic follower of Jeremiah such as Baruch. 52:31-34, at least, would favor the latter alternative.

# Historical Appendix

## Jeremiah 52

Jeremiah 52 is a historical appendix parallel to 2 Kings 24:18 – 25:30 (omitting 25:22-26). Whether this chapter was taken directly from 2 Kings or a common source is not demonstrable. The structure and terminology of 52:1-3 are so characteristic of 2 Kings that it is highly unlikely that the editor of Kings copied Jeremiah 52 (see 2 Kings 21:1-2, for example). Jer. 51:64 suggests that this appendix is the work of someone other than Jeremiah himself. The chapter relates some of the details concerning the rebellion of Zedekiah, the fall of Jerusalem, the sacking of the temple, the disposition of the Israelites, the number of those taken captive, and the subsequent fortunes of Jehoiachin.

### AN ACCOUNT OF THE SIEGE, FALL, AND SACKING OF JERUSALEM 52:1-27

¹ Zedeki'ah was twenty-one years old when he became king; and he reigned eleven years in Jerusalem. His mother's name was Hamu'tal the daughter

of Jeremiah of Libnah. ² And he did what was evil in the sight of the LORD, according to all that Je-hoi'akim had done. ³ Surely because of the anger of the LORD things came to such a pass in Jerusalem and Judah that he cast them out from his presence.

And Zedeki'ah rebelled against the king of Baby-lon. ⁴ And in the ninth year of his reign, in the tenth month, on the tenth day of the month, Nebuchad-rez'zar king of Babylon came with all his army against Jerusalem, and they laid siege to it and built siege-works against it round about. ⁵ So the city was be-sieged till the eleventh year of King Zedeki'ah. ⁶ On the ninth day of the fourth month the famine was so severe in the city, that there was no food for the people of the land. ⁷ Then a breach was made in the city; and all the men of war fled and went out from the city by night by the way of a gate between the two walls, by the king's garden, while the Chalde'ans were round about the city. And they went in the direction of the Arabah. ⁸ But the army of the Chal-de'ans pursued the king, and overtook Zedeki'ah in the plains of Jericho; and all his army was scattered from him. ⁹ Then they captured the king, and brought him up to the king of Babylon at Riblah in the land of Hamath, and he passed sentence upon him. ¹⁰ The king of Babylon slew the sons of Zedeki'ah before his eyes, and also slew all the princes of Judah at Riblah. ¹¹ He put out the eyes of Zedeki'ah, and bound him in fetters, and the king of Babylon took him to Babylon, and put him in prison till the day of his death.

¹² In the fifth month, on the tenth day of the month — which was the nineteenth year of King Neb-uchadrez'zar, king of Babylon — Nebu'zarad'an, the

captain of the bodyguard who served the king of Babylon, entered Jerusalem. ¹³ And he burned the house
of the LORD, and the king's house and all the houses
of Jerusalem; every great house he burned down.
¹⁴ And all the army of the Chalde'ans, who were with
the captain of the guard, broke down all the walls
round about Jerusalem. ¹⁵ And Nebu'zarad'an the
captain of the guard carried away captive some of
the poorest of the people and the rest of the people
who were left in the city and the deserters who had
deserted to the king of Babylon, together with the
rest of the artisans. ¹⁶ But Nebu'zarad'an the captain
of the guard left some of the poorest of the land to
be vinedressers and plowmen.

¹⁷ And the pillars of bronze that were in the house
of the LORD, and the stands and the bronze sea that
were in the house of the LORD, the Chalde'ans broke
in pieces, and carried all the bronze to Babylon. ¹⁸ And
they took away the pots, and the shovels, and the
snuffers, and the basins, and the dishes for incense,
and all the vessels of bronze used in the temple service; ¹⁹ also the small bowls, and the firepans, and
the basins, and the pots, and the lampstands, and
the dishes for incense, and the bowls for libation.
What was of gold the captain of the guard took away
as gold, and what was of silver, as silver. ²⁰ As for the
two pillars, the one sea, the twelve bronze bulls which
were under the sea, ᶻ and the stands, which Solomon
the king had made for the house of the LORD, the
bronze of all these things was beyond weight. ²¹ As for
the pillars, the height of the one pillar was eighteen
cubits, its circumference was twelve cubits, and its
thickness was four fingers, and it was hollow. ²² Upon

ᶻ Heb lacks the sea

it was a capital of bronze; the height of the one capital was five cubits; a network and pomegranates, all of bronze, were upon the capital round about. And the second pillar had the like, with pomegranates. 23 There were ninety-six pomegranates on the sides; all the pomegranates were a hundred upon the network round about.

24 And the captain of the guard took Serai'ah the chief priest, and Zephani'ah the second priest, and the three keepers of the threshold; 25 and from the city he took an officer who had been in command of the men of war, and seven men of the king's council, who were found in the city; and the secretary of the commander of the army who mustered the people of the land; and sixty men of the people of the land, who were found in the midst of the city. 26 And Neb-u'zarad'an the captain of the guard took them, and brought them to the king of Babylon at Riblah. 27 And the king of Babylon smote them, and put them to death at Riblah in the land of Hamath. So Judah was carried captive out of its land.

1-3 A number of features of the narrative deserve special comment. The judgment on Zedekiah is significant (v. 2), for, according to 2 Kings, the king sets the moral and religious tone for his people and is responsible to Yahweh for their spiritual welfare. The catastrophic end of Judah, like that of Israel before her, was due to the "anger" of Yahweh casting the people from His presence (v. 3; 2 Kings 17:18). Jeremiah, however, also emphasized the presence of Yahweh in exile. (29:7)

4-16 An abbreviated form of 52:4-16 appears in 39:1-2, 4-10, where further comment is made. The additional information concerning a severe famine during

369

the siege of Jerusalem (v. 6) is confirmed by the ominous note of Jer. 37:21 (cf. Lam. 2:20; 4:1-20). Jer. 52:12 also supplies the date when Nebuzaradan, the captain of the guard, entered the city of Jerusalem to pillage it.

**17-23** The removal of the temple vessels and furnishings was considered intolerable sacrilege. Some of these utensils had been captured earlier, an action that gave rise to false predictions about Israel's return (27:16-22; 28:1-16). A second description of the temple furnishings is given in 1 Kings 7:13-51. In the preaching of Jeremiah, however, the temple and its accouterments had become barriers against, rather than a means for, fostering a dynamic relationship between Israel and Yahweh (cf. 7:1-14). The stripping of Solomon's temple was therefore a vindication of Jeremiah's message. The absence of any reference to the ark of the covenant in this catalog of furnishings may argue for the fact that it had been removed at some earlier date. In any case it was no longer vital for Jeremiah's theology. (Compare the comment on 3:16.)

**24-27** The leading personnel of Jerusalem were taken into exile to deprive Judah of any good leadership and thereby prevent further revolt (cf. 2 Kings 24:15). The leaders mentioned in 52:24-27, moreover, were violently opposed to Babylonian rule. Seraiah was the grandfather to Jeshua, the great high priest after the exile (1 Chron. 6:14; Ezra 3:2), and a forefather of Ezra (Ezra 7:1). Although Jeremiah had contact with Zephaniah (v. 24) several times, there is no indication of a sharp clash between the two men as such (21:1; 29:24-32; 37:3). In addition to the personnel connected directly with the temple and the king, the text mentions 60 of "the people of the land" (v. 25). This expression seems to have reference to full male citizens who were responsible representatives of their various communities and occupied a rung immediately below the princes and priests in the social ladder (cf. Jer. 34:19 also). These captives were executed at Nebuchadnezzar's campaign headquarters at Riblah (in Syria).

## A POSTSCRIPT ON THE NUMBERS
## TAKEN CAPTIVE                           52:28-30

28 This is the number of the people whom Nebuchadrez'zar carried away captive: in the seventh year, three thousand and twenty-three Jews; 29 in the eighteenth year of Nebuchadrez'zar he carried away captive from Jerusalem eight hundred and thirty-two persons; 30 in the twenty-third year of Nebuchadrez'zar, Nebu'zarad'an the captain of the guard carried away captive of the Jews seven hundred and forty-five persons; all the persons were four thousand and six hundred.

Jeremiah's postscript giving the numbers of the three deportations offers a valuable footnote to the history of this period (vv. 28-30). This note reveals that the deportation of 598/7 B. C. involved more than three thousand citizens of Judah, but the one connected with the actual destruction of Jerusalem in 587 B. C. included only 832 persons. The third deportation took place in 582 B. C., apparently as a punitive measure after the assassination of the governor Gedaliah (cf. 41:1-2). These modest figures illustrate that there were probably many more inhabitants left in Judah than is generally assumed, and that although most of the recognized leaders, officials, and artisans were taken captive, an active Israelite community of worshipers survived

371

(cf. 41:5), one segment of which fled to Egypt (43:1-7). We are not certain how these figures were calculated. 2 Kings 24:14 speaks of ten thousand captives taken into exile by Nebuchadnezzar.

## A Postscript on the Release
## of Jehoiachin                                    52:31-34

[31] And in the thirty-seventh year of the captivity of Jehoi'achin king of Judah, in the twelfth month, on the twenty-fifth day of the month, E'vil-mer'odach king of Babylon, in the year that he became king, lifted up the head of Jehoi'achin king of Judah and brought him out of prison; [32] and he spoke kindly to him, and gave him a seat above the seats of the kings who were with him in Babylon. [33] So Jehoi'-achin put off his prison garments. And every day of his life he dined regularly at the king's table; [34] as for his allowance, a regular allowance was given him by the king according to his daily need, until the day of his death as long as he lived.

The second postscript of Jer. 52 describes the re-lease of Jehoiachin from the confinement of prison by Evilmerodach (Amel-marduk in Babylonian), the son of Nebuchadnezzar. Jehoiachin had been taken captive by Nebuchadnezzar in the 598/7 campaign against Jerusalem and was still regarded by many as the legiti-mate king of the people of Judah inasmuch as his suc-cessor, Zedekiah, had been set on the throne by a Baby-lonian monarch. The honor afforded Jehoiachin was undoubtedly interpreted by the exiles as a sign of divine favor and a portent of greater things to come. As such it perhaps offers a fitting conclusion to both the Book of Jeremiah and the Books of Kings. The interest in Jehoiachin is all the more surprising inasmuch as this king ruled only three months (see the comment on 22:24-30). Nevertheless, in the hearts of many the honor of the Davidic line was still important for the name and hope of Israel. For Jeremiah, however, the recognition of Yahweh's kingship, will, and undeserved forgiveness even during the exile was far more significant. God's people dare not fix their hope primarily on political Davidic rulers. The future of God's people lay in God's own new covenant of grace.

# Lamentations

# INTRODUCTION

*The Occasion for the Book*

The city of Jerusalem fell into the unfriendly hands of the Babylonian soldiers in 587 B. C. Its walls were broken down, its temple was looted and destroyed, its leaders killed or taken into exile, and most of its buildings burned to the ground (see Jer. 39). The fall of that city was a traumatic experience for all those people who had trusted in Jerusalem as the symbol of security. Yahweh had chosen that city for His royal abode. Many people therefore believed it was indestructible. As soon as it had fallen, their faith was virtually shattered. Questions of doubt poured from their lips. Are we still the people of God? Why did all this happen? Has the covenant with Yahweh been terminated? Is there any hope for mercy in the future? In his own way the poet of Lamentations reaches for answers and tries to evoke Yahweh's compassion despite the ugly situation – and because of it. In a series of emotional but formal dirges and laments he recounts the miseries of Jerusalem's downfall and searches for something more than comfort from the God whom he holds responsible for the humiliation of His people. The writer is apparently living among the broken and humiliated survivors in Judah, for whom the ruins of Jerusalem were a constant reminder of their disgrace and apparent rejection by God. They idealized its former glory (4:1-7) and remained bitter about its present condition (1:12-17). In the midst of this anguish the author of Lamentations captures the mood of his suffering people and tries to bring their concerns before God in a constructive way.

*The Author of the Book*

The author of Lamentations is left anonymous. The RSV preserves a superscription that stems from a preface to the Greek translation but does not appear in the Hebrew original. The tradition that Jeremiah was the author of Lamentations is therefore an ancient one. The evidence of the book, however, cannot provide us with a conclusive answer as to the author's identity. He was apparently an eyewitness like Jeremiah and one who was willing to express the trials of his faith in a manner similar to that of Jeremiah (see Jer. 15:15-21; 20:7-18). He pulls no punches! The terminology employed differs from that of Jeremiah but the mood is often similar. The portrait of a suffering individual of Ch. 3 seems to be written with the person of Jeremiah in mind. Like Jeremiah the author exercises the prophetic function of challenging God's drastic action and interceding as the representative of his people in order to evoke God's sympathy. In view of this there is no reason to see a radical conflict between Jeremiah's perspective and the attitude toward Israel's leaders (4:7, 20), Egypt (4:17), and the temple worship (2:6) reflected in Jeremiah. In general, however, Lamentations shows a marked simi

378

larity with certain psalms (e. g., 129; 77; 102) and parts of Is. 40–55. The tradition that Jeremiah created these poems in Lamentations is supported by the statement of 2 Chron. 35:25 that Jeremiah wrote laments for King Josiah that are recorded in a certain book of laments.

*The Structure of the Book*

Each of the five chapters of Lamentations has a carefully worked out structure. It is immediately apparent that Chs. 1–2 and 4–5 have 22 verses each while Ch. 3 has 66 verses. This is not accidental. The Hebrew alphabet has 22 letters, and the number 22 comes to designate the idea of completeness. More explicitly, however, Chs. 1–4 are known as acrostics. That is, the verses begin with successive letters of the Hebrew alphabet. In the case of Ch. 3, three verses begin with the first letter of the alphabet, three verses with the second, and so on through the alphabet. Some have suggested that this form was employed as an aid to memorizing the poems. But this is uncertain. Perhaps the monotonous ritual of going through the entire alphabet reflects the mournful regularity of ancient lamentation and wailing. In this way the poet expresses the fullness of human suffering from A to Z. In addition Chs. 1, 2, and 4 are dirges similar to those repeated at the death of an individual. The pitiful "How . . ." is a common way of introducing dirges (1:1; 2:1; 4:1; cf. 2 Sam. 1:19, 25, 27). Chapter 4 is basically the lament of an individual, but Ch. 5 is a lament for the community. Individual and communal laments were part of the temple worship of Jerusalem and are known to us from the Psalter (e. g., 39; 79; 80). Further, the four acrostics of Lamentations also have a fixed rhythm of three beats plus two for each line. This is the accepted rhythm to express the doleful monotony of the wailing rites of ancient Israel.

### The Message of the Book

The message of Lamentations is a sympathetic word with the broken and downtrodden. It is a divine word with a people of God who stand under the judgment of God, the divine verdict of death. The poet of Lamentations is part of a people who have been violently crushed under the condemnation of God. Part of his therapy is to recount and highlight the atrocities associated with the downfall of his people. He does not hide the truth. What happened was ugly. But what happened was the fault of God's people. The poet dispels any popular notion that Judah or Jerusalem had been faithful to the will of God and hence deserved a better fate. Zion deserved what she got. In judgment God had kept His word. The threat of the covenant curse had been imposed, and the righteousness of Yahweh was vindicated. Zion suffered because of "the multitude of her transgressions," Jerusalem had "sinned grievously," and "therefore she became filthy" (1:5, 8). "I have rebelled against his word," she cries (1:18). Yahweh dealt justly with Zion because of her transgressions (1:22). The poet does not even allude to the optimistic reform of Josiah, which preceded the fall of Jerusalem by less than 40 years (2 Kings 23). That reform was apparently no basis for expecting an extended era of blessing. Jeremiah described the whole reform program as a sham (see the comment of Jer. 3:10). The people of God had no redress. Their punishment was completely just even if unusually harsh. (Lam. 4:6)

The poet of Lamentations speaks of Zion and for Zion, the temple mountain that came to be the symbol of God's chosen covenant people. The popular tradition arose that because Yahweh had selected Zion for His sacred city among His people, its walls were invulnerable and its destruction impossible. With God almighty on her side, Zion was safe forever, they believed. "The kings of the earth did not believe . . . that foe or enemy could enter the gates of Jerusalem," writes the poet (4:12). But Zion, "the perfection of beauty, the joy of all the earth" (2:15), did fall. The reason for her destruction, however, does not lie in the inability of Yahweh to defend her or in the unexpected power of her foes but in the broken relation between Yahweh and His beloved daughter Zion. "This was for the sins of her prophets and the iniquity of her priests" (4:13). "The Lord gave full vent to his wrath, he poured out his hot anger" (4:11). The writer belongs to that circle of citizens who, like Yahweh, loved Zion. With nostalgia he describes her "holy stones," her "precious sons," and her glorious princes. But with sincere confession he acknowledges that her subsequent misery is wrought by God as punishment for her iniquity (4:22). The people of Zion have suffered the curses for breach of covenant allegiance which had been enunciated in Deuteronomy 28. Compare Lam. 1:5, 18 and Deut. 28:41; Lam. 1:9 and Deut. 28:43; Lam. 2:20 and Deut. 28:53; where the poet seems to make direct reference to curses imposed because of covenant disobedience. The people of God, the inhabitants of Zion, fell on the day of the Lord (1:12, 21). Their misery was not due to historical accident. Their destruction was a planned act of Yahweh which had been announced in advance (1:21). This was the day of decisive intervention that Jeremiah and other prophets had announced; this was the day of "his fierce anger" (1:12), when Yahweh would demonstrate His justice and vindicate His name.

This writer does not describe Zion's plight as an act of self-pity. His cry is a confession of guilt to Yahweh and an appeal for grace from His hand. He yearns for the past joys of Zion and in so doing expresses the hope that one day Yahweh will reverse her fortunes. The ground of his hope lies in the very nature of Zion's destruction. Yahweh Himself had afflicted her. He remains her Lord, therefore, and has the power to rebuild her future. By recounting all the gruesome details of Judah's devastation and by highlighting the glories of her past, the poet is reaching for divine compassion. He dwells on the revolting details of the siege of Jerusalem until they become nauseating. He acknowledges that God's people are nothing but a "filthy thing," (1:17), the "offscouring and refuse among the peoples" (3:45). This catalog of miseries is designed to cause Yahweh to "remember" His inheritance and to act accordingly (5:1). Ultimately His love will become evident to those under the condemnation of His wrath. His "steadfast love never ceases" and "He does not willingly afflict" His sons (3:22, 33). Even in judgment and death the sons of Zion remain His people and the city of Zion His city. The closing lines of the book summarize the attitude and hope of the writer admirably. He intends to challenge God to display His concern for His destroyed people precisely because He is the King of earth. In this challenge the faith of the poet in the vindication of Yahweh's mercy through the restoration of His city is forcefully illustrated. There must be a plan of God in the punishment of His people; otherwise His punishment is futile.

*Bibliographical Aids*

*Studies in the Book of Lamentations* by Norman Gottwald is No. 14 in a series entitled *Studies in Biblical*

*Theology* (Chicago: Allenson, 1954). This book is an excellent topical analysis of the form and theology of Lamentations. Gottwald is also the author of the fine article on Lamentations in the *Interpreter's Dictionary of the Bible* (Nashville: Abingdon, 1962), Vol. 2.

Volume 12 of the *Layman's Bible Commentary* by Howard Kuist (Richmond: John Knox Press, 1960) is brief but valuable.

Among the more technical commentaries in English which the average layman could read with profit we would suggest T. Meek in *The Interpreter's Bible*, Vol. 6 (Nashville: Abingdon, 1956), and A. S. Herbert in the new *Peake's Commentary on the Bible* (London: Nelson, 1962).

# OUTLINE

# The Misery of Fallen Zion

## Lamentations 1

¹ How lonely sits the city
  that was full of people!
How like a widow has she become,
  she that was great among the nations!
She that was a princess among the cities
  has become a vassal.

² She weeps bitterly in the night,
  tears on her cheeks;
among all her lovers
  she has none to comfort her;
all her friends have dealt treacherously with her,
  they have become her enemies.

³ Judah has gone into exile because of affliction
  and hard servitude;
she dwells now among the nations,
  but finds no resting place;
her pursuers have all overtaken her
  in the midst of her distress.

⁴ The roads to Zion mourn,
 for none come to the appointed feasts;
all her gates are desolate,
 her priests groan;
her maidens have been dragged away,ᵃ
 and she herself suffers bitterly.

⁵ Her foes have become the head,
 her enemies prosper,
because the LORD has made her suffer
 for the multitude of her transgressions;
her children have gone away,
 captives before the foe.

⁶ From the daughter of Zion has departed
 all her majesty.
Her princes have become like harts that find no
 pasture;
they fled without strength
 before the pursuer.

⁷ Jerusalem remembers
 in the days of her affliction and bitterness ᵇ
all the precious things
 that were hers from days of old.
When her people fell into the hand of the foe.
 and there was none to help her,
the foe gloated over her,
 mocking at her downfall.

⁸ Jerusalem sinned grievously,
 therefore she became filthy;
all who honored her despise her,
 for they have seen her nakedness;

---

ᵃ Gk Old Latin: Heb *afflicted*    ᵇ Cn: Heb *wandering*

yea, she herself groans,
and turns her face away.

9 Her uncleanness was in her skirts;
she took no thought of her doom;
therefore her fall is terrible,
she has no comforter.
"O LORD, behold my affliction,
for the enemy has triumphed!"

10 The enemy has stretched out his hands
over all her precious things;
yea, she has seen the nations
invade her sanctuary,
those whom thou didst forbid
to enter thy congregation.

11 All her people groan
as they search for bread;
they trade their treasures for food
to revive their strength.
"Look, O LORD, and behold,
for I am despised."

12 "Is it nothing to you,$^c$ all you who pass by?
Look and see
if there is any sorrow like my sorrow
which was brought upon me,
which the LORD inflicted
on the day of his fierce anger.

13 "From on high he sent fire;
into my bones $^d$ he made it descend;
he spread a net for my feet;
he turned me back;

$^c$ Heb uncertain     $^d$ Gk: Heb bones and

389

he has left me stunned,
    faint all the day long.

¹⁴ "My transgressions were bound ᵉ into a yoke;
    by his hand they were fastened together;
they were set upon my neck;
    he caused my strength to fail;
the Lord gave me into the hands
    of those whom I cannot withstand.

¹⁵ "The LORD flouted all my mighty men
    in the midst of me;
he summoned an assembly against me
    to crush my young men;
the Lord has trodden as in a wine press
    the virgin daughter of Judah.

¹⁶ "For these things I weep;
    my eyes flow with tears;
for a comforter is far from me,
    one to revive my courage;
my children are desolate,
    for the enemy has prevailed."

¹⁷ Zion stretches out her hands,
    but there is none to comfort her;
the LORD has commanded against Jacob
    that his neighbors should be his foes;
Jerusalem has become
    a filthy thing among them.

¹⁸ "The LORD is in the right,
    for I have rebelled against his word;
but hear, all you peoples,
    and behold my suffering;

ᵉ Cn: Heb uncertain

my maidens and my young men
  have gone into captivity.

19 "I called to my lovers
  but they deceived me;
my priests and elders
  perished in the city,
while they sought food
  to revive their strength.

20 "Behold, O LORD, for I am in distress,
  my soul is in tumult,
my heart is wrung within me,
  because I have been very rebellious.
In the street the sword bereaves;
  in the house it is like death.

21 "Hear *f* how I groan;
  there is none to comfort me.
All my enemies have heard of my trouble;
  they are glad that thou hast done it.
Bring thou *g* the day thou hast announced,
  and let them be as I am.

22 "Let all their evil doing come before thee;
  and deal with them
as thou hast dealt with me
  because of all my transgressions;
for my groans are many
  and my heart is faint."

*f* Gk Syr: Heb *they heard*    *g* Syr: Heb *thou hast brought*

1-11 The opening chapter of Lamentations is a dirge over the city of Jerusalem, which fell in 587 B. C. after a three-year siege by Nebuchadnezzar of Babylon.

391

Verses 1-11 are a description of Zion personified as "a widow" who has been humiliated and forsaken by those nations and states who had been her "friends" (v. 2) or "lovers" (v. 19) in the revolt against Babylon. Zion, the hill on which the temple was built, represents God's people, who were punished by Yahweh Himself (vv. 5, 8) when they were sent into exile (v. 3). In her disgrace Zion remembers her former condition (v. 7), the loneliness of her downfall (vv. 7, 9), the desecration of the temple "sanctuary" and the misery of famine during the final siege (v. 10-11). Zion is condemned and forsaken because of the enormity of her sins (vv. 5, 8). Hence she has become a "filthy thing" so detestable that others are utterly disgusted and disdainful. "She has no comforter" (v. 9). The princess has become like a "vassal," a slave. (V. 1)

**12-22** In these verses we hear Zion offering a lament in her own words. She is acutely conscious that the day of her destruction was the day of the Lord prophesied by prophets like Amos (5:18) and Jeremiah (4:5-9). That day was the decisive "day of his fierce anger" (v. 12), "the day thou hast announced" (v. 21). The foreboding word of the prophets had been vindicated. But there was no consolation. God's wrath was like a "fire" (v. 13), or a hunter's "net" (v. 13), or a "yoke" made from her own sin (v. 14) or like being crushed as grapes in "a wine press," (v. 15). She confesses that Yahweh is quite "right" or righteous in his punishment. She had rebelled "against his word," and she has no excuse (v. 18). She knows that her extreme anguish is the result of her extreme rebelliousness (v. 20). But that knowledge affords no comfort. Her misery is excruciating. Her public disgrace is unbearable (v. 12, 16, 17, 21). Hence she cannot refrain from screaming for God's vengeance against her enemies (v. 22). If God is just, other wicked nations should also suffer, she cries. Dirges normally conclude with a prayer such as that of vv. 20-22. Compare also the end of Lam. 2.

# The Felling of Majestic Zion

## Lamentations 2

[1] How the Lord in his anger
   has set the daughter of Zion under a cloud!
He has cast down from heaven to earth
   the splendor of Israel;
he has not remembered his footstool
   in the day of his anger.

[2] The Lord has destroyed without mercy
   all the habitations of Jacob;
in his wrath he has broken down
   the strongholds of the daughter of Judah;
he has brought down to the ground in dishonor
   the kingdom and its rulers.

[3] He has cut down in fierce anger
   all the might of Israel;
he has withdrawn from them his right hand
   in the face of the enemy;
he has burned like a flaming fire in Jacob,
   consuming all around.

⁴ He has bent his bow like an enemy,
  with his right hand set like a foe;
  and he has slain all the pride of our eyes
    in the tent of the daughter of Zion;
  he has poured out his fury like fire.

⁵ The Lord has become like an enemy,
  he has destroyed Israel;
  he has destroyed all its palaces,
    laid in ruins its strongholds;
  and he has multiplied in the daughter of Judah
    mourning and lamentation.

⁶ He has broken down his booth like that of a garden,
    laid in ruins the place of his appointed feasts;
  the LORD has brought to an end in Zion
    appointed feast and sabbath,
  and in his fierce indignation has spurned
    king and priest.

⁷ The Lord has scorned his altar,
    disowned his sanctuary;
  he has delivered into the hand of the enemy
    the walls of her palaces;
  a clamor was raised in the house of the LORD
    as on the day of an appointed feast.

⁸ The LORD determined to lay in ruins
    the wall of the daughter of Zion;
  he marked it off by the line;
    he restrained not his hand from destroying;
  he caused rampart and wall to lament,
    they languish together.

⁹ Her gates have sunk into the ground;
    he has ruined and broken her bars;

her king and princes are among the nations;
    the law is no more,
and her prophets obtain
    no vision from the LORD.

<sup></sup>10 The elders of the daughter of Zion
    sit on the ground in silence;
they have cast dust on their heads
    and put on sackcloth;
the maidens of Jerusalem
    have bowed their heads to the ground.

11 My eyes are spent with weeping;
    my soul is in tumult;
my heart is poured out in grief [h]
    because of the destruction of the daughter of my
      people,
because infants and babes faint
    in the streets of the city.

12 They cry to their mothers,
    "Where is bread and wine?"
as they faint like wounded men
    in the streets of the city,
as their life is poured out
    on their mother's bosom.

13 What can I say for you, to what compare you,
    O daughter of Jerusalem?
What can I liken to you, that I may comfort you,
    O virgin daughter of Zion?
For vast as the sea is your ruin;
    who can restore you?

14 Your prophets have seen for you
    false and deceptive visions;

[h] Heb *to the ground*

they have not exposed your iniquity
  to restore your fortunes,
but have seen for you oracles
  false and misleading.

15 All who pass along the way
  clap their hands at you;
they hiss and wag their heads
  at the daughter of Jerusalem;
"Is this the city which was called
  the perfection of beauty,
  the joy of all the earth?"

16 All your enemies
  rail against you;
they hiss, they gnash their teeth,
  they cry: "We have destroyed her!
Ah, this is the day we longed for;
  now we have it; we see it!"

17 The LORD has done what he purposed,
  has carried out his threat;
as he ordained long ago,
  he has demolished without pity;
he has made the enemy rejoice over you,
  and exalted the might of your foes.

18 Cry aloud [i] to the Lord!
  O [j] daughter of Zion!
Let tears stream down like a torrent
  day and night!
Give yourself no rest,
  your eyes no respite!
19 Arise, cry out in the night,
  at the beginning of the watches!

[i] Cn: Heb *Their heart cried*  [j] Cn: Heb *O wall of*

Pour out your heart like water
    before the presence of the Lord!
Lift your hands to him
    for the lives of your children,
who faint for hunger
    at the head of every street.

20 Look, O LORD, and see!
    With whom hast thou dealt thus?
Should women eat their offspring,
    the children of their tender care?
Should priest and prophet be slain
    in the sanctuary of the Lord?

21 In the dust of the streets
    lie the young and the old;
my maidens and my young men
    have fallen by the sword;
in the day of thy anger thou hast slain them,
    slaughtering without mercy.

22 Thou didst invite as to the day of an appointed feast
    my terrors on every side;
and on the day of the anger of the LORD
    none escaped or survived;
those whom I dandled and reared
    my enemy destroyed.

**1-10** Lamentations 2 is also a dirge over Zion, but the speaker throughout is the poet. This dirge opens with the same typical "how" (cf. 1:1; 4:1). The first half of the dirge (vv. 1-10) is a vivid description of how Jerusalem fell. The poet was apparently an eyewitness who sees her as a fallen star (v. 1; cf. Is. 14:12-15) "cast down" by God. Majestic Zion had been felled! God had forgotten His own "footstool," that is, the temple He had chosen for His earthly throne (v. 1). God "had become like an enemy" (v. 5); He had destroyed the cities of Judah, humiliated its leaders (v. 2), broken down His "booth," the temple (see Ps. 76:2), rejected its anointed leaders (v. 6), and even surrendered the sacred altar itself into the hands of the pagan foe (v. 7). Thus all the cherished and appointed means of worship and life in the community of Israel had been eliminated. Not only was the city in ruins, but God Himself had left her, and none of the traditional ways of communicating with God had survived. There was no religious leadership, no "law" from the priests, and no "vision" from the prophets (v. 9). There seemed to be no hope, for God had apparenly terminated the established religious practices of Israel. God seemed to have no mercy left. The historical figure of Babylon who had actually destroyed Jerusalem is almost incidental in this portrait; Yahweh is the real foe behind the scenes.

**11-17** In vv. 11-22 the poet tries to evoke God's sympathy by describing the suffering and anguish of His people when Jerusalem was being captured. The poet thinks of the babes and infants fainting in the city squares because their mother's breasts are dry and the famine has begun (vv. 11-12). The ruin of Zion is as wide as the ocean. It is beyond comparison (v. 13). The prophets who should have known better and exposed her guilt before it was too late had made glib promises about peace and prosperity (v. 14: cf. Jer. 8:11; 23:16-17). Yahweh carried out the threat which His persecuted prophets (like Jeremiah) had delivered. This doom had been planned long ago; Zion's destruction was not a sudden unannounced catastrophe. She had no excuse! (V. 17)

**18-22** In an effort to move God and gain His ear, the poet urges Zion to weep and wail incessantly until God listens to her (vv. 18-19). Then the poet offers his own appeal for compassion. He tells God to take a good look at what He has done. It is disgusting: women eating their own children and murder in the temple! God slaughtered without mercy. The day of the Lord's wrath (see 1:12, 21) was like a feast when all the guests were the victims (cf. Zeph. 1:7). Surely God could not remain untouched by these terrible sights for which He was responsible. Despite what God had done the poet knows that God alone could begin to remedy the situation. In a sense, therefore, this dirge is also a confession of penitence and a plea for restoration. Yahweh is still Zion's God. (Vv. 20-22)

# A Suffering Servant of Zion

## Lamentations 3

¹ I am the man who has seen affliction
    under the rod of his wrath;
² he has driven and brought me
    into darkness without any light;
³ surely against me he turns his hand
    again and again the whole day long.

⁴ He has made my flesh and my skin waste away,
    and broken my bones;
⁵ he has besieged and enveloped me
    with bitterness and tribulation;
⁶ he has made me dwell in darkness
    like the dead of long ago.

⁷ He has walled me about so that I cannot escape;
    he has put heavy chains on me;
⁸ though I call and cry for help,
    he shuts out my prayer;
⁹ he has blocked my ways with hewn stones,
    he has made my paths crooked.

¹⁰ He is to me like a bear lying in wait,
  like a lion in hiding;
¹¹ he led me off my way and tore me to pieces;
  he has made me desolate;
¹² he bent his bow and set me
  as a mark for his arrow.

¹³ He drove into my heart
  the arrows of his quiver;
¹⁴ I have become the laughingstock of all peoples,
  the burden of their songs all day long.
¹⁵ He has filled me with bitterness,
  he has sated me with wormwood.

¹⁶ He has made my teeth grind on gravel,
  and made me cower in ashes;
¹⁷ my soul is bereft of peace,
  I have forgotten what happiness is;
¹⁸ so I say, "Gone is my glory,
  and my expectation from the LORD."

¹⁹ Remember my affliction and my bitterness,ᵏ
  the wormwood and the gall!
²⁰ My soul continually thinks of it
  and is bowed down within me.
²¹ But this I call to mind,
  and therefore I have hope:

²² The steadfast love of the LORD never ceases,ˡ
  his mercies never come to an end;
²³ they are new every morning;
  great is thy faithfulness.
²⁴ "The LORD is my portion," says my soul,
  "therefore I will hope in him."

ᵏ Cn: Heb *wandering*  ˡ Syr Tg: Heb *we are not cut off*

²⁵ The LORD is good to those who wait for him,
   to the soul that seeks him.
²⁶ It is good that one should wait quietly
   for the salvation of the LORD.
²⁷ It is good for a man that he bear
   the yoke in his youth.

²⁸ Let him sit alone in silence
   when he has laid it on him;
²⁹ let him put his mouth in the dust—
   there may yet be hope;
³⁰ let him give his cheek to the smiter,
   and be filled with insults.

³¹ For the LORD will not
   cast off for ever,
³² but, though he cause grief, he will have compassion
   according to the abundance of his steadfast love;
³³ for he does not willingly afflict
   or grieve the sons of men.

³⁴ To crush under foot
   all the prisoners of the earth,
³⁵ to turn aside the right of a man
   in the presence of the Most High,
³⁶ to subvert a man in his cause,
   the LORD does not approve.

³⁷ Who has commanded and it came to pass,
   unless the LORD has ordained it?
³⁸ Is it not from the mouth of the Most High
   that good and evil come?
³⁹ Why should a living man complain,
   a man, about the punishment of his sins?

⁴⁰ Let us test and examine our ways,
   and return to the LORD!

403

⁴¹ Let us lift up our hearts and hands
    to God in heaven:
⁴² "We have transgressed and rebelled,
    and thou hast not forgiven.

⁴³ "Thou hast wrapped thyself with anger and pursued
        us,
    slaying without pity;
⁴⁴ thou hast wrapped thyself with a cloud
    so that no prayer can pass through.
⁴⁵ Thou hast made us offscouring and refuse
    among the peoples.

⁴⁶ "All our enemies
    rail against us;
⁴⁷ panic and pitfall have come upon us,
    devastation and destruction;
⁴⁸ my eyes flow with rivers of tears
    because of the destruction of the daughter of my
        people.

⁴⁹ "My eyes will flow without ceasing,
    without respite,
⁵⁰ until the LORD from heaven
    looks down and sees;
⁵¹ my eyes cause me grief
    at the fate of all the maidens of my city.

⁵² "I have been hunted like a bird
    by those who were my enemies without cause;
⁵³ they flung me alive into the pit
    and cast stones on me;
⁵⁴ water closed over my head;
    I said, 'I am lost.'

⁵⁵ "I called on thy name, O LORD,
    from the depths of the pit;

⁵⁶ thou didst hear my plea, 'Do not close
   thine ear to my cry for help!' ᵐ
⁵⁷ Thou didst come near when I called on thee;
   thou didst say, 'Do not fear!'

⁵⁸ "Thou hast taken up my cause, O LORD,
   thou hast redeemed my life.
⁵⁹ Thou hast seen the wrong done to me, O LORD;
   judge thou my cause.
⁶⁰ Thou hast seen all their vengeance, all their devices
      against me.

⁶¹ "Thou hast heard their taunts, O LORD,
   all their devices against me.
⁶² The lips and thoughts of my assailants
   are against me all the day long.
⁶³ Behold their sitting and their rising;
   I am the burden of their songs.

⁶⁴ "Thou wilt requite them, O LORD,
   according to the work of their hands.
⁶⁵ Thou wilt give them dullness of heart;
   thy curse will be on them.
⁶⁶ Thou wilt pursue them in anger and destroy them
   from under thy heavens, O LORD." ⁿ

   ᵐ Heb uncertain
   ⁿ Syr Compare Gk Vg: Heb *the heavens of the LORD*


The third chapter of Lamentations is an unusual kind
of lament with a variation of the acrostic form discussed
in the introduction above. At first the anonymous
"man" speaks in the first person (vv. 1-39), then the communal "we" is employed (vv. 40-47), and finally the
individual "I" appears again (vv. 48-66). If the "man"
is not Jeremiah himself, he is either playing the role of

the suffering prophet Jeremiah or some similar persecuted prophet of that day. His character is similar in many respects to that of the suffering servant in Is. 53. The experiences of this man are more than personal. The community of God's people is also involved, as vv. 40-48 clearly imply. The prophet represents his people before God; he is the spokesman on their behalf and reflects their need. The intercessions of Jeremiah have a similar basis (see 4:10, 19-22; 8:18 – 9:3). Thus Lamentations 3 is concerned with the same subject as the rest of the book: the meaning of God's severe punishment in the destruction of Jerusalem.

**1-18** The first part of the lament (vv. 1-18) is a cry of anguish against God and what He has done. God drove this "man" into the depths of agony and "darkness." He mutilated his body and broke his spirit (vv. 4-6). He left him no way of escape or redress (vv. 7-9). He treated him like prey (vv. 10-12). He made him the butt of international jokes (vv. 13-15). And last but not least, He removed both his dignity and his hope of God's compassion (vv. 16-18). The tone and theme of this cry is quite similar to that of Job 16:6-17. The primary difference is that this prophet acknowledges his guilt, whereas Job does so only belatedly.

**19-39** After the outburst of hopelessness in v. 18, the lament continues with a cry of hope (vv. 19-39). Suddenly the speaker seems passively resigned to his fate. He seems to be repeating the traditional message of comfort that God's covenant people have always known. He is listening to the answer he knows to be true but finds hard to accept, because his extreme misery is always on his mind (vv. 19-21). He knows about Yahweh's faithfulness to the covenant (His "steadfast love"), and he knows about God's eternal compassion

(vv. 22-24). He knows, too, that God will eventually work things out for the good of those who "wait," that is, patiently trust in Him. Every young man benefits from a "yoke" of hardships, he tells himself. But all of this is hard to accept calmly (vv. 25-27). He is aware that ideally a man should swallow insults without retaliating (vv. 28-30). He is convinced that in the end God will show His true character as a loving and compassionate Overlord, "for he does not willingly afflict" (v. 33). In other words, the cruel suffering that God inflicts is a necessary evil and not something God enjoys doing. In the last analysis God is a God of love and mercy, but nothing, whether "good or evil," happens without God's approval or plan. "Why should a living man complain?" asks the poet. Things will all work together for good in the long run. But in the meantime it is difficult not to be impatient and miserable in the face of severe affliction. (Vv. 31-39)

**40-47** Having reaffirmed the message of comfort, which all men should theoretically accept without protest, he pleads with the people of God (who had suffered the humiliation of the fall of Jerusalem) to join in a common prayer of repentance (vv. 40-47). To "return" to Yahweh (v. 40) means to repent and change one's attitude. God's people should acknowledge their rebellion and sin. While they remain belligerent, there is no forgiveness and consequent restoration possible (v. 41-42). They also recognize that God's anger has made them the "offscouring" of the earth, the object of public derision because of their downfall (vv. 43-47), and such a confession is also a plea for help.

**48-66** The lament of Lamentations 3 concludes with personal prayer for deliverance (vv. 48-66). The poet repeats his assertion that he will weep until God sees his state and acts. He reminds God that he is in the "pit" of agony, very close to death (vv. 49-54). He keeps telling God that God has, after all, heard his prayers and pronounced a word of comfort, "Do not fear," even if He has not acted as yet (vv. 55-57). He is convinced that God has taken up his case and that his life is therefore safe, or "redeemed." But the poet's condition belies this fact. He needs public verification and restoration. Hence he pleads for God to act; "Judge thou my cause," he cries (vv. 58-59). Public vindication of his own redemption and of God's righteousness will be seen when full retribution falls on those who cause the poet's disgrace. They deserve the curse of God's anger for the enormity of their crimes. (Vv. 60-66)

# The Desecration of Holy Zion

## Lamentations 4

1 How the gold has grown dim,
   how the pure gold is changed!
The holy stones lie scattered
   at the head of every street.

2 The precious sons of Zion,
   worth their weight in fine gold,
how they are reckoned as earthen pots,
   the work of a potter's hands!

3 Even the jackals give the breast
   and suckle their young,
but the daughter of my people has become cruel,
   like the ostriches in the wilderness.

4 The tongue of the nursling cleaves
   to the roof of its mouth for thirst;
the children beg for food,
   but no one gives to them.

5 Those who feasted on dainties
   perish in the streets;
those who were brought up in purple
   lie on ash heaps.

6 For the chastisement[o] of the daughter of my people
has been greater
than the punishment[p] of Sodom,
which was overthrown in a moment,
no hand being laid on it.[q]

7 Her princes were purer than snow,
whiter than milk;
their bodies were more ruddy than coral,
the beauty of their form[r] was like sapphire.[s]

8 Now their visage is blacker than soot,
they are not recognized in the streets;
their skin has shriveled upon their bones,
it has become as dry as wood.

9 Happier were the victims of the sword
than the victims of hunger,
who pined away, stricken
by want of the fruits of the field.

10 The hands of compassionate women
have boiled their own children;
they became their food
in the destruction of the daughter of my people.

11 The LORD gave full vent to his wrath,
he poured out his hot anger;
and he kindled a fire in Zion,
which consumed its foundations.

12 The kings of the earth did not believe,
or any of the inhabitants of the world,
that foe or enemy could enter
the gates of Jerusalem.

[o] Or *iniquity* [p] Or *sin* [q] Heb uncertain [r] Heb uncertain
[s] Heb *lapis lazuli*

<sup>13</sup> This was for the sins of her prophets
    and the iniquities of her priests,
who shed in the midst of her
    the blood of the righteous.

<sup>14</sup> They wandered, blind, through the streets,
    so defiled with blood
that none could touch
    their garments.

<sup>15</sup> "Away! Unclean!" men cried at them;
    "Away! Away! Touch not!"
So they became fugitives and wanderers;
    men said among the nations,
    "They shall stay with us no longer."

<sup>16</sup> The LORD himself has scattered them,
    he will regard them no more;
no honor was shown to the priests,
    no favor to the elders.

<sup>17</sup> Our eyes failed, ever watching
    vainly for help;
in our watching <sup>t</sup> we watched
    for a nation which could not save.

<sup>18</sup> Men dogged our steps
    so that we could not walk in our streets;
our end drew near; our days were numbered;
    for our end had come.

<sup>19</sup> Our pursuers were swifter
    than the vultures in the heavens;
they chased us on the mountains,
    they lay in wait for us in the wilderness.

<sup>t</sup> Heb uncertain

²⁰ The breath of our nostrils, the LORD'S anointed,
   was taken in their pits,
  he of whom we said, "Under his shadow
  we shall live among the nations."

²¹ Rejoice and be glad, O daughter of Edom,
   dweller in the land of Uz;
  but to you also the cup shall pass;
   you shall become drunk and strip yourself bare.

²² The punishment of your iniquity, O daughter of
   Zion, is accomplished,
  he will keep you in exile no longer;
  but your iniquity, O daughter of Edom, he will
   punish,
  he will uncover your sins.

1-10 Lamentations 4 is a dirge similar to Ch. 2. In both chapters the former glory of the holy city stands in stark contrast to circumstances that surrounded her destruction at the hands of the Babylonians. The first unit (vv. 1-10) offers a concrete account of the siege and fall of the city. The past condition of Zion is idealized; she was pure gold, her sons were worth their weight in gold (vv. 1-2), her princes "purer than snow" (v. 7), and her daughters were compassionate (v. 10). Now everything is just the opposite. The holy city is desecrated (v. 1), the people have become cruel like heartless ostriches who desert their young (v. 3), the rich are now beggars sitting in ashes (v. 5), the princes are shriveled up by famine (v. 8), and the mothers boiled their own children for food when the famine was severe (v. 10). The fall of Sodom was nothing compared with this. (V. 6)

11-16 The second unit (vv. 11-16) of this lament exposes the guilty leaders. The ultimate cause of Zion's

412

downfall was the burning anger of Yahweh (v. 11). But everyone thought that Zion was inviolable; she was the city Yahweh had chosen to make His own. He would not destroy His own special abode (v. 12). The blame for Zion's downfall is then placed on the prophets and priests. They had not conscientiously spoken God's will but had exploited the people to keep them quiet. Thus they have blood on their hands. The blood of those murdered in the fall is also their responsibility. Now they have become like lepers, separated and "unclean." God Himself has rejected them. They must now wander on the earth as fugitives like Cain. (Vv. 13-16)

**17-22** The third section (vv. 17-22) depicts the futile hope of the people during the siege of Jerusalem. They had vainly hoped for Egypt (see Jer. 37:5-10) to come and relieve the siege, but their dreams were soon shattered (v. 17). The people knew their end was inevitable and they could not escape. The enemy was ready like a vulture to grab any who tried to flee to the mountains or the wilderness (v. 18-19). King Zedekiah, "the Lord's anointed" and the one in whom the people hoped for safety, did flee (Jer. 39:4-7) but was caught in the enemies' "pits," like an animal (v. 20). The lament closes with a taunt song against Edom, who had apparently taken advantage of Jerusalem's downfall. Edom was a traditional enemy of Judah (see Is. 34:1-17; Jer. 49: 7-22; Obad. 1-21). There was some consolation for Zion in the thought that Edom's turn was coming. And if that is true, there is always the hope when God is jealous against Edom, He will be as jealous for Judah and reverse the exile (cf. Jer. 30:12-17). When that happens, Zion's punishment will be terminated. (Vv. 21-22)

# A Prayer for the Remnant of Zion

## Lamentations 5

[1] **Remember, O LORD, what has befallen us;**
  **behold, and see our disgrace!**
[2] **Our inheritance has been turned over to strangers,**
  **our homes to aliens.**
[3] **We have become orphans, fatherless;**
  **our mothers are like widows.**
[4] **We must pay for the water we drink,**
  **the wood we get must be bought.**
[5] **With a yoke** [u] **on our necks we are hard driven;**
  **we are weary, we are given no rest.**
[6] **We have given the hand to Egypt,**
  **and to Assyria, to get bread enough.**
[7] **Our fathers sinned, and are no more;**
  **and we bear their iniquities.**
[8] **Slaves rule over us;**
  **there is none to deliver us from their hand.**
[9] **We get our bread at the peril of our lives,**
  **because of the sword in the wilderness.**

[u] Symmachus: Heb lacks *with a yoke*

414

¹⁰ Our skin is hot as an oven
    with the burning heat of famine.
¹¹ Women are ravished in Zion,
    virgins in the towns of Judah.
¹² Princes are hung up by their hands;
    no respect is shown to the elders.
¹³ Young men are compelled to grind at the mill;
    and boys stagger under loads of wood.
¹⁴ The old men have quit the city gate,
    the young men their music.
¹⁵ The joy of our hearts has ceased;
    our dancing has been turned to mourning.
¹⁶ The crown has fallen from our head;
    woe to us, for we have sinned!
¹⁷ For this our heart has become sick,
    for these things our eyes have grown dim,
¹⁸ for Mount Zion which lies desolate;
    jackals prowl over it.

¹⁹ But thou, O LORD, dost reign for ever;
    thy throne endures to all generations.
²⁰ Why dost thou forget us for ever,
    why dost thou so long forsake us?
²¹ Restore us to thyself, O LORD, that we may be
        restored!
    Renew our days as of old!
²² Or hast thou utterly rejected us?
    Art thou exceedingly angry with us?

Lamentations concludes with a prayer or lament
of God's people after the fall of Jerusalem. A similar
communal prayer is found in 3:40-47. The remnant of
the nation of Israel prays for mercy. God is invited to
consider the plight of His people, who are more like
orphans than God's children (vv. 1-3). The poet and

415

his community are apparently the survivors in Judah, who are struggling to survive under the disgrace and oppression of their conquerors (v. 4). They must wear a "yoke" like slaves; yet those who rule them are really "slaves" of their Babylonian masters (vv. 5, 8). Fugitives have appealed to countries in the East (of which Assyria is typical) and in the West (of which Egypt is typical) to find food and refuge (v. 6). The survivors in Palestine feel that their lot is the end result of the sins of their predecessors; the children feel they are taking the rap for the guilt of their fathers (v. 7). This was a prevalent gripe which Ezekiel discusses in detail (Ch. 18). Ignominy is aggravated by anarchy and insult; famine, rape, murder, and exploitation of children are rampant (vv. 9-13). Feelings of frustration, hopelessness, misery, despair, and guilt have taken all the joy out of life. Zion is desolate; God seems to have abandoned His people forever (vv. 14-18). Judah's crown has fallen; she is no longer a nation (v. 16). God, of course, never loses His crown. He rules forever! This fact gives the poet fresh reason to appeal. Hence he closes his prayer and the book with a ringing challenge to God. Similar bold questions conclude laments and prayers elsewhere in the Old Testament (cf. Jer. 14:8-9; 15:18). These questions are designed to stir God to action and are based on the right of a prophet to intercede with boldness for His covenant people. He is their mediator. He challenges God's right to ignore His people for so long. He screams for restoration. And he throws back in God's face the horrible possibility that God has rejected His people forever. Surely God could not ignore a challenge like that! (Vv. 19-21)

www.ingramcontent.com/pod-product-compliance
Lightning Source LLC
Chambersburg PA
CBHW020351100426
42812CB00001B/24